Penguin Handbooks
The Philosopher in the Kitchen

Jean-Anthelme Brillat-Savarin (1755–1826)
was born at the town of Belley in France,
where he was elected Mayor in 1793. The
outbreak of the Revolution drove him abroad,
to Switzerland and then to America, where
he earned his living by giving French
lessons and by playing in the orchestra at
the New York Theatre. In 1796 he returned
to France. His book *La Physiologie du goût*
appeared a year before his death.

The Philosopher in the Kitchen
Jean-Anthelme Brillat-Savarin

Translated by Anne Drayton

Penguin Books

Penguin Books Ltd, Harmondsworth,
Middlesex, England
Penguin Books Inc., 3300 Clipper Mill Road,
Baltimore, Md 21211, U.S.A.
Penguin Books Australia Ltd, Ringwood,
Victoria, Australia

La Physiologie du goût first published 1825
This translation published by Penguin Books 1970
Copyright © Anne Drayton, 1970

Made and printed in Great Britain by
Cox & Wyman Ltd,
London, Reading and Fakenham
Set in Intertype Baskerville

Contents

Introduction

No professional likes being outclassed by an amateur, and chefs and restaurateurs still find it hard to reconcile themselves to the fact that the man whose name is the synonym of culinary excellence and the author of the gourmets' Bible was not a cook in some great gastronomic capital but a magistrate in a sleepy French province.

Brillat-Savarin was born on 2 April 1755 into a family of lawyers in Belley, the chief town of the region of Bugey, which with Bresse and Gex had been incorporated in France by the 1601 Treaty of Lyons. The area was one famed, not only for its picturesque scenery, but also for its food and drink. As Lucien Tendret, a relative of Brillat-Savarin and another Belley lawyer, once wrote:

No region offers a greater variety of provisions for the table. Our beef is of prime quality, the flesh of the sheep reared in our mountains has the succulent flavour of that of the lambs of Pré-Salé, the hams cooked in our homes are as highly appreciated as the most famous in the world, and the traditional Belley sausage is as good as the Bologna mortadello. Our turkeys never grow as big as those in Berry, but their flesh is tastier and more delicate. In our markets you will find plump capons, chickens, and ducks. Crayfish, trout, and pike abound in our rivers, and the Lake of Bourget provides us with lavaret, perch, and char. On our hillsides and in our woods and meadows you will find winged game of all kinds, and the saddle of a hare from the Combe à la Done or the Rocher de Talbacon is tastier than a haunch of venison. There is a profusion of truffles, morels, and mushrooms in our woods. We envy neither Isigny butter nor the choicest cheeses, and our fruit and vegetables have a flavour acquired only in certain latitudes of the temperate zone. The wines of Virieu, Manicle, Pontet, and Culoz take longer to grow old than ourselves, and if they lack the bouquet of the great wines of Burgundy and Bordeaux, they still have a delightful aroma and leave the mouth fresh and the head clear.

Brillat-Savarin's native region was not only celebrated for its foodstuffs but also for the dishes the people of Bugey produced from the raw material nature provided in such abundance: the *noix de veau aux morilles noires* of Le Valromey, the *filet de bœuf aux truffes noires* which was the speciality of Vieu, or the *écrevisses à la Nantua* of which our author wrote that they were a dish 'worthy to be set before the angels if they still travelled on earth as in the time of Lot'.

It is small wonder that Jean-Anthelme Brillat-Savarin (his second name was that of the patron saint of Belley Cathedral) became addicted to good food and wine at an early age. His father, Marc-Anthelme Brillat-Savarin, *procureur du roi* at Belley, and his mother, who was known as 'fair Aurore', were both great gourmets, as were his two brothers, one of whom became colonel of the 134th infantry regiment and the other the deputy public prosecutor at Belley. So, undoubtedly, was his sister Pierrette, who died in her hundredth year, sitting up in bed, having just finished a good dinner and calling loudly for dessert. As for his other two sisters, Marie and Gasparde, who unlike Pierrette remained unmarried, they were so devoted to the task of providing Anthelme's creature comforts that they used to remain in bed during the ten months he spent in Paris every year, husbanding their strength for their brother's return.

At the age of twenty-three Anthelme went to Lyons, according to some authorities to obtain his degree in law after a dissertation on Domat and Justinian's *Institutes*, although other sources claim that he finished his law studies at Dijon. Whatever the truth of the matter, as soon as he was qualified he obtained a post as magistrate at Belley. He spent the next few years in agreeable style, carrying out his not too onerous duties, hunting, reading, making music with a local society of amateurs, and enjoying such gastronomic delights as his mother's pâté known as the *oreiller de la belle Aurore* (fair Aurore's pillow).

Talleyrand once said that nobody who had not lived before the Revolution knew how sweet life could be, and this was doubly true in the French provinces. But for Brillat-Savarin that sweet life was soon to be disturbed, for in 1789 he was elected by the Third Estate of Belley to represent them at Versailles. There was nothing of the revolutionary in his make-up, and indeed it is said that in the Constituent Assembly he opposed the division of the country into departments, the introduction of the jury system, and the abolition of capital punishment. At the end of his term as a representative, on 30 September 1791, he returned home as president of the civil tribunal of the newly created department of the Ain, only to be deposed as a royalist when the monarchy was abolished in 1792. However, he was so popular with his fellow citizens that they elected him Mayor of Belley, and for a year he did his utmost to protect his native town against the excesses of the Revolution. Then, in 1793, with the institution of the Terror, he found himself in imminent danger, and, as he relates in *The Philosopher in the Kitchen*, only love of music, which he shared with the wife of the sinister Representative Frôt, saved him from the guillotine.

Despite this narrow escape, he was still in deadly danger, so he decided to flee the country, first to Cologne and then to Switzerland, where he spent several pleasant months enjoying Swiss hospitality and cooking, and learning the art of making a good *fondue*.

In Lausanne he met a canon of Notre-Dame de Paris who invited him to join him as his aide-de-camp, but soon afterwards Brillat-Savarin set off for the United States, where, as he tells his readers, he 'found refuge, work, and peace'.

In New York he earned his living giving French lessons and playing the violin in a theatre orchestra. Among his most cherished memories of his stay in the United States was the famous evening at Little's in which he and two other French émigrés beat two Englishmen in a drinking-bout, and a delightful hunting expedition in Connecticut which is likewise recounted in *The Philosopher in the Kitchen*. In 1796, deciding that the situation in France had improved sufficiently, he left the United States where, as he later wrote, 'my time had gone so pleasantly that all I asked of heaven (and my prayer was answered), in the emotion of departure, was that I might be no unhappier in the Old World than I had been in the New'.

On his return to France he was struck off the list of émigrés and appointed to the staff of the future Marshal Augereau, who was then fighting on the Rhine. By this time he had obviously acquired a certain reputation as a gourmet, for he was promptly put in charge of catering for the general staff, a task which he performed to the delighted satisfaction of his fellow officers.

When the campaign was over, the Directory appointed him government commissioner on the Versailles Court of Criminal Justice, and after the fall of the Directory he became a judge on the Supreme Court of Appeal. In 1808, as a final honour, Napoleon made him a Chevalier de l'Empire, in recognition of the courage and humanity he had shown as Mayor of Belley at the height of the Revolution.

For the rest of his life Brillat-Savarin was to lead a peaceful, satisfying existence, performing his judicial functions conscientiously, entertaining his friends, playing the violin – he could now afford a Stradivarius – which had earned him his living in America, and spending two months of each year in his beloved Bugey. Every year too, on 26 June, his name-day, he would invite any young men from Bugey who happened to be in Paris to dinner at his house in the rue Richelieu, treating them to a wine from their native province which was brought from the Côte Grêle specially in a barrel on the back of his old mare Babet. His dinners in Paris were now famous for their excellence, and some of them were graced by the presence of his beautiful cousin, Juliette Récamier, who is given an honoured place in *The Philosopher in the Kitchen*. Madame Récamier had a great affection for Brillat-Savarin, whom she asked for advice at the height of her passion for Chateaubriand, and who was himself in love with her. So at least we may assume from the references to her in his great work, and from the dedication he wrote in the copy he sent her just before he died:

'Madame, receive kindly and read indulgently the work of an old man. It is a tribute of a friendship which dates from your childhood and, perhaps, the homage of a more tender feeling. . . . How can I tell? At my age a man no longer dares interrogate his heart.'

For many years one of Brillat-Savarin's leisure occupations had been writing. He was the author of a history of duelling and a number of rather racy short stories, most of which appear to have been lost, and also spent many evenings writing and revising what he called his 'gastronomical meditations'. These eventually became his most absorbing preoccupation, and he would even take the manuscript with him to the Palais de Justice, where he would work on it as an antidote to the more tedious legal arguments of learned counsel.

Occasionally after dinner Brillat-Savarin would read extracts from his great work to a few friends, including Baron Richerand, and in his preface to *The Philosopher in the Kitchen* he reproduces what purports to be a conversation with Richerand in which the baron urged him to publish his meditations. Other friends also gave him encouragement, notably Henrion de Pansey, the President of the Supreme Court of Appeal, a gourmet who once told Brillat-Savarin: 'I shall never consider the sciences to be sufficiently honoured or suitably represented until a cook sits in the Institut.'

Yielding to these exhortations, Brillat-Savarin finally published *The Philosopher in the Kitchen* at his own expense in December 1825, but without the author's name. Despite this modest precaution, all Paris soon knew who had written the remarkable work everyone was talking about. But Brillat-Savarin did not enjoy the pleasures of fame for long. On 18 January he received an invitation to the expiatory ceremony commemorating the death of Louis XVI in a letter which concluded with the acid comment: 'Your presence will be all the more welcome in that it will be the first time.' Although he was suffering from a severe cold, Brillat-Savarin obediently attended the ceremony at Saint-Denis, was chilled by the draughts in the basilica, and died of pneumonia on 2 February.

Brillat-Savarin was dead, but his work lived on, winning more readers and higher praise as the years went by. It had, of course, its detractors, and the remarkable private collection of the Paris restaurateur Monsieur Raymond Oliver contains an autographed copy in which Brillat-Savarin's rival in gourmandise, the Marquis de Cussy, has tried to improve on his aphorisms. One of the chief reproaches levelled at the author in his time was that the cooking he admired and recommended was middle-class and provincial. But that, of course, was its great merit, for the upper classes ate poorly in early-nineteenth-century France: their food was often cold by the time it reached the table from faraway kitchens, and they generally sacrificed quality for show. Only in provincial middle-class homes were meals not only copious but cooked with loving artistry, since, as Balzac pointed out, the lack of occupation and monotony of life in the provinces concentrated attention on the kitchen.

Most authorities, however, were and still are loud in their praises of *The Philosopher in the Kitchen*. It was recognized as a work without precedent in any literature, a unique combination of recipes and aphorisms, reflections and reminiscences, history and philosophy, which raised gastronomy to the level of an art. Hoffmann's noble tribute to it is as valid today as when it was first written: 'A divine book, which illuminates the art of eating with the light of genius.'

ANNE DRAYTON

Aphorisms

By the Professor to serve as a prologue to his work and an eternal foundation for his Science

I. The world is nothing without life, and all that lives takes nourishment.

II. Animals feed: man eats: only the man of intellect knows how to eat.

III. The fate of nations depends on the way they eat.

IV. Tell me what you eat: I will tell you what you are.

V. The Creator, who made man such that he must eat to live, incites him to eat by means of appetite, and rewards him with pleasure.

VI. Gourmandism is an act of judgement, by which we give preference to things which are agreeable to our taste over those which are not.

VII. The pleasures of the table belong to all times and all ages, to every country and every day; they go hand in hand with all our other pleasures, outlast them, and remain to console us for their loss.

VIII. The table is the only place where the first hour is never dull.

IX. The discovery of a new dish does more for the happiness of mankind than the discovery of a star.

X. Drunkards and victims of indigestion do not know how to eat or drink.

XI. The right order of eating is from the most substantial dishes to the lightest.

XII. The right order of drinking is from the mildest wines to the headiest and most perfumed.

XIII. To maintain that one wine may not be drunk after another is heresy; a man's palate can be saturated, and after the third glass the best of wines produces only a dull impression.

XIV. Dessert without cheese is like a pretty woman with only one eye.

xv. A man can become a cook, but he has to be born a *rôtisseur*.

xvi. The most indispensable quality in a cook is punctuality; it is also that of a guest.

xvii. To wait too long for an unpunctual guest is an act of discourtesy towards those who have arrived in time.

xviii. The man who invites his friends to his table, and fails to give his personal attention to the meal they are going to eat, is unworthy to have any friends.

xix. The mistress of the house must always see to it that the coffee is excellent, and the master that the liqueurs are of the first quality.

xx. To entertain a guest is to make yourself responsible for his happiness so long as he is beneath your roof.

Dialogue between the Author and his Friend

(after the usual compliments)

THE FRIEND: At breakfast this morning, my wife and I decided in our wisdom that you should publish your Gastronomical Meditations at the earliest opportunity.

THE AUTHOR: *What woman wills, God wills.* There, in five words, you have the whole of Parisian law. But I'm not a Parisian, and I'm a bachelor . . .

THE FRIEND: Why, you bachelors are just as much in women's power as the rest of us, and sometimes to our cost. But here your unmarried state won't save you, for my wife claims the right to be obeyed, on the ground that it was at her house in the country that you wrote your first few pages.

THE AUTHOR: My dear doctor, you know my regard for the fair sex; more than once you have praised my submission to their orders; you were even among those who said I would make an excellent husband. . . . And yet I hesitate to publish my book.

THE FRIEND: But why?

THE AUTHOR: Because, after all my serious researches, I'm afraid that people who only know my book by its title may take me for just a trifler.

THE FRIEND: You've no reason to be afraid of that. Aren't your thirty-six years of public service enough to give you a very different reputation? Besides, my wife and I are convinced that everyone will want to read your book.

THE AUTHOR: Really?

THE FRIEND: Men of learning will read it to discover the truths which you have only hinted at till now.

THE AUTHOR: I admit that that might be so.

THE FRIEND: Women will read it, of course, because they will see that . . .

THE AUTHOR: My dear fellow, I am an old man and I have mended my ways: *Miserere mei.*

THE FRIEND: Gourmands will read you, because you will do them justice and give them at last the position in society which is their due.

THE AUTHOR: There at least you speak the truth! It is inconceivable that they should have been slighted and ignored so long! I love those dear gourmands as if they were my children! They are so good-natured! They have such sparkling eyes!

THE FRIEND: Besides, haven't you often said your work is one all our libraries need?

THE AUTHOR: I have said so, and it's a fact, and I'd choke rather than take my words back.

THE FRIEND: Well, since you agree with me, come with me at once to . . .

THE AUTHOR: No, no! An author's path is sometimes very pleasant, but it has its thorny places, and I intend to leave them to my heirs to deal with.

THE FRIEND: But if you do that you'll be disinheriting your friends, your acquaintances, your contemporaries. Have you the courage to do such a thing?

THE AUTHOR: My heirs! My heirs! The spirits of the dead, so I have heard, are regularly flattered by the praises of the living; and that is a kind of bliss I wish to save up for the next world.

THE FRIEND: But are you sure those praises will reach you there? And are you convinced that you can rely on your heirs?

THE AUTHOR: Why, I have no reason to think them capable of neglecting a duty in virtue of which I would excuse them a great many others.

THE FRIEND: But will they, can they, feel a father's love for your brainchild, or give it an author's fond attention, without which any work looks a little awkward to the public?

THE AUTHOR: But my manuscript will be corrected and neatly written, finished in every particular: there'll be nothing left to do but print it.

THE FRIEND: And what about accidents? Alas, countless precious works have been lost in this way, like that of the celebrated Lecat on the state of the soul during sleep, his whole life's work!

THE AUTHOR: No doubt that was a grievous loss, and I am far from aspiring to be the cause of such regrets.

THE FRIEND: Believe me, heirs have quite enough to do, what with the Church and the Law and the Medical Faculty; and with the best will in the world they may have no time to attend to different things which must be done before, during, and after the publication of even the slimmest volume.

THE AUTHOR: But the title! And the subject! And the fun people will make of it!

THE FRIEND: The mere word *gastronomy* makes everyone prick up his ears: the subject is in fashion, and jokers have as much of the gourmand in them as anyone else. So you can put your mind at rest on that score. Besides, have you forgotten that the gravest personages have given us light reading sometimes? Monsieur de Montesquieu, for example.[1]

THE AUTHOR: Why, so he has! He wrote *The Temple of Cnidos*; and it can be argued that a more useful purpose is served by meditating upon what is the principal necessity, pleasure, and occupation of all our days, than by recording the sayings and doings of a pair of brats two thousand years ago in the groves of ancient Greece, and how one pursued and the other tried hard not to escape.

THE FRIEND: So at last you give in?

THE AUTHOR: Give in? Not a bit of it. That was just the author showing his cloven hoof for a moment; and that reminds me of an amusing scene in an English comedy, the

---

1. Monsieur de Montucla, known for an admirable *History of Mathematics*, also compiled a *Dictionary of Culinary Geography*; he showed me some fragments of it during my stay at Versailles. And it is said that Monsieur Berryat Saint-Prix, the distinguished Professor of Legal Procedure, has written a novel in several volumes.

play called *The Natural Daughter* unless I am mistaken. But judge for yourself.

The play is about the Quakers, and, as you know, members of that sect call everyone thee and thou, wear simple clothes, never go to war, never swear, behave with great restraint, and above all are forbidden to lose their temper.

Well, the hero of the play is a handsome young Quaker, who appears on the stage wearing a brown coat and a large broad-brimmed hat, and with his hair uncurled; which doesn't prevent him from falling in love.

He has a rival in the person of a fop, who, encouraged by his appearance, and taking it as an indication of his character, makes fun of him, mocks him, and insults him: to such good effect that the young man, gradually growing angrier, finally loses his temper and thrashes his impudent tormentor in masterly fashion.

When the deed is done, he suddenly resumes his former bearing, meditates for a moment, and then remarks sadly: 'Alas, I fear the flesh was too strong for the spirit!'

So it was with me, and after an understandable lapse I come back to my original decision.

THE FRIEND: It is too late now; by your own confession you have shown your cloven hoof. The game's up, and you are coming with me to a publisher's. More than one of them have already got wind of your secret.

THE AUTHOR: You had better be careful, for I will put you in my book, and who knows what I might say of you?

THE FRIEND: What could you say? Don't imagine you can frighten me!

THE AUTHOR: I shall not say that your native town, which is also mine,[1] is proud of having given birth to you, nor that at the age of twenty-four you had already brought out a work on the elements of medicine which has remained a classic ever since; that your reputation, which is well de-

1. Belley, the chief town of Bugey, a pleasant land of mountains, hills, rivers, limpid streams, waterfalls, and gorges – a real garden of a hundred square leagues in area. Here, before the Revolution, the third estate, by the local constitution, had ascendancy over the two other orders.

served, wins your patients' confidence; that your appearance
reassures them; that your skill astounds them; that your
sympathetic manner comforts them – everyone knows that.
But I shall reveal to all Paris [*drawing myself up*], to all
France [*puffing my chest out*], to the whole world, the one
fault which I know you to possess!

THE FRIEND [*earnestly*]: And what is that, may I ask?

THE AUTHOR: An ingrained fault, which all my reproaches
have failed to cure.

THE FRIEND [*alarmed*]: Tell me! Don't keep me on ten-
terhooks any longer!

THE AUTHOR: You eat too fast.[1]

[*Upon which the friend picks up his hat and goes out smiling, certain that he has been preaching to the converted.*]

1. Fact, not fiction. The friend in this dialogue is Doctor Richerand.

Preface

The decision to submit the present work to the public did not involve me in any considerable labour; merely the setting in order of material long since gathered together. This was an amusing occupation which I had saved up for my old age.

When I came to consider the pleasures of the table in all their aspects, I soon perceived that something better than a mere cookery book might be made of such a subject, and that there was a great deal to be said about such a basic everyday function, bearing so closely upon our health, our happiness, and even our work.

Once this central idea had been established, the rest was plain sailing; I looked about me and took note of what I saw, and often at the most sumptuous banquets I have been saved from boredom by the pleasure I derived from my observations.

That is not to deny that in order to perform the task I had set myself, I had to be a physicist, a chemist, a physiologist, and even something of a scholar. But I had made these researches without the slightest intention of becoming an author; a praiseworthy spirit of curiosity spurred me on, together with a fear of being behind the times, and a desire to be able to hold my own in conversations with men of science, whose company I have always enjoyed.[1]

Medicine is indeed my favourite hobby, almost to the point of mania; and one of my happiest memories is how one day I went in by the door reserved for the professors, in their

1. 'Come and dine with me next Thursday,' Monsieur de Greffulhe said to me one day. 'I will arrange a dinner with scientists or men of letters, whichever you prefer.' 'My choice is made,' I replied: 'we will dine twice.' Which we did, and the meal with the men of letters was notably the choicer and more delicate of the two. (See Meditation 12.)

company, to hear a dissertation by Doctor Cloquet, and had the pleasure of hearing a murmur of curiosity run round the amphitheatre, as each student asked his neighbour who the important stranger could be who had honoured the assembly with his presence.

Yet I think there is another day which I recall just as fondly, when I exhibited my *irrorator* to the Board of the Society for the Encouragement of National Industry: this was an invention of mine which was simply a compression-fountain adapted for spraying scent indoors. I had brought my apparatus in my pocket, fully charged: I turned on the tap, and a fragrant cloud escaped with a hiss, rose to the ceiling and fell in tiny drops on the spectators and their papers. Then with indescribable delight I saw the wisest heads in the capital bow down beneath my *irroration*; and I nearly swooned with joy when I observed that the wettest were also the happiest.

Sometimes when I think of the solemn lucubrations into which I have been drawn by the wide range of my subject, I am genuinely afraid of having been a bore; for I too have sometimes yawned over the works of other people.

I have done everything in my power to avoid this reproach: I have only touched upon those subjects which seem to lay themselves open to it; I have scattered anecdotes throughout my work, some of them taken from my own experience; I have left out many strange and extraordinary facts which the reason is bound to reject; I have called attention to certain truths which the learned seem to have kept to themselves, and made them intelligible to a wider public. If, despite all my efforts, I have not presented my readers with a dish of science which is easily digestible, I shall none the less sleep soundly, because I know the majority will absolve me on the score of my intentions.

Another reproach which might be levelled at me is that I sometimes let my pen run away with me, and tend to turn garrulous when I have a tale to tell. But is it my fault if I am old? Is it my fault if I am like Ulysses, who had seen the cities and ways of life of many peoples? Am I to be blamed for including a little of my own biography? Besides, I would remind the reader that I am letting him off my 'Political Reminiscences', which he would certainly have had to read like so many others, seeing that for the last thirty-six years I have occupied the front seat at the passing show of men and events.

Above all, let no one class me in the ranks of the compilers: if I had been reduced to that pass, my pen would have stopped writing, and I would have lived no less happily as a result.

I have said with Juvenal:

Semper ego auditor tantum! numquamne reponam?[1]

and those who know will readily perceive that, accustomed to both the tumult of society and the silence of the study, I have taken the best of what each of those two extremes has to offer.

Finally, I have given myself much personal satisfaction; I have mentioned several of my friends, who have no idea that they are in my book; I have recalled a number of pleasant memories, and made permanent a number which seemed likely to escape me; and as the homely phrase goes, 'I have drunk my coffee'.

Perhaps there will be one of my readers of the disdainful sort who will cry: 'What do I care if . . . What can he be thinking of, to say . . . etc., etc.?' But I am sure the rest will call him to order, and that an impressive majority will treat my effusions kindly on account of the praiseworthy sentiment that inspires them.

Something remains to be said about my style: for 'the style's the man', according to Buffon. But let no one think I am about to claim an indulgence which is never granted to those who need it; I merely wish to offer a few words in explanation.

I ought to write marvellously well, for Voltaire, Jean-Jacques, Fénelon, Buffon, and later Cochin and d'Aguesseau have been my favourite authors; I know them by heart.

1. 'Am I always to be only a listener and never make reply?' [Ed.]

But it may be the gods have otherwise ordained: and if that is the case, this is the reason for their decision:

I am more or less conversant with five modern languages, and thus have at my command a vast repertoire of words of every sort. When I am in need of an expression, and cannot find it in the French storehouse, I take it from the next one, and leave it to the reader to translate my phrase or guess my meaning: such is his fate. No doubt I could manage otherwise; but I am prevented from doing so by a theory to which I am firmly attached.

I am convinced that French, the language which I employ, is comparatively poor in resources. What is to be done in such a case? I must borrow, or steal. I do both, since these borrowings are not subject to an order for restitution, and the theft of words is not a punishable offence.

The reader will have some idea of my audacity when he learns that I call a man I send on an errand *volante* (from the Spanish), and that I was determined to gallicize the English verb *to sip*, which is equivalent to our own *boire à petites reprises*, if I had not disinterred the old French *siroter*, which used to have much the same meaning.

Naturally, I expect the purists will call upon the names of Bossuet, Fénelon, Racine, Boileau, Pascal, and others of the time of Louis XIV: I seem to hear them already, raising a terrible outcry.

To which I shall reply, quite calmly, that I am far from denying the merit of the authors I have named, or of others that I might have named; but what follows from their example? ... Nothing, except that having done so well with so wretched an instrument, they would have done incomparably better with a finer one. Just as it is reasonable to believe that Tartini would have been a better violinist if his bow had been as long as Baillot's.

It will be seen that I am on the side of the Neologists, and indeed of the Romantics: for the latter are discoverers of hidden treasure, while the former may be likened to explorers who travel to the ends of the earth to look for the provisions we need.

In this respect the Northern races, and especially the English, have the advantage of us: their genius is never at a loss for an expression, but coins words or borrows them. The result is that our translations, particularly those made from works of some depth or vigour, are never more than pale and colourless copies of their originals.

I remember once listening at the Institut to a very elegant discourse on the dangers of the neologism and the necessity of preserving our language in the form in which it was established by the authors of our Augustan Age.

As a chemist, I passed this work of art through the retort; and this is all that was left: *We have done so well that there is no possibility of doing better, nor of doing otherwise.*

Well, I have lived long enough to know that the same is said by every generation, and that the next generation never fails to make fun of its writings. Besides, how should words fail to change, when customs and ideas are continuously undergoing modification? If we do the same things that the ancients did, we do them in a different way, and there are whole pages in certain French books which it would be impossible to translate into either Latin or Greek.

Every tongue has its birth, its zenith, and its decline; and all those spoken between the time of Sesostris and the time of Philippe-Auguste now exist only as inscriptions on monuments.

The same fate awaits our own tongue, and in the year 2825 I shall only be read with the help of a dictionary, if I am read at all ...

I once had an argument on this subject with my good friend Monsieur Andrieux, of the Académie Française. I attacked in good order and pressed him hard, and would have forced him to surrender if he had not beaten a prompt retreat, which I did not attempt to hinder, because I remembered, luckily for him, that he was responsible for a letter in the new dictionary.

I have a final observation to make, which I have saved till the end because of its importance.

When I write and speak of myself in the singular, the

reader may assume that I am taking part in a conversation with him; he may ask questions, argue, be sceptical, and even laugh. But when I arm myself with the formidable *We*, I become the Professor; and he must listen in respectful silence.

> I am Sir Oracle
> And when I ope my lips, let no dog bark.

Shakespeare, *Merchant of Venice*, I, I.

Part One

Gastronomical
Meditations

1. On the Senses

The senses are the organs through which man communicates with external objects.

1. Number of the Senses

The number of the senses is not fewer than six, namely:

Sight, which embraces space, and, through the medium of light, reveals to us the existence and colour of the bodies which surround us;

Hearing, which through the medium of the air receives the vibrations set up by noisy or sonorous bodies;

Smell, which enables us to discern the odours of those bodies which are endowed with them;

Taste, by means of which we approve anything which is edible and palatable;

Touch, which determines the consistency and surface of bodies;

And lastly, the sense of *physical desire,* which brings the two sexes together, and whose aim is the reproduction of the species.

It is an astonishing fact that this important sense went unrecognized until almost the time of Buffon, having been confused, or rather associated, until then with the sense of touch.

However, the two have nothing in common; the organism of the sixth sense is as complete as are the mouth or eyes; and it has this peculiarity, that although both sexes are fully equipped to feel sensation through it, they must be joined together before the purpose Nature has set itself can be attained. And if taste, whose purpose is the preservation of the individual, is indisputably one of the senses, the same title must surely be given to those organs whose function is the preservation of the species.

Let us grant then to physical desire that *sensual* position which cannot be denied it, and bequeath to our heirs the responsibility of giving it its proper rank.

2. Action of the Senses

If we may be allowed to go back, in imagination, to the earliest moments of the history of the human race, it is also permissible to believe that the first sensations of man were absolutely direct, that is to say, that he saw without precision, heard without clarity, ate without discernment, and made love without tenderness.

But since all these sensations have a common centre in the soul, the special attribute of mankind and the ever active cause of perfectibility, they were considered, compared, and judged in the soul; and soon all the senses were led to help one another, for the use and benefit of the *sensitive ego*, or, to call it by another name, the *individual*.

Thus touch corrected the errors of sight; sound, by means of the spoken word, became the interpreter of every feeling; sight and smell gave added powers to taste; hearing compared sounds and judged distances; and physical desire influenced the organs of all the other senses.

The torrent of time, flowing onwards over the human race, has constantly brought new improvements, the cause of which, almost imperceptible but continually active, can be found in the claims made by each of our senses in turn to be agreeably occupied.

Thus sight gave birth to painting, sculpture, and spectacles of every sort;

Sound, to melody, harmony, the dance, and music in all its branches and methods of execution;

Smell, to the discovery, cultivation, and use of scents;

Taste, to the production, selection, and preparation of everything capable of serving as food;

Touch, to every art, every skill, every industry;

Physical desire, to all that can prepare for or embellish the union of the sexes, and since the days of Francis the First, to romantic love, coquetry, and fashion; especially to co-quetry, which was born in France, and has no name in any other language, so that every day the élite of foreign nations comes for lessons in *coquetterie* to the capital of the world.

Strange as the proposition may appear at first sight, it can be easily verified; for it would be impossible to talk intelligibly about those three great motive forces of present-day society in any of the languages of antiquity.

I had composed a dialogue on the subject, which might not have been without its attractions; but I have suppressed it, in order to give my readers the pleasure of making one up for themselves; this is a task on which they can expend their wit and learning for a whole evening.

We said above that the sense of physical desire had influenced the organs of all the other senses: its effect on the sciences has been no less profound, for a close examination will show that all the most delicate and ingenious achievements of science are due to the hope or desire of one sex to be united with the other.

Such then, in reality, is the genealogy of even the most abstract sciences: they are simply the immediate result of the continuous efforts we have made to gratify our senses.

3. Perfectioning of the Senses

Our senses, which we look upon with great fondness, are nevertheless far from being perfect. I shall not waste time in proving this statement, but merely observe that sight, the most ethereal of them all, and touch, at the other end of the scale, have acquired in the course of time a remarkable accession to their powers.

By means of *spectacles* the eye escapes, so to speak, from the senile decay which afflicts most of our other organs.

The *telescope* has discovered stars which were previously unknown and inaccessible to all our faculties of measurement; it has penetrated to regions so remote as to reveal luminous and obviously enormous bodies which appear to us as no more than nebulous and almost imperceptible spots.

The *microscope* has given us knowledge of the interior configuration of bodies; it has shown us plants, and indeed a whole vegetation, whose very existence was unsuspected. We have seen animals a hundred thousand times smaller than the smallest which can be observed by the naked eye; and yet these tiny creatures move and feed and reproduce themselves, which implies the existence of organs more minute than anything we can imagine.

On the other hand, machinery has multiplied strength; man has turned his every conception into fact, and moved burdens which Nature had made too heavy for his puny powers.

With the help of weapons and the lever man has subjugated Nature: he has made her minister to his pleasures, his needs, his very whims: he has altered the surface of the earth, and a feeble biped has become lord of creation.

Sight and touch, with their powers so greatly increased, might well be attributes of a species far superior to man; or rather, the human species would be very different if all our senses had improved likewise.

It should be added, however, that although touch has developed enormously in terms of muscular power, yet civilization has done almost nothing for it as a sensitive organ; but all things are possible, and it must be remembered that the human species is still quite young, and that a great many centuries must pass before the senses can extend their dominion.

For example, it is only about four centuries since the invention of harmony, that heavenly science which is to sound what painting is to colour.[1]

1. We are aware that the contrary has been maintained; but there is no support for such a theory.

If the ancients had known harmony some precise notions regarding it would have been preserved in their writings; whereas all that can be adduced is a few obscure phrases which lend themselves to any interpretation.

Moreover it is impossible to trace the birth and progress of harmony in those monuments of antiquity which have come down to us; we are

No doubt the ancients sang to the accompaniment of instruments played in unison, but their knowledge went no further than that; they were incapable of separating sound from sound, or of appreciating the relationship between one sound and another.

It was not until the fifteenth century that the tonic scale was fixed, the arrangement of chords regulated, and use made of these innovations to reinforce the means of vocal expression.

By this tardy but perfectly natural discovery the power of hearing has been doubled; it has been shown to include two faculties in some degree independent of each other, one which receives sounds and one which appreciates their resonance.

German doctors maintain that persons sensitive to harmony possess an additional sense.

As for those to whom music is nothing but a jumble of confused sounds, it is worth noting that they almost all sing out of tune; and we must conclude, either that their hearing apparatus is so constructed as to receive only short and waveless vibrations, or more probably, that their two ears do not have the same compass, and their component parts, being of different length and sensibility, can transmit only an obscure and indeterminate sensation to the brain; just as two instruments played in different keys and in different time could not produce a coherent melody.

The last few centuries have also seen important advances in the sphere of taste; the discovery of sugar and its various uses, alcohol, ices, vanilla, tea, and coffee have provided our palate with hitherto unknown sensations.

Who knows but that touch may have its turn, and some happy chance may open up a source of new delight? This is all the more likely in that the tactile sense exists all over the body, and consequently can be excited at any point.

---

indebted to the Arabs, who presented us with the organ, which by making several continuous notes audible at once, gave birth to the first idea of harmony.

4. Powers of Taste

We have seen how physical love has influenced all the sciences, exercising that tyranny which is its invariable characteristic.

The more prudent and measured, though no less active, faculty of taste has attained the same end, but with a slowness which ensures its lasting success.

At a later stage we shall examine its progress in detail; but at this point we can already remark that whoever has been a guest at a sumptuous banquet, in a hall adorned with mirrors, paintings, statues, and flowers, a hall balmy with scents, beautified by the presence of pretty women, and filled with the strains of sweet music – that man, we say, required no great effort of the imagination to be convinced that all the sciences have been pressed into service to enhance and set off the pleasures of taste.

5. Aim of the Action of the Senses

Let us now examine the system of our senses taken as a whole. We shall see that the Author of Creation had two aims, one of which is the consequence of the other, namely the preservation of the individual and the continuation of the species.

Such is the destiny of man, considered as a sensitive being; it is towards this dual goal that all his activities are directed.

The eye perceives external objects, reveals the marvels with which man is surrounded, and teaches him that he is part of a great whole.

Hearing perceives sounds, not only as an agreeable sensation, but also as a warning of the movement of potentially dangerous bodies.

Feeling, in the form of pain, gives immediate notice of all bodily wounds.

The hand, that faithful servant, not only prepares man's withdrawal from danger, and protects him on his way, but also lays hold by choice of those objects which instinct tells it are most suitable for making good the losses caused by the maintenance of life.

Smell investigates those objects: for noxious substances almost always have an evil odour.

Then taste makes its decision, the teeth are set to work, the tongue joins with the palate in savouring, and soon the stomach begins its task of assimilation.

And now a strange languor invades the body, objects lose their colour, the body relaxes, the eyes close, everything disappears, and the senses are in absolute repose.

When he awakes, man sees that nothing has changed in his surroundings, but a secret fire is aflame in his breast, a new faculty has come into play; he feels an urge to share his existence with another being.

This disturbing and imperious urge is common to both sexes; it brings them together, and unites them; and when the seed of a new existence has been sown, they can sleep in peace; they have just fulfilled their most sacred duty, by ensuring the perpetuation of the species.[1]

Such are the general philosophical observations which I have thought fit to lay before my readers, before proceeding to a more detailed examination of the organ of taste.

1. Monsieur de Buffon has portrayed, with all the charm of the most brilliant eloquence, the earliest moments of Eve's existence. Having to treat a very similar subject, we have made no attempt to provide more than a brief sketch: our readers will find it easy to add the colouring.

2. On Taste

6. Definition of Taste

Taste is that one of our senses which puts us in contact with palatable bodies by means of the sensation which they arouse in the organ designed to judge them.

Taste, which is excited by appetite, hunger, and thirst, is the seat of several operations, resulting in the growth, development, and preservation of the individual, and the making good of losses caused by natural wastage.

Organized bodies do not all obtain nourishment in the same way: the Author of Creation, whose methods are as varied as they are sure, has provided them with different means of subsistence.

Vegetables, at the lower end of the scale of living things, obtain nourishment through their roots, which are implanted in the native soil, and, by the operation of a special mechanism, select those substances which have the property of stimulating their growth and maintaining their existence.

Mounting a little higher, we encounter bodies endowed with animal life, but without the means of locomotion; they are born in surroundings favourable to their existence, and special organs extract from those surroundings whatever is needed to sustain them during their allotted span; they do not seek their food, their food seeks them.

A third method has been ordained for the preservation of those animals which move about the earth, and of which man is incontestably the most perfect. A special instinct warns him that he is in need of food; he goes in search of it; he seizes those objects which he suspects possess the property of supplying his needs; he eats, and is restored, and so pursues in life the career which is his lot.

Taste may be considered under three heads:

In the physical man, it is the apparatus by means of which he enjoys whatever is palatable;

In the moral man, it is the sensation aroused in the centre of feeling by the action of a palatable body on the relevant organ;

Lastly, considered in its material context, it is the property possessed by a given body of acting upon the organ and giving rise to the sensation.

It appears that taste has two principal uses:

1. It invites us, by means of pleasure, to make good the losses which we suffer through the action of life.

2. It helps us to choose, from the various substances offered us by Nature, those which are suitable as food.

In the exercise of this choice, taste has a powerful ally in smell, as we shall see later; for it may be stated as a general maxim that nutritious substances are repugnant to neither taste nor smell.

7. *Operation of Taste*

It is no easy matter to determine the precise nature of the organ of taste. It is more complicated than it seems at first sight.

Clearly, the tongue plays an important part in the mechanism of degustation; for, endowed as it is with a certain amount of muscular energy, it serves to crush, revolve, compress, and swallow food.

In addition, through the numerous papillae scattered over its surface, it absorbs the sapid and soluble particles of the substances with which it comes into contact; but all that is not enough to complete the sensation, which requires the cooperation of several adjacent parts, namely the cheeks, the palate, and above all the nasal fossae, to which physiologists have perhaps not paid sufficient attention.

The cheeks furnish saliva, which is equally essential to mastication, and to the formation of the alimentary bolus; they, as well as the palate, are endowed with the faculty of appreciation; I am even inclined to think that in certain cases the gums have a little themselves; and without the *odoration* which takes place at the back of the mouth, the sensation of taste would be dull and incomplete.

Persons born without a tongue, or whose tongue has been cut out, are not completely deprived of the sensation of taste. Examples of the former case are to be found in all the text-books; and I learned something of the latter case from a poor wretch whose tongue had been cut out by the Algerians as a punishment for having attempted to escape from their clutches, together with some of his comrades in captivity.

This man, whom I met in Amsterdam, where he earned his living as a messenger, had received a reasonable education, and it was quite easy to carry on a conversation with him in writing.

After noting that all the front part of his tongue, as far as the string, had been removed, I asked him if he still found any enjoyment in what he ate, and if the sensation of taste had survived the cruel operation he had undergone.

He replied that what caused him the greatest fatigue was the act of swallowing, which he only performed with difficulty; that he had retained the faculty of taste to a fair degree; that he could still enjoy good food as well as any man, provided the taste was not too strong; but that very acid or bitter substances caused him intolerable pain.

He further informed me that cutting out the tongue was a common punishment in the African states; that it was particularly inflicted on persons suspected of being the leaders in any conspiracy; and that there were special instruments designed for the purpose. I would have liked him to describe them to me; but he showed so painful a repugnance on the subject that I pressed him no further.

I reflected on what he had told me, and, going back to the ignorant times when the tongues of blasphemers were pierced or cut out, and to the period when such punishments were laid down by law, I felt justified in concluding that they were of African origin, and had been introduced by the returning Crusaders.

We have already seen how the sensation of taste is principally situated in the papillae of the tongue. Now, anatomy teaches that all tongues are not equally provided with these papillae, and that one tongue may possess three times as many as another. This circumstance explains how it is that of two guests seated at the same banqueting table, one displays the liveliest pleasure, while the other seems to be eating only under constraint; the reason is that the second guest has a poorly equipped tongue, and that the empire of taste also has its blind and deaf subjects.

8. Sensation of Taste

Five or six opinions have been expressed concerning the mode of operation of the sensation of taste; I have my own, which is as follows:

The sensation of taste is a chemical process operating through the medium of humidity, as we used to say in the old days; in other words, the sapid molecules must be dissolved in some fluid or other, in order to be absorbed by the nervous projections, papillae, or suckers, which cover the surface of the tasting apparatus.

This theory, new or not, is supported by physical and almost palpable proofs.

Pure water causes no sensation of taste, because it contains no sapid particles whatever. But dissolve a grain of salt in it, or a few drops of vinegar, and the sensation will occur.

Other drinks, on the contrary, give us a sensation of taste, because they are simply solutions more or less heavily charged with appreciable particles.

It would be useless to fill the mouth with particles of an insoluble substance; the tongue would experience the sensation of touch, but not of taste.

As for substances which are solid and savoury, they must be divided up by the teeth, saturated with saliva and the other gustative fluids, and pressed against the palate by the tongue until they exude a juice which, being then sufficiently charged with sapidity, is appreciated by the papillae, which deliver to the triturated substance the pass-port it needs for admittance into the stomach.

This theory, which will be further developed, easily answers the principal tests which can be applied to it.

For if it be asked what is meant by sapid bodies, the answer is that they are soluble bodies suitable to be absorbed by the organ of taste.

And if it be asked how the sapid body operates, the answer is that it acts whenever it is in a state of dissolution which allows it access to the cavities charged with receiving and transmitting the sensation.

In short, nothing is sapid but what is either already dissolved or imminently soluble.

9. Of the Savours

The number of savours is infinite, for every soluble body has a special savour which is not quite like any other.

The savours are also differentiated by simple, double, and multiple combinations, so that it is impossible to classify them, from the most attractive to the most intolerable, from the strawberry to the colocynth. No attempt to do so has been completely successful.

There is nothing surprising about this failure; for if it is granted that there exists an indefinite number of series of basic savours, all capable of being modified by an infinite number of combinations, it follows that a new language would be needed to express all the resultant effects, mountains of folio volumes to define them, and undreamed-of numerical characters to label them.

Now, since no circumstance has so far arisen in which any savour could be appreciated with scientific exactitude, we have been forced to make do with a few general terms, such as *sweet, sugary, acid, bitter,* and so on, which are all contained, in the last analysis, in the two expressions, *agreeable* or *disagreeable* to the taste, and which suffice for all practical purposes to indicate the gustatory properties of whatever sapid body is in question.

Our successors will know more about all this than we do, and there can be no doubt that chemistry will reveal to them the causes and basic elements of the savours.

10. Influence of Smell upon Taste

The moment has arrived when, in accordance with the plan I have laid down for my work, I must accord due approbation to the sense of smell, and recognize the important services it renders in the appreciation of the savours; for among all the authors I have come across, I have found none who seemed to me to do it full and entire justice.

For my part I am not only convinced that without the cooperation of smell there can be no complete degustation, but I am also tempted to believe that smell and taste are in fact but a single sense, whose laboratory is the mouth and whose chimney is the nose; or to be more precise, in which the mouth performs the degustation of tactile bodies, and the nose the degustation of gases.

My theory could be vigorously defended; but as I make no claim to be the founder of a new school of thought, I simply offer it for the consideration of my readers, and as proof that I have made a close study of my subject. Now, I shall proceed with my demonstration of the importance of smell, if not as a constituent part of taste, at least as its essential accessory.

All sapid bodies are necessarily odorous, and thus have a place in the empire of smell no less than in the empire of taste.

We eat nothing without being conscious of its smell, either at once or upon reflection; and towards unknown foodstuffs the nose always acts as an advance sentry, crying: 'Who goes there?'

When smell is intercepted, taste is paralysed: this is proved by three experiments which anyone may perform with equal success.

First Experiment: When the nasal membrane is irritated by a violent *coryza*, or cold in the head, taste is completely obliterated; no savour is discernible in what is swallowed, even though the tongue remains in its normal state.

Second Experiment: If the nose is held between finger and thumb during the act of eating, the sense of taste becomes curiously dulled and imperfect; by this means the most repulsive medicine may be taken almost without noticing.

Third Experiment: The same effect will be observed if, at the moment of swallowing, the tongue is kept pressed against the palate instead of being allowed to return to its normal position; in this case, the circulation of air is intercepted, the sense of smell is not aroused, and gustation does not take place.

Each of these effects is due to the same cause, the lack of cooperation from the sense of smell, with the result that only the succulent qualities of the sapid body are perceived, and not the odour which emanates from it.

11. Analysis of the Sensation of Taste

On the basis of the foregoing principles, I consider it certain that taste gives rise to sensations of three distinct orders, namely, *direct* sensation, *complete* sensation, and *considered* sensation.

The *direct* sensation is the first impression arising out of the immediate action of the organs of the mouth, while the substance to be tasted is still resting on the front part of the tongue.

The *complete* sensation is composed of the first impression, and the impression which follows when the food leaves its initial position and passes to the back of the mouth, assailing the whole organ with its taste and perfume.

Lastly, the *considered* sensation is the judgement passed by the brain on the impressions transmitted to it by the organ.

Let us put this theory to the test by observing what takes place when a man eats or drinks.

A man who eats a peach, for example, is first of all agreeably impressed by the smell emanating from it; he puts it into his mouth and experiences a sensation of freshness and acidity which incites him to continue; but it is not until the moment when he swallows, and the mouthful passes beneath the nasal channel, that the perfume is revealed to him, completing the sensations which every peach should cause. And finally, it is only after he has swallowed that he passes judgement on the experience, and says to himself 'That was delicious!'

The same is true of a man who drinks a glass of wine: while the wine is in his mouth he receives a pleasant but imperfect impression; it is only when he finishes swallowing it that he can really appreciate the taste and detect the particular bouquet of each kind of wine; and a few moments must elapse before the gourmand can say: 'That's good, or passable, or bad. ... Damn! It's Chambertin! ... Good grief! It's Suresnes!'

It is thus clearly in accordance with principle and following standard practice that your true connoisseur *sips* his wine; for as he pauses after each mouthful, he obtains the sum total of pleasure he would have experienced if he had emptied his glass at a single draught.

The same process occurs, but in a much more violent form, when the sense of taste is due to be disagreeably affected.

Consider the unfortunate patient forced by his doctor to drink a huge glass of black medicine, such as was normally prescribed in the days of Louis XIV.

Smell, that faithful sentry, warns him of the repulsive taste of the poisonous liquid; his eyes grow round as at the approach of danger; disgust shows on his lips, and his stomach begins to heave in anticipation. But the doctor urges him to be brave, he steels himself for the ordeal, rinses his throat with brandy, holds his nose, and drinks ...

So long as the pestiferous brew is in his mouth and lining the organ, the sensation is vague and his condition tolerable: but with the final mouthful an after-taste develops, the nauseous odours take effect, and every feature of the patient expresses a horror and distaste which nothing but the fear of death could make him face.

On the other hand, when an insipid drink is swallowed, such as a glass of water, for example, there is neither taste nor after-taste: we experience nothing and think nothing; we drink, and that is all.

12. *Order of the Different Impressions of Taste*

Taste is not as richly endowed as hearing, which can receive and compare several sounds at once; the action of taste is simple, that is to say it cannot be impressed by two flavours at the same time.

But it may be double and even multiple in succession; that is to say that in the same act of gutturation it is possible to experience a second and even a third sensation, one after the other, each fainter than the last, which we refer to by the words after-taste, bouquet, or fragrance; just as, when a key-note is struck, the trained ear can distinguish one or more series of consonances, the number of which has not yet been discovered for certain.

The careless, hasty eater never discerns the impressions of the second category; they are the exclusive apanage of a chosen few, who by this means can classify in order of excellence the various substances submitted for their approval.

These fugitive impressions linger for a long time in the organ of taste; the Professors, without being aware of it, take up an appropriate position, and it is always with neck out-stretched and nose to larboard that they utter their decrees.

13. *Pleasures Occasioned by Taste*

Let us now cast a philosophical glance at the pleasure or pain of which taste may be the occasion.

We are faced first of all with the application of that sad but universal truth, that man is far better equipped for suffering than for pleasure.

Thus the injection of tart, sour, or bitter substances can

produce sensations of extreme pain and anguish. It is even said that hydrocyanic acid only kills so swiftly because it causes a pain so acute that the vital forces cannot endure it without extinction.

Agreeable sensations, on the other hand, cover a very limited range; and although there is an appreciable difference between what is insipid and what pleases our taste, the interval is not very wide between what is acknowledged to be good and what is considered excellent; for example, in the first category, a tough, dry piece of boiled beef; in the second, a piece of veal; in the third, a pheasant cooked to a turn.

And yet of all our senses, taste, such as Nature has created it, remains the one which, on the whole, gives us the maximum of delight: ·

1. Because the pleasure of eating is the only one which, enjoyed in moderation, is not followed by weariness;

2. Because it is of all times, all ages, and all conditions;

3. Because it recurs of necessity at least once a day, and may without inconvenience be repeated twice or three times within the same space of time;

4. Because it can be enjoyed in company with all our other pleasures, and can even console us for their absence;

5. Because the impressions which it receives are at once more durable and more dependent on our will;

6. And lastly because, when we eat, we experience an indefinable and peculiar sensation of well-being, arising out of an instinctive awareness that through what we are eating we are repairing our losses and prolonging our existence.

This theme will be more fully developed in a chapter in which we shall particularly discuss the pleasures of the table, taken at the point to which modern civilization has brought them.

14. The Supremacy of Man

We were brought up in the comfortable belief that of all walking, swimming, crawling, or flying creatures, man has the most perfect sense of taste.

This faith is in danger of being undermined.

Doctor Gall, relying on I know not what evidence, maintains that there are animals in which the gustative apparatus is more fully developed, and therefore more perfect than man's.

This is an unwelcome doctrine to our ears, and smacks of heresy.

Man, by divine right King of all Nature, for whose benefit the earth was covered and made populous, must necessarily be equipped with an organ capable of enjoying the sapidity of all his subjects.

The low intelligence of animals is matched by the crudity of their tongues: the fish's tongue is no more than a mobile bone; that of birds, for the most part, membraneous cartilage; in quadrupeds it often has a rough or scaly surface, and is incapable of circumflex movements.

The tongue of man, on the contrary, by its delicate texture and the various membranes with which it is closely surrounded, clearly reveals the sublime nature of the functions for which it is intended.

Moreover, I have found it to be capable of at least three distinct movements, namely *projection, rotation,* and *exploration.* The first takes place when the tip of the tongue emerges from between the lips; the second, when the tongue makes a circular movement within the space bounded by the inside of the cheeks and the palate; the third when it curves upwards or downwards to pick up fragments of food lodged in the semicircular canal formed by the lips and gums.

Animals are limited in their tastes: some live on nothing but vegetables, others eat only flesh, others again feed exclusively on grain; not one of them has any notion of composite savours.

Man, on the contrary, is *omnivorous*; everything that is edible is at the mercy of his vast appetite; hence, as an immediate consequence, he must possess powers of degustation proportionate to the extensive calls due to be made on them. Sure enough, the machinery of taste attains a rare perfection in man; and to be convinced of the fact, let us watch it in action.

As soon as an esculent substance is introduced into the mouth, it is confiscated, gas and juice, beyond recall.

The lips cut off its retreat; the teeth seize it and crush it; it is soaked with saliva; the tongue kneads it and turns it over; an intake of breath pushes it towards the gullet; the tongue lifts it to help it on its way; its fragrance is enjoyed by the sense of smell as it goes by, and down it plunges to the stomach, there to undergo further transformations; and throughout the whole of this operation not one particle, not one drop, not one atom had escaped the attention of the apparatus of taste.

It is this perfection which makes man the only gourmand in the whole of Nature.

This gourmandism is even contagious, and man transmits it readily enough to the animals which he has appropriated for his own use, and which have become to some extent his companions, such as elephants, dogs, cats, and even parrots.

If certain animals have a thicker tongue, a more developed palate, or a wider throat, it is because their tongue, in its muscular function, is destined to lift heavier weights, their palate to compress and their throat to swallow larger mouthfuls; but by no acceptable analogy can it be deduced from this that their sense of taste is more perfect.

Moreover, since taste can only be gauged by the nature of the sensations it transmits to the centre of feeling, the impression received by an animal is not to be compared with that received by a man; the latter, being at once the clearer and more precise of the two, necessarily implies that his transmitting apparatus is of superior quality.

Finally, what more can be desired of a faculty so delicate that the gourmands of ancient Rome were able to distinguish, by the difference in taste, a fish caught between the bridges from one caught lower down the river? Have we not men among us today who have discovered the peculiar savour of the leg on which a partridge rests its weight while it sleeps? And are we not surrounded by gourmands who can tell the latitude in which the grapes of any given wine

ripened as surely as any pupil of Biot or Arago can foretell
an eclipse?

What follows from all this? Why, that we must render
unto Caesar that which is Caesar's, proclaim man the *great
gourmand of Nature*, and not be astonished if now and again
the good doctor followed the example of Homer: *Auch
zuweilen schläfert der gute Gott.*[1]

15. Method Adopted by the Author

So far we have only considered taste in respect of its physical
constitution; and apart from certain anatomical details, of
which few readers will regret the absence, we have been
scrupulously scientific. But our self-imposed task is by no
means ended there, for it is above all from its moral history
that this restorative sense derives its importance and its
glory.

Accordingly, we have made a careful analysis of that
history, and arranged the theories and facts of which it is
composed in such a way as to provide instruction without tears.

Thus in the chapters which follow we shall show how the
sensations, by dint of repetition and reflection, have improved the organ and extended the range of its powers; and
how the necessity of eating, which at first was just an instinct, has become a very passion, and obtained considerable
influence over everything to do with society.

We shall also describe how all the sciences which are concerned with the composition of things have classified and set
apart those things which affect the organ of taste, and how
travellers have moved towards the same goal, by offering us
substances which Nature seemed to have intended never to
combine.

We shall follow chemistry into our subterranean laboratories, where that science enlightened our cooks, established principles, created new methods, and revealed
hitherto hidden causes.

1. 'God also sleeps at times.' [Ed.]

Finally, we shall see how by the combined power of time and experience a new science suddenly arose to nourish, restore, preserve, persuade, and console us; a science which, not content with strewing flowers in the path of the individual, also contributes in no small measure to the strength and prosperity of empires.

If in the midst of these solemn lucubrations an amusing anecdote, a happy memory, or some adventure recalled from a stormy life, should appear at the tip of our pen, we shall let it flow, to offer our attentive readers a moment's respite. The number of those readers does not alarm us: on the contrary, we shall take pleasure in conversing with them, for if they are men, we feel sure that they are as indulgent as they are cultured, and if they are women, they must needs be charming.

Here the Professor, full of his subject, lowered his hand and ascended to the upper regions.

He went back down the ages, and visited in their cradles the sciences which minister to the gratification of taste. He followed their progress through the night of time, and perceiving that, for the delights they had to offer, former ages were less fortunate than those which came after them, he seized his lyre, and chanted, in the Dorian manner, the historical Elegy which will be found among the *Miscellanea* at the end of this work.

3. On Gastronomy

16. Origin of the Sciences

The sciences are not like Minerva, who sprang fully armed from the brain of Jupiter; they are daughters of time, and take shape imperceptibly, first by the combination of methods learned from experience, and later by the discovery of principles deduced from the combination of those methods.

Thus, the first greybeards whose wisdom caused them to be summoned to the bedsides of the sick, and whose compassion led them to dress the sores of the afflicted, were also the first doctors.

The Egyptian shepherds who observed that certain stars, at the end of a certain period of time, returned to the same positions in the sky, were the first astronomers.

The man who first expressed in characters the simple proposition *two plus two equals four* created mathematics, that mighty science which raised man to the throne of the universe.

In the course of the last sixty years several new sciences have been added to our system of knowledge, among them stereotomy, descriptive geometry, and the chemistry of gases.

All these sciences are the product of countless generations, and they will progress all the more steadily in the future in that printing will preserve them from all risk of regression. Who knows, for example, but that the chemistry of gases may eventually master those rebel elements, combine them one with another in hitherto untried proportions, and so obtain substances and results which would greatly extend the limit of our powers?

17. *Origin of Gastronomy*

Gastronomy arose in her turn, and all her sisters gathered round to welcome her.

For what could be refused to her who supports us from the cradle to the grave, who lends new delights to love, strengthens the bonds of friendship, disarms hatred, facilitates the conduct of affairs, and offers us, during our brief span of life, the only pleasure which, having no aftermath of weariness, remains to refresh us after all the rest?

So long as the preparing of food was exclusively entrusted to paid servants, and the secrets of those preparations confined below stairs; so long as cooks kept their knowledge to themselves and only recipes were made public, the results of such labours were simply the products of an art.

But then at last, perhaps too late, men of science came upon the scene.

They examined, analysed, and classified all foodstuffs, and reduced them to their basic elements.

They plumbed the mysteries of assimilation, followed inert matter through all its metamorphoses, and saw how it might come to life.

They observed the effects of diet, both passing and permanent, for a day, a month, or a whole lifetime.

They noted its influence even on the faculty of thought, whether the mind was affected by the senses, or responded itself without the cooperation of its organs; and out of all these labours a grand theory emerged, embracing all mankind and that part of creation which can be made animal.

While these things were happening in the laboratories of learned men, people took to saying in the salons that a science which nourished men was at least as valuable as that which taught how to kill them; poets sang the pleasures of the table, and books with good cheer as their subject offered their readers views of greater depth and maxims of more general interest.

Such were the circumstances which preceded the advent of Gastronomy.

18. Definition of Gastronomy

Gastronomy is the reasoned comprehension of everything connected with the nourishment of man.

Its aim is to obtain the preservation of man by means of the best possible nourishment.

It attains this object by giving guidance, according to certain principles, to all who seek, provide, or prepare substances which may be turned into food.

Gastronomy, in fact, is the motive force behind farmers, vinegrowers, fishermen, and huntsmen, not to mention the great family of cooks, under whatever title they may disguise their employment as preparers of food.

Gastronomy pertains:

To natural history, through its classification of foodstuffs;

To physics, through its examination of the composition and qualities of foodstuffs;

To chemistry, through the various processes of analysis and decomposition to which it subjects them;

To cookery, through the art of preparing dishes and making them agreeable to the taste;

To commerce, through its quest for the means of buying what it consumes at the lowest possible price, and of retailing what it has to sell at the highest possible price;

Finally, to political economy, through its value as a source of revenue and a means of exchange between nations.

Gastronomy governs the whole life of man; for the tears of the new-born child are for its nurse's breast, and the dying man derives pleasure from the final potion, which, alas, he will never digest.

Its influence is felt by all classes of society; for while it is gastronomy which rules the banquets of kings, it is also gastronomy which stipulates how many minutes a humble egg should be boiled.

The material subject of gastronomy is everything which can be eaten; its immediate object, the preservation of the individual; and its methods of attaining that object, cultivation which produces foodstuffs, commerce which exchanges them, industry which prepares them, and experience which devises the means of turning them to the best possible account.

19. Various Objects of Gastronomy

Gastronomy examines taste as an organ of both pleasure and pain; it has discovered the gradual increase of excitement to which taste is liable, regulated the rate of that increase, and fixed upon a limit beyond which no self-respecting person should go.

It also examines the effect of food on man's character, his imagination, his wit, his judgement, his courage, and his perceptions, whether he be awake or asleep, active or at rest.

It is gastronomy which determines the point of esculence of every foodstuff, for they are not all palatable in identical circumstances.

Some are best taken before attaining their final stage of development, such as capers, asparagus, sucking-pigs, spoon-fed pigeons, and other animals normally eaten very young; some when they have reached their full degree of perfection, such as melons, the majority of fruits, mutton, beef, and the flesh of all full-grown animals; some when decomposition has set in, such as medlars, woodcock, and above all pheasant; and finally some, like potatoes and the manioc plant, after their noxious qualities have been removed.

It is gastronomy too which classifies all these substances according to their various qualities, indicates those which may be eaten together, and by measuring their different degrees of ability, distinguishes those which should form the basis of our meals from those which are simply accessories, and those again which, without being essential to our existence, none the less form an agreeable distraction, and have become the indispensable accompaniment to any convivial gathering.

It is no less closely concerned with the various drinks which fall to our lot, according to time, place, and climate.

It teaches us how to prepare and preserve them, and above all, the order in which we should imbibe them in order to obtain a steady increase of enjoyment, up to the point where pleasure ends and excess begins.

It is gastronomy which makes a study of men and things, in order to transport everything that deserves to be known from one place to another, so that a well-ordained banquet seems like an epitome of the world, every part of which is duly represented.

20. Uses of Gastronomical Knowledge

Some knowledge of gastronomy is necessary to all men, since it adds to the sum of human pleasures; its usefulness increases in so far as it is applied to the higher ranks of society, and it is indispensable to persons with considerable incomes who entertain on a large scale, whether they do so for political reasons, or following their own inclination, or in obedience to the laws of fashion.

They derive this special advantage from their knowledge, that something of their own personality goes into the way in which their table is kept; up to a certain point they can supervise those persons in whom they must necessarily place their trust, and in many cases they can even direct operations.

The Prince de Soubise decided to hold a reception one day; it was to end with a supper, and he sent for the bill of fare.

His steward appeared at his bedside in the morning with an ornate card on which the first item to meet the prince's eye was 'fifty hams'.

'Bertrand,' he said, 'have you gone mad? Fifty hams! Do you want to regale the whole of my regiment?'

'No, Your Highness; only one ham will appear on the table; but I shall need all the rest for my brown sauce, my stock, my garnishings, my ...'

'Bertrand, you're a thief, and I shan't pass that item.'

'But Your Highness,' answered the artist, hardly able to

contain his anger, 'you don't know our resources! You have only to say the word, and I'll take all those fifty hams you object to and put them into a crystal phial no bigger than my thumb!'

What answer could be made to so positive an assertion? The prince smiled, nodded, and the item was allowed to pass.

21. Influence of Gastronomy on Affairs

It is well known that among men whose way of life is still close to the state of nature, no affair of importance is discussed anywhere but at table; it is in the midst of their feasts that savages decide the question of peace or war; and without going so far afield, we can see our villagers conducting all their business at the inn.

This fact has not escaped the notice of those who frequently have occasion to deal with affairs of importance; they are aware of the difference between a hungry man and a man well fed, and know that the table establishes a kind of tie between the two parties to a discussion: after a meal a man is more apt to receive certain impressions, to submit to certain influences; and this is the origin of political gastronomy. Meals have become a means of government, and the fate of nations has often been sealed at a banquet. This is neither a paradox nor even a novelty, but a plain statement of fact. Read the historians, from Herodotus down to our own day, and you will see that there has never been a great event, not even excepting conspiracies, which was not conceived, worked out, and organized over a meal.

22. An Academy of Gastronomes

Such, at a glance, is the realm of gastronomy, a domain fertile in all manner of results, and certain to be enriched in the future by the discoveries and labours of the men of learning who will cultivate it; for there can be no doubt that before many years have passed, gastronomy will have its own academicians, universities, professors and prizes.

First, some rich and zealous gastronome will institute periodical meetings beneath his own roof, where the most learned theorists will gather together with practising artists to discuss and examine the various aspects of the science of *food*.

Soon (for such is the history of all academies) the Government will intervene to offer its patronage and lay down rules, seizing the occasion to give the people compensation for all the children made fatherless by guns and all the Ariadnes saddened by the call to arms.

Happy the man who shall give his name to that academy! That name will go down from age to age, linked with those of Noah, Bacchus, Triptolemus, and all the other bene-factors of humanity; he will be among ministers what Henri IV is among kings, and his praise will be in every *mouth*, without any law to make that obligatory.

4. On Appetite

23. Definition of Appetite

Movement and life are the cause of a continuous wastage of substance in every living body; and the human body, that complicated machine, would soon break down if Providence had not equipped it with a device for warning it when its strength is no longer equal to its needs.

This warning device is appetite. That is the name we give to the first indication of the need for food.

Appetite is heralded by a certain languor in the stomach and a slight feeling of fatigue.

At the same time the brain dwells on objects analogous to its needs; the memory recalls things which have been pleasant to the taste; the imagination pictures them, as it were in a dream. This condition is not without charm; and we have heard thousands of adepts exclaim joyously: 'Oh, what a pleasure it is to have a good appetite, when you know that an excellent meal is waiting for you!'

In the meantime, the whole machinery of nourishment is set in motion: the stomach grows sensitive; the gastric juices rise, the internal gases are noisily displaced; the mouth fills with saliva; and all the digestive powers are up in arms, like soldiers only waiting for the word of command to go into action. A few moments more, and spasmodic movements will begin; there will be yawning, stomach pangs, and finally hunger.

It is possible to observe every phase of these various conditions in any room where people are being kept waiting for dinner.

They are so natural that the most exquisite politeness cannot disguise the symptoms; and hence my aphorism, 'The most indispensable quality in a cook is punctuality.'

24. Anecdote

I shall illustrate this solemn maxim by recalling certain observations I once made at a dinner party, *quorum pars magna fui*, and where the pleasure of observing saved me from the agonies of suffering.

I was invited one day to dinner at the house of an important public official. The invitation was for half past five, and at the proper time everyone had arrived, for it was well known that our host liked his guests to be punctual, and sometimes scolded late-comers.

On arrival I was struck by the air of consternation which reigned among the company; people were whispering into one another's ears and looking out of the window into the courtyard, and some faces wore an expression of stupefaction. Something extraordinary had obviously occurred.

I went up to one of the guests, whom I thought the most likely to be able to satisfy my curiosity, and asked him what was happening. 'Alas,' he replied, in tones of deepest affliction, 'his Grace has been summoned to a Council of State; he left a moment ago, and who knows when he may be back?' 'Is that all?' I replied, with an air of unconcern which was far from revealing what I really felt. 'Why, that's a matter of a quarter of an hour at the most; some piece of information must be needed which only he can supply; they know that this is an official dinner, and they have no reason to keep us fasting.' So I spoke; but in my heart of hearts I was ill at ease, and I would have preferred to be almost anywhere else.

The first hour went by quickly enough; friends and acquaintances sat down together, exhausted the trivial subjects of conversation, and speculated as to the reason for our good host's summons to the Tuileries.

During the second hour, symptoms of impatience began to appear; anxious glances were exchanged, and the first murmurs of complaint were heard, coming from three or four guests who, having found nowhere to sit down, were not in the best position for waiting.

By the third hour discontent was rife, and everyone was complaining. 'When will he be back?' said one. 'What can he be thinking of?' said another. 'This will be the death of me,' said a third. And every guest kept asking himself the unanswerable question: 'To leave, or not to leave?'

With the fourth hour the symptoms became more pronounced; arms were stretched, to the peril of neighbours' eyes; loud yawns could be heard on all sides; every face was flushed with concentration; and no one listened when I ventured to say that he whose absence was the cause of our misery was doubtless the unhappiest of us all.

Attention was momentarily distracted by an apparition. One of the guests, who was on closer terms with our host than the rest, penetrated as far as the kitchens; he came back breathless and looking as if the end of the world were at hand. Almost inarticulate, in that muffled tone of voice which is a compromise between fear of making a noise and the desire to be heard, he exclaimed: 'His Grace left without giving any instructions, and however long he is away, dinner will not be served before his return.' He spoke; and the consternation caused by his speech will not be surpassed by the effect of the trumpet of the Last Judgement.

Among all these martyrs, the unhappiest was the worthy d'Aigrefeuille, well known to all Paris in those days; his whole body was a mass of suffering, and the anguish of Laocoön was visible on his features. Pale, distracted, seeing nothing, he perched on a chair, folded his little hands across his great belly, and closed his eyes, not to sleep but to wait for death.

But death did not come. About ten o'clock we heard a carriage rolling into the courtyard; everyone stood up spontaneously. Sadness was turned to joy, and five minutes later we were seated at table.

But the time for appetite was past. It was as if we were surprised to find ourselves beginning dinner at such an untimely hour; our jaws failed to work with those isochronous movements which mark an accustomed task, and I later learned that this was a source of some discomfort to several of the guests.

The recommended procedure in such a case is to avoid eating immediately after the hindrance is removed; a glass of sugared water or a cup of broth should be swallowed first, to soothe the stomach; then an interval of ten or fifteen minutes should elapse, or else the constricted organ will be crushed by the load of food thrust upon it.

25. Large Appetites

When we read in early literature of the preparations made for the entertainment of two or three persons, and the enormous helpings of food offered to a single guest, it is difficult to avoid the belief that the men who lived nearer than ourselves to the cradle of the world were also endowed with appetites far larger than our own.

Appetites in those days were supposed to increase in proportion to the dignity of the individual; and a man who was served with the entire back of a five-year-old bull would drink from a cup so heavy that he could scarcely lift it.

A few individuals living in more recent times have borne witness to what was done in the past; and historical records are full of examples of almost incredible voracity, applied even to the most repugnant objects.

I will spare my readers these somewhat disgusting details, and instead relate two particular feats of which I myself was a witness, and which call for no blind faith on their part.

About forty years ago I paid a flying visit to the parish priest of Bregnier, a man of great stature, whose appetite was renowned throughout the region.

Although it was barely midday when I arrived, I found him already seated at table. He had finished the soup and boiled beef, and these two inevitable courses had been followed by a leg of mutton *à la royale*, together with a fine capon and a copious salad.

As soon as I appeared he offered to have a place laid for me, but I declined, and I did well as it turned out; for alone and unaided he briskly put away all there was, namely, the leg of mutton down to the ivory, the capon down to the bone, and the salad down to the bottom of the dish.

A large white cheese was then placed before him, in which he made an angular breach of ninety degrees, washing it down with a bottle of wine and a jug of water; then he took a rest.

What particularly pleased me was that throughout this operation, which lasted about three quarters of an hour, the venerable priest seemed quite unhurried. The huge mouthfuls he tossed into his great maw did not prevent him from laughing and talking; and he devoured everything that had been put before him with no more fuss than if he had been eating a brace of larks.

It was the same with General Bisson, who used to drink eight bottles of wine every morning at breakfast without turning a hair; he had a larger glass than anyone else, and he emptied it more often; but he gave the impression that he did so without thinking, and the business of imbibing two gallons of liquid no more prevented him from joking and issuing his orders than if it had been a glass of water.

General Bisson reminds me of my fellow countryman, the gallant General Prosper Sibuet, who died on the field of honour in 1813 at the passage of the Bober, after serving for many years as chief *aide-de-camp* to General Masséna.

Prosper was eighteen years old, and the possessor of one of those splendid appetites by which Nature proclaims that she is building up a fine specimen of manhood, when one evening he entered the kitchen of a certain Genin, the host of an inn where the old men of Belley used to meet to eat chestnuts and drink the new white wine of the district, the so-called *vin bourru*.

A magnificent turkey, golden brown, and done to a turn, had just been taken off the spit; the smell of it would have tempted a saint.

The old men, who were no longer hungry, paid little attention to it; but young Prosper's digestive powers were immediately affected. His mouth began to water, and he exclaimed: 'I have only just risen from table, but I'll wager I can eat that fat turkey alone and unaided.'

'*Sez vosu mezé, z'u payo*,' retorted Bouvier du Bouchet, a stout farmer who was present, '*è sez vas caca en rotaz, i-zet vo ket pairé et may ket mezarai la restaz*.'[1]

The operation began forthwith. The young athlete neatly detached a wing, swallowed it in two mouthfuls, cleaned his teeth by eating the neck of the bird, and drank a glass of wine by way of an interlude.

Next he attacked a leg, ate it as calmly as the wing, and tossed down a second glass of wine to smooth the way for the rest of the fowl.

The second wing then followed the first; and the officiant, growing more and more animated, was seizing the last remaining limb, when the unfortunate farmer cried out in dismay:

'*Hai! ze vaie praou qu'izet fotu; m'ez, monche Chibouet, poez kaet zu daive paiet, lessé m'en a m'en mesiet on mocho*.'[2]

Prosper was as good a fellow then as he afterwards became a good soldier; he granted the request of his antagonist, who was left with the still considerable carcase of the fowl, and paid for both food and drinks with a good grace.

General Sibuet was very fond of relating this feat of youthful prowess; he used to say that he had only granted the farmer's request as a matter of courtesy, and that he felt perfectly capable of winning the wager without this assistance. Certainly what remained of his appetite at the age of forty left no doubt as to the truth of this assertion.

1. 'If you eat it straight off, I'll pay for it, but if you give up on the way, you'll pay, and I'll eat what is left.'

2. 'Alas! I see that I've lost; but, Monsieur Sibuet, since I've got to pay, at least leave me a morsel to eat.'

I am glad to quote this sample of the dialect of Bugey, in which the *th* of the Greeks and English is used, and, in *praou* and other similar words, a diphthong which exists in no other language, and the sound of which cannot be expressed by any known character. (See the third volume of the *Transactions of the Society of French Antiquaries*.)

5. On Food in General

26. Definitions

What do we mean by food?

POPULAR REPLY: Food is whatever provides nourishment.

SCIENTIFIC REPLY: By food we mean those substances which, on being submitted to the stomach, can be animalized by digestion, and so repair the losses suffered by the human body through the wear and tear of life.

Thus the distinctive quality of food consists in the property of undergoing animal assimilation.

27. Analytical Studies

The animal world and the vegetable world are those which have so far provided food for the human race. From minerals, only remedies and poisons have been extracted as yet.

Since the time when analytical chemistry became an exact science, a great deal has been discovered about the dual nature of the elements composing our bodies and the substances which Nature seems to have created to repair the losses we suffer.

There was a close analogy between these two lines of research, since man is largely composed of the same substances as the animals he eats; and it was also essential to seek in vegetables the affinities which made them, too, capable of animalization.

The most detailed and praiseworthy researches have been carried out in these two spheres, and it has been found possible to break down both the human body and the foodstuffs by which it is strengthened, first into their secondary parts, and then into their basic elements; beyond that point we have not so far been allowed to penetrate.

Here I had originally intended to insert a little treatise on the chemistry of food, and to inform my readers into how many thousandths of carbon, hydrogen, etc., they themselves and the food which nourishes them could be reduced; but I was prevented from doing so by the reflection that I could scarcely fulfil such a task without copying out the excellent chemical treatises which are already available to everyone. I was also afraid of boring my readers with a list of barren details; I have therefore confined myself to a reasoned nomenclature, reserving the right to insert here and there a few chemical formulae in less complicated and more intelligible terms.

28. Osmazome[1]

The most signal service rendered by chemistry to the science of food is the discovery, or rather the precise comprehension of osmazome.

Ozmazome is that highly sapid part of meat which is soluble in cold water, as distinct from the extractive parts, which are only soluble in boiling water.

It is in osmazome that the principal merit of a good soup resides; the brown of roast meat is due to the caramelization of osmazome; and it is osmazome that gives its rich flavour to venison and game.

It is found chiefly in full-grown animals with dark flesh, or *chairs faites,* and scarcely ever in the lamb, the sucking pig, the chicken, or even in the white meat of the larger birds; this is why the true connoisseur has always preferred the fleshy thigh, or *entrecuisse*: the instinct of taste anticipated science.

It was a similar foreknowledge of osmazome that led to many a cook's dismissal, for tampering with the first

1. *Osmazome,* the name given by the French chemist Jacques Thénard to what was in fact creatin, was a word as fashionable in Brillat-Savarin's day as *vitamin* a century later. [Translator]

bouillon; it was the same prescience which made the reputation of the richest soups, and gave rise to the use of *croûtes au pot* to fortify a broth; and it also led Canon Chevrier to invent pans provided with lock and key, that famous canon whose Friday spinach was always cooked on the previous Sunday, and put back on the fire every day with a new dressing of fresh butter.

Finally, the importance of husbanding this substance, even before it was known to exist, led to the coining of the maxim that to make a good broth, the pot must only *smile,* a curiously refined expression for its country of origin.

Osmazome, only discovered after delighting our forefathers for countless ages, can be compared with alcohol, which made many generations drunk before it was found that it could be extracted in its crude state by distillation.

Osmazome, after treatment by boiling water, leaves what is called extractive matter; and it is this latter product, combined with osmazome, which forms meat gravy.

Elements of Food

Fibre is what forms the tissue of flesh and is visible after cooking. It resists boiling water, and preserves its shape although stripped of part of its outer covering. To carve meat cleanly care must be taken to keep a right angle, or very near it, between the fibre and the blade of the knife; meat so carved has a more pleasing appearance, tastes better, and is more easily chewed.

Bones are chiefly composed of gelatine and phosphate of lime.

The quantity of gelatine diminishes with advancing years. By the age of seventy, the bones are only a sort of flawed marble; this is what renders them so brittle, and makes it incumbent on old people to avoid any risk of falling.

Albumen is found in both flesh and blood, it congeals at a temperature of less than 122 degrees; the scum on the surface of beef broth is formed of it.

Gelatine occurs equally in the bones and the soft and cartilaginous parts of the body; its distinctive quality is that of congealing at the normal temperature of the atmosphere; two and a half parts in a hundred of hot water are enough to produce this result.

Gelatine is the basis of all fat and lean jellies, blancmanges, and other similar preparations.

Fat is a concrete oil which forms in the interstices of the cellular tissue; in certain animals, such as pigs, fowls, ortolans, and garden warblers, either through a natural predisposition or by artificial means, it coheres in a mass; and in some of these animals, losing its insipidity, it acquires a delicate and extremely pleasant aroma.

Blood is composed of an albuminous serum, fibrin, a little gelatine, and a little osmazome; it congeals in hot water, and becomes a highly nutritious food (e.g. black pudding).

All the elements we have just listed are common to man and the animals he is accustomed to eat. It is thus not at all surprising that an animal diet should be eminently invigorating and fortifying; for its component parts, being very similar to our own, and already animalized, can be easily animalized a second time when they are subjected to the vital action of our digestive organs.

29. The Vegetable World

The vegetable world, however, offers no less variety and resources in the way of nourishment.

Starch is admirably nourishing, especially when it is unmixed with foreign elements.

By starch we mean the flour or powder obtained from cereal grain, leguminous plants, and several kinds of root, of which the potato is as yet the most important.

Starch is the basis of bread, cakes, and all sorts of mash, and thus forms a most important part of the nourishment of almost every race on earth.

It has been remarked that a diet of starch softens a man's fibres, and even robs him of courage. The Indians, who live almost exclusively on rice, and have never resisted any attempt to subjugate them, are often cited as a case in point.

Almost all domestic animals eat starch greedily, and they, on the contrary, are singularly fortified by it, because it is a more substantial food than the dried or green vegetables on which they are accustomed to feed.

Sugar is no less important, whether taken as a food or as a medicine.

This substance, which was once confined to the Indies and the colonies, became indigenous here at the beginning of this century. It has been found in the grape, the turnip, the chestnut, and above all the beetroot; so that it is not too much to say that Europe could be self-supporting in this respect, and independent of America or the Indies. This is an eminent service rendered by science to society, and may well have more extensive results in the future. (See the section on 'Sugar'.)

Sugar, both in its solid form and in the various plants in which Nature has secreted it, is extremely nutritious; animals are fond of it, and the English, who give a great deal of it to their racehorses, have found that it improves their staying-power in the various tests to which they are subjected.

In the days of Louis XIV sugar was only to be found in apothecaries' shops, but it has since given rise to a number of lucrative trades, such as those of pastrycook, confectioner, and soft-drink manufacturer.

Sweet oils are also derived from the vegetable world; they do not become esculent until mixed with other substances, and should be regarded chiefly as seasoning.

Gluten, which is particularly found in wheat, contributes greatly to the fermentation of the bread of which it forms part; chemists have gone so far as to declare it to be animal in nature.

There are cakes made in Paris for children and birds, and in some parts of France for adults, in which gluten predominates, due to part of the starch having been extracted by means of water.

Mucilage owes its nutritious quality to the various substances of which it is the vehicle.

Gum can be taken as food, when the need arises; which is not surprising, since it contains very nearly the same elements as sugar.

The vegetable gelatine which is extracted from several kinds of fruit, notably apples, gooseberries, quinces, and a few more, can also be used as food; it is improved by the addition of sugar, but is never as valuable as the jellies made from bones, horns, calves' feet, and fish-glue. This food is generally light, emollient, and wholesome; as a result it is nearly always to be found in kitchen or pantry.

Difference between Feasting and Fasting

With the exception of gravy, which, as we have seen, is composed of osmazome and extractive matter, we find in fish most of the substances mentioned above as occurring in the land-animals, such as fibrin, gelatine, and albumen; so that it would be fair to say that it is gravy that distinguishes feasting from fasting.

Another peculiarity of the fasting diet is that fish also contain a notable quantity of phosphorus and hydrogen, that is to say of the most combustible elements in nature. Whence it follows that ichthyophagy is a heating diet; and this suggests that there was some justification for the praise given in the past to certain religious orders, whose diet was directly contrary to the most fragile of their vows.

30. A Personal Observation

I shall say no more about this physiological question; but I must not omit to mention an observation of mine which can easily be verified.

A few years ago I went to see a country house in a little hamlet on the outskirts of Paris, situated on the banks of the Seine facing the island of Saint-Denis, and consisting mainly of eight fishermen's huts. I was struck by the number of children whom I saw swarming about on the road.

I expressed my surprise to the boatman who was ferrying me across the river.

'Sir,' he replied, 'there are only eight families of us, and we have fifty-three children, forty-nine of them girls, and only four boys; of those four one is mine, and there he is.' So saying, he stood up with an air of triumph, and showed me a little fellow of five or six, lying in the bows of the boat and eating raw crayfish. The name of that little hamlet is —.

From this observation, which goes back more than ten years, and from a few others which I cannot describe so easily, I have come to believe that the effect of a fish diet on sexual activity is probably more stimulating than substantial; and my opinion is supported by the fact that quite recently Doctor Bailly proved, by a series of observations extending over nearly a century, that whenever the annual census of births contains a much larger number of girls than boys, the superabundance of females has always been due to debilitating circumstances. This might well be the origin of the jokes which from time immemorial have been made at the expense of the husband whose wife gives birth to a daughter.

Much more might be said on the subject of foodstuffs in general and the various modifications which they may be made to undergo by admixture; but I hope that what I have already said will more than satisfy the majority of my readers. The others I will refer to the *ex professo* treatise, and I will conclude with two considerations which are not devoid of interest.

The first is that animalization takes place in much the same way as vegetation; in other words, the flow of restorative matter created by digestion is absorbed in various ways through the sieves and suckers with which our organs are equipped, and becomes flesh, nail, bone, or hair, just as the same soil sprinkled with the same water produces a radish, a lettuce, or a dandelion, depending on the seeds sown by the gardener.

The second is that in the organism of life we do not obtain the same results as in absolute chemistry; for the organs whose function is to produce life and movement act powerfully on the elements subjected to them.

But Nature, who likes to wrap herself in veils and halt us on the very threshold of discovery, has concealed the laboratory in which she works her transformations; and considering that the human body contains lime, sulphur, phosphorus, iron, and a dozen other substances besides, it is hard to explain how all this can be sustained and renewed for several years on nothing but bread and water.

6. Specialities

31. Introduction

When I began to write, my list of contents was already drawn up, and my book complete in my head; but my progress has none the less been slow, because part of my time is devoted to more serious labours.

Meanwhile certain aspects of the subject which I believed to be my private province have been touched on by others; elementary books on chemistry and medicine have been made available to the general public, and doctrines which I expected to be the first to teach have become popular; for example, I had devoted several pages to the chemistry of the *pot-au-feu*, the substance of which is now to be found in several recently published works.

In consequence, I have had to revise that part of my book, reducing it to a few elementary principles, some theories which cannot be repeated too often, and certain observations culled from long experience, which will, I hope, be new to the majority of my readers.

32. Pot-au-feu, Potage, etc.

We apply the phrase *pot-au-feu* to a piece of beef boiled in slightly salted water in order to extract its soluble parts.

The liquid which is left at the end of the operation is called *bouillon*.

Finally, the meat from which the soluble part has been extracted is known as *bouilli*.

The water first of all dissolves part of the osmazome; then the albumen, which congeals just below 145 degrees, forming a scum which is usually removed; then the remainder of the osmazome, with the extractive matter of juice; and finally, a few portions of the outer covering of the fibres, which have come away under the continual pressure of the boiling liquid.

To make good *bouillon*, the water has to come to the boil slowly, to prevent the albumen from coagulating inside the meat before extraction; and it should boil almost imperceptibly, so that the various parts which are successively dissolved may be easily and thoroughly united.

Vegetables are added to the *bouillon* to bring out the flavour, and bread or noodles to make it more nutritious; the result is called *potage*.

Potage is a wholesome, light, nutritious food which agrees with everyone; it delights the stomach and stimulates its receptive and digestive faculties. Persons inclined to obesity, however, should take only *bouillon*.

It is generally agreed that nowhere can such good *potage* be obtained as in France; and my own travels have confirmed the truth of this saying. Not that there is anything surprising about that; for *potage* is the basis of the French national diet, and the experience of centuries has inevitably brought it to perfection.

33. On Bouilli

The *bouilli* is wholesome food, which rapidly appeases hunger, and is easy enough to digest; but it has little strength in itself, because the meat has lost part of its animalizable juices in the boiling.

As a general rule, it is found that beef which has been boiled has lost half its weight.

Persons who eat *bouilli* may be divided into four categories, as follows:

1. Victims of habit, who eat it because their parents ate it before them, and hope that their children will imitate them with the same implicit obedience;

2. Impatient persons, who detest inactivity at table, and have accordingly contracted the habit of falling upon the first foodstuff that comes to hand (*materiam subjectam*);

3. Careless persons, whom heaven has not blessed with the sacred flame; they regard meals as just part of the day's work, and put all dishes on the same level, sitting at table like oysters on an oyster-bank;

4. Greedy persons, who in an attempt to conceal the extent of their appetites, hastily cast a first victim into their stomach, to appease the devouring gastric fire within and to pave the way for the various consignments they intend to dispatch to the same destination.

Professors never eat *bouilli*, both out of respect for the principles of gastronomy and because they have often preached this undeniable truth to their pupils: 'Bouilli is meat without its juice.'[1]

34. On Poultry

I am a great partisan of secondary causes, and devoutly believe that the whole race of fowls was solely created to fill our larders and enrich our banquets.

It is undeniable that from quail to turkey-cock, wherever we meet with a member of this large family, we may be sure of finding food that is both light and savoury, and agrees equally with the convalescent and the man in the best of health; for who among us, after being condemned by a doctor to the diet of a desert father, has not revelled in a nice wing of chicken, the herald of his long-awaited return to social life?

We have not been content, however, with the natural qualities of the gallinaceous species; art has laid hands on them, and under the pretext of improving them, has condemned them to martyrdom. Not only do we take away their means of reproduction, but we keep them in solitary confinement, cast them into darkness, force them to eat willy-nilly, and so blow them up to a size for which they were never intended.

1. This truth is beginning to penetrate, and *bouilli* is no longer served by the self-respecting host; it has been replaced by a roast fillet, a turbot, or a *matelote*.

It must be admitted that this unnatural rotundity is also delicious, and that the tender succulence which makes them worthy of our finest tables is due to those reprehensible practices which we have just mentioned.

Thus improved, fowls are to the kitchen what his canvas is to the painter, or to charlatans the cap of Fortunatus; they are served up to us boiled, roasted, fried, hot or cold, whole or in pieces, with or without sauce, boned, skinned, or stuffed, and always with equal success.

Three districts of old-world France dispute the honour of furnishing the best fowls, namely, Caux, Le Mans, and Bresse.

As regards capons there is some doubt as to which is superior, and as a rule the one we are eating seems better than the rest; but as for pullets, there are none to compare with those of Bresse, known as *poulardes fines*; they are round as an apple, and all too rare in Paris, where they never come except in votive hampers.

35. On the Turkey

The turkey is undoubtedly one of the handsomest presents which the New World has offered to the Old.

Those people who insist on knowing more than anyone else maintain that the Romans were partial to the turkey, that it was served at Charlemagne's wedding-feast, and that it is therefore incorrect to praise the Jesuits for this savoury import.

One could answer these paradoxes with two simple facts:

1. The French name of the bird, *coq d'Inde*, clearly betrays its origin: for in the old days America was known as the West Indies;
2. The appearance of the bird, which is clearly outlandish.

No scientist could have any doubts on the question.

However, although for my part I was thoroughly convinced, I conducted extensive research into the subject, which I shall spare the reader, and which led me to the following conclusions:

1. That the turkey appeared in Europe towards the end of the seventeenth century;
2. That it was imported by the Jesuits, who bred it in large numbers, especially on one of their farms in the neighbourhood of Bourges;
3. That from there it gradually spread over the whole of France; which is why in many regions the popular word for turkey was and still is *jésuite*;
4. That America is the only place where the turkey has been found wild and in a state of nature (there are none in Africa);
5. That in North America, where it is very common, it is reared either from eggs which are found and hatched out, or from young birds which are caught in the forest and tamed; reared in this way it is nearer to the natural state, and retains its primitive plumage.

Convinced by these points, I would like to observe that we owe a double debt of gratitude to the good Fathers, for they were also responsible for the importation of quinine, which in English is called Jesuit's-bark.

In the course of my researches I also discovered that the acclimatization of the species in France was a gradual process. Enlightened students of the subject have informed me that about the middle of the last century, out of every twenty turkeys hatched, not more than ten grew to maturity; whereas today, all things being equal, the proportion is fifteen in twenty. Rain-storms are particularly fatal to them. The heavy rain-drops, driven by the wind, beat upon their soft, unprotected skulls and kill them.

36. On Turkey-Lovers

The turkey is the largest of our domestic fowls, and if not the most delicately flavoured at least the most savoury.

It has also the unique merit of attracting all classes of society.

When the vine-grower or the ploughman wants a treat on some long winter evening, what do we see roasting over a bright fire in the kitchen where the table is laid? A turkey.

When the hard-working artisan invites a few friends to his house to enjoy a holiday which is all the more precious for being rare, what is sure to be the principal dish of the feast? A turkey, stuffed with sausages or Lyons chestnuts.

And in the high places of gastronomy, at those select gatherings where politics are forced to give way to dissertations upon taste, what do the guests hope for and long for as the second course? A truffled turkey!... And my secret memoirs contain a note to the effect that its potent juices have often brought a glow to eminently diplomatic features.

37. *Influence of the Turkey on Finance*

The importation of turkeys has produced a considerable accretion to the public purse, and given rise to an important trade.

By rearing turkeys, the farmer can pay his rent more easily, and his daughters can often save up enough for their dowries; for city dwellers must pay well if they wish to feast on that foreign flesh.

The financial importance of the truffled turkey deserves special mention.

I have reason to believe that from the beginning of November to the end of February three hundred truffled turkeys are consumed in Paris every day, or thirty-six thousand in the whole period.

The ordinary price of a turkey so prepared is at least 20 francs, which gives a total of 720,000 francs – a tidy sum to be in circulation. To this must be added an equivalent sum for chickens, pheasants, and partridges, likewise truffled, which are displayed every day in the food shops, to the agony of those beholders who cannot afford to buy them.

38. An Exploit of the Professor

During my stay at Hartford, in Connecticut, I had the good fortune to shoot a wild turkey. Such an exploit is worthy to be handed down to posterity, and I shall recount it all the more readily in that I am the hero of the tale.

A worthy old American farmer, who lived in the back-woods, had asked me to join him for a few days' shooting, promising me partridges, grey squirrels, and wild turkeys, and inviting me to bring along a friend or two.

Accordingly, one fine day in October 1794, Mr King and I set out on a couple of hired hacks, in the hope of arriving by nightfall at Mr Bulow's farm, situated five mortal leagues from Hartford, Connecticut.

Mr King was a peculiar sort of sportsman; he was passionately fond of shooting; but whenever he killed a bird he used to curse himself as a murderer and give vent to elegies and moral reflections on the fate of the victim; after which he would repeat the offence.

Although the road was little more than a rough track, we reached our destination without mishap, and were welcomed with that quiet but cordial hospitality which is expressed in deeds rather than words; that is to say, in a few moments suitable greetings had been extended to us and comforts provided for men, horses, and dogs.

We devoted about two hours to an inspection of the farm and its outbuildings; I could describe it all if I wished, but I prefer to introduce my readers to Mr Bulow's four buxom daughters, for whom our arrival was a great event.

Their ages ranged from sixteen to twenty; they were radiant with freshness and health, and there was a simplicity and natural grace about them which lent a thousand charms to their most ordinary actions.

Shortly after our return from the tour of inspection, we sat down to a copious meal. There was a superb piece of corned beef, a stewed goose, a magnificent leg of mutton, a vast selection of vegetables, and at either end of the table two huge jugs of a cider so excellent that I could have gone on drinking it for ever.

When we had shown our host that we were true sportsmen, at least as far as appetite was concerned, he turned to the object of our visit; he indicated to us as best he could the places where we might expect to find game, the landmarks which would guide us on our way back, and above all the farms where we could obtain refreshment.

During this conversation the young ladies had made some excellent tea, of which we drank several cups; after which we were shown to a room with two beds, where we soon fell asleep under the influence of exercise and good cheer.

The next day we set out rather late in the morning, and, once past the limit of Mr Bulow's clearings, I found myself for the first time in virgin forest, where the sound of an axe had never been heard.

I walked along in delight, observing the benefits and ravages of time the creator and destroyer, and following with interest the successive phases in the life of an oak, from the moment when it emerges from the soil with a couple of leaves to the time when nothing is left of it but a long dark stain, the dust of its heart.

Mr King, however, scolded me for my daydreaming, and we set about our sport. Our first victims were a few of those pretty little grey partridges which are so plump and tender. Then we brought down six or seven grey squirrels, which are highly prized in those parts; and finally our lucky star brought us into the middle of a flock of turkeys.

They flew off at short intervals one after another, flapping their wings noisily, and screaming raucously. Mr King fired first and ran after his bird; the rest all appeared to be out of range, but then a straggler rose, not ten paces from where I stood; I fired at him above a clearing, and he fell stone-dead.

Only a sportsman can understand the joy I felt at that perfect shot. I took that glorious bird and had been turning him this way and that for a full quarter of an hour when I heard Mr King calling for help. I ran to join him, and found that he only wanted me to help him in the search for a turkey which he swore that he had shot, but which had none the less disappeared completely.

I put my dog on the trail, but he led us into some undergrowth which was so dense and prickly that it would have stopped a snake, and we were forced to abandon the search; this put my companion into a bad temper which lasted until he reached home.

The remainder of our day's sport was not worth recording. Going home, we lost our way in those boundless woods, and we were resigning ourselves to a night in the open, when we heard the silvery voices of our hostesses and the deep bass of their papa; they had been kind enough to come to meet us, and our troubles were over.

The four sisters were ready for us: best dresses, new sashes, pretty bonnets, and dainty shoes showed that they had gone out of their way to please; and for my part, when one of them came up to me and took my arm, for all the world as if she were my wife, I resolved to show her every courtesy.

When we reached the farm we found supper waiting for us; but before tackling it, we sat down for a moment in front of a blazing fire which had been lit for us, despite the mildness of the weather. We felt a lot better for it, and our tiredness vanished as if by magic.

This practice had no doubt been borrowed from the Indians, who always keep a fire burning in their tents. Or perhaps it has come down to us from Saint Francis of Sales, who said that a fire was a good thing for twelve months in the year. (*Non liquet.*)

We ate like starving men; a generous bowl of punch helped us to round off the evening, and our conversation, to which our host contributed more freely than the previous day, lasted far into the night.

We spoke of the War of Independence, in which Mr Bulow had served as a senior officer; of Monsieur de la Fayette, whose memory grows ever dearer in the hearts of all Americans, who never speak of him but by his title, as the Marquis; of agriculture, which at that time was bringing great prosperity to the United States; and lastly of our own dear France, which I loved more than ever since I had been forced to leave her shores.

By way of an interlude, Mr Bulow would turn now and then to his eldest daughter and say, 'Maria, give us a song.' She never needed to be asked a second time, but with a charming air of embarrassment sang the national tune of 'Yankee Doodle', 'Queen Mary's Elegy', and 'Major André's Lament', all popular songs in that country. Maria had taken a few lessons, and in those remote parts passed for something of a *virtuosa*; but the chief merit of her singing lay in the quality of her voice, which was soft, unaffected, and clear.

Next morning we took our leave, despite our host's friendly insistence that we should stay. While the horses were being saddled, Mr Bulow took me to one side, and spoke the following remarkable words:

'If there is a happy man under heaven, my dear sir, you see that man in me; everything around you, and everything you have seen in my house, comes from my own property. These stockings were knitted by my daughters; my shoes and clothing came from my animals, and they together with my garden and my poultry-yard provide me with my plain but ample fare; and, which is greatly to the credit of our Government, Connecticut contains thousands of farmers as happily placed as I am, and whose doors, like mine, are never locked.

'The taxes here are almost nothing, and so long as they are paid we can sleep in peace. Congress does everything in its power to help our budding industry; agents travel the country in every direction to purchase what we have to sell; and I have now enough money for a long time to come, for I have just been paid twenty-four dollars a ton for flour which I usually give away at eight.

'All this comes from the liberty which we have won by force of arms and based on good laws. I am my own master, and you will not be surprised to learn that the sound of the drum is never heard here, and that except on the Fourth of

July, the glorious anniversary of our independence, neither soldiers, uniforms, nor bayonets are ever to be seen.'

During the whole of our homeward journey I was absorbed in deep reflection; it will perhaps be thought that my mind was full of Mr Bulow's parting words, but in fact the subject of my thoughts was quite different; I was thinking of how I would cook my turkey, and I was worried by the fear that Hartford would be unable to furnish all my needs; for I wished to make my mark by using my spoils to the best possible advantage.

I am making a painful sacrifice in omitting the details of the trouble I took to prepare a distinguished meal for the American guests I had invited. It must suffice to say that the partridge wings were served *en papillote* and the grey squirrels stewed in Madeira.

As for the turkey, which was our only roast dish, it was charming to behold, pleasing to smell, and delicious to taste. And so, until the last morsel was consumed, from all round the table came cries of 'Very good!' 'Exceedingly good!' 'My dear sir, what a glorious dish!'[1]

39. On Game

The term *game* includes all animals which live in a state of natural liberty in fields and woods, and which are fit to be eaten.

We say 'fit to be eaten', because some animals do not come under the category of game. Such are foxes, badgers, crows, magpies, owls, etc., which we call *vermin*.

Game is divided into three classes:

1. The flesh of the wild turkey has more colour and flavour than that of the domestic variety.

It gave me great pleasure to learn that my esteemed colleague, Monsieur Bosc, had shot turkeys in Carolina, and that he had found them excellent, and far superior to those we rear in Europe. He accordingly advises breeders to allow the birds as much liberty as possible, letting them range the fields and even the woods, in order to enhance their flavour and bring them to their original condition. (*Annales d'Agriculture*, 28 February 1821.)

The first begins with the thrush, and includes, in a descending scale, all the lesser birds.

The second begins with the corncrake and includes the woodcock, the partridge, the pheasant, the rabbit, and the hare; this is game in the proper sense of the term – ground game and marsh game, furry game and feathered game.

The third is more generally known by the name of venison, and comprises the wild boar, the roe deer, and all the other hoofed animals.

Game is one of our favourite foods, being wholesome, tasty, full-flavoured, and easily digestible by all except the aged.

But these qualities are not so inherent as to be independent of the cook's skill. Throw a pinch of salt, some water, and a piece of beef into the pot, and you will obtain *potage* and *boulli*. Repeat the process, but with wild boar or deer instead of the beef, and you will be disappointed by the result; in this instance, the advantage lies with the butcher's meat.

But in the hands of a skilled cook, game undergoes a great many modifications and transformations, and provides most of the full-flavoured dishes which constitute transcendental cookery.

A great part of the merit of game is due to the nature of its breeding-ground; the taste of a red Périgord partridge is not the same as that of a red partridge from Sologne; and while a hare shot in the plains around Paris makes only a mediocre dish, a leveret born in the parched highlands of Valromey or Upper Dauphiné is perhaps the most savoury of all quadrupeds.

Among the small birds, the first in order of excellence is beyond question the warbler.

It grows at least as fat as the robin or the ortolan, and Nature has further endowed it with a unique flavour of such exquisite bitterness that it stimulates, satisfies, and delights the organ of taste. If the warbler were as large as a pheasant, it would easily command the price of an acre of land.

It is a great pity that this privileged bird is such a rarity in

Paris; it is true that a few are to be found in the capital, but they lack that plumpness which is their whole merit, and can scarcely be said to bear any resemblance to those of the eastern or southern regions of France.[1]

Few people know how to eat a small bird; here is the method, as it was privately revealed to me by Canon Charcot, a born gourmand, who was a perfect gastronome some thirty years before the word was invented.

Take a plump little bird by the beak, sprinkle him with a little salt, remove the gizzard, thrust him boldly into your mouth, bite him off close to your fingers, and chew hard; this will produce enough juice to wet the whole organ, and you will taste a delight unknown to the common herd:

Odi profanum vulgus et arceo.[2] (Horace)

Among game properly so called, the quail is the daintiest and most delightful. A plump quail is equally appealing in taste, shape, and colour. It is an admission of ignorance to serve it up otherwise than roasted or *en papillote*, because its flavour is extremely ephemeral, and, if the animal comes into contact with any liquid, it dissolves, evaporates, and is lost.

The woodcock is another very distinguished bird; but few people are aware of all its charms. A woodcock is never in all

---

1. In my youth tales were still told at Belley of the Jesuit Father Fabi, a native of that diocese, and his passion for warblers.

No sooner did the hawkers start selling them in the streets than people said: 'Here are the warblers! Father Fabi must be on his way!' Sure enough, he never failed to arrive on the first of September with a friend; they came to feast on warblers as long as the season lasted; everyone in the region made a point of inviting them to a meal, and they left about the twenty-fifth.

So long as he was in France, he never missed his annual ornithophilical excursions, which only came to an end when he was in Rome, where he died in the office of Penitentiary in 1688.

Father Fabi (Honoré) was a man of great learning; he published various works on theology and physics, in one of which he sought to prove that he had discovered the circulation of the blood before or at least as early as Harvey.

2. 'I hate the ignorant crowd and keep it off.' [Ed.]

its glory except when róasted under the eye of a sportsman, and preferably the sportsman who killed it; then the dish is prepared in accordance with the rules, and the mouth grows moist in the anticipation of delight.

But over all these birds, and all others too, the pheasant takes precedence; yet few mortals know how to present it to perfection.

A pheasant eaten within a week of its death is not as grand as a partridge or a chicken, for its whole merit lies in its aroma.

Science has investigated the expansion of that aroma, experiment has turned theory into practice, and a pheasant cooked at the right moment is a dish worthy of the most exalted gourmands.

The reader will find in the *Miscellanea* a description of the manner of roasting pheasants called *à la Sainte Alliance*. The time has come for this method, hitherto confined to a small circle of friends, to be made known far and wide for the happiness of mankind. A truffled pheasant is not as good as might be imagined; the bird has too little moisture to anoint the tuber; and moreover, the flavour of the one and the fragrance of the other neutralize each other, or rather are incompatible.

40. On Fish

Certain sages, of somewhat unorthodox tendencies, maintain that the Ocean was the common cradle of all existing things; that the human race itself was born in the sea; and that it owes its present condition only to the influence of the air and the habits it has been forced to acquire in order to live in this unfamiliar element.

Be that as it may, it is at least certain that the watery realm contains a vast number of creatures of all shapes and sizes, endowed with vital properties in widely differing proportions, on a system totally unlike that which governs the warm-blooded animals.

It is also certain that at all times and in all parts of the world, it furnishes a vast quantity of foodstuffs, and that, in the present state of science, it provides our tables with a most agreeable variety of dishes.

Fish, being less nutritious than flesh and more succulent than vegetables, is a *mezzo termine* which suits almost every temperament, and may be allowed even to convalescents.

The Greeks and Romans, though less advanced than ourselves in the art of seasoning fish, nevertheless prized it highly, and carried delicacy to the point of being able to tell by the taste in which waters their fish had been caught.

They kept fish alive in tanks; and the reader will doubtless know of the cruel practice of Vadius Pollo, who killed his slaves to feed their corpses to his eels: a practice of which the Emperor Domitian strongly disapproved, although he regrettably failed to punish the offender.

There has been a great deal of argument about the rival merits of sea fish and freshwater fish.

The question will probably never be decided for as the Spanish proverb says, *sobre los gustos, no hai disputa*.[1] Everyone is affected after his own manner; such sensations are too ephemeral to be expressed by any known character, and there is no scale to determine whether a cod, a sole, or a turbot is superior to a salmon trout, a fine pike, or even a six- or seven-pound tench.

It is certain, however, that fish is much less nourishing than meat, either because it contains no osmazome, or because, being much lighter in weight, it contains less matter in the same volume. Shell-fish, and especially oysters, provide little nourishing substance; and this is the reason why so many can be eaten immediately before a meal without any harmful effects.

In the old days, a meal of any note usually began with oysters, and there were always a good many guests who did not stop before they had swallowed a gross (twelve dozen, a hundred and forty-four). Wishing to know the weight of this advance-guard, I investigated the matter, and found that a

1. 'One can't argue about tastes.' [Ed.]

dozen oysters, water included, weighed four ounces, and a gross, therefore, three pounds. Now, I am convinced that the same individuals, who were not prevented by the oysters from eating a copious meal, would have been completely sated if they had eaten a like quantity of meat, even if it had only been chicken.

Anecdote

In 1798 I was at Versailles as a commissioner of the Directory, and had fairly frequent dealings with Monsieur Laperte, who was secretary to the tribunal of the department; he was extremely fond of oysters, and used to complain of never having eaten enough of them, or, as he put it, 'had his bellyful of them'.

I decided to provide him with that satisfaction, and to that end invited him to dinner.

He came; I kept him company as far as the third dozen, after which I let him go on alone. He went up to thirty-two dozen, taking more than an hour over the task, for the servant was not very skilful at opening them.

Meanwhile, I was inactive, and as that is a distressing condition to be in at the table, I stopped my guest when he was still in full career. 'My dear fellow,' I said, 'it is not your fate to eat your bellyful of oysters today; let us have dinner.'

We dined: and he acquitted himself with the vigour and appetite of a man who had been fasting.

41. *Muria and Garum*

The ancients extracted two very choice sauces from fish, namely *muria* and *garum*.

The first was simply brine of tunny-fish, or to be more precise, the liquid substance drawn from that fish by the addition of salt.

About *garum*, which was costlier, much less is known to us today. It is said to have been obtained by pressure from the soused entrails of mackerel or scomber; but if this were so, there would be no reason for its high price. There are some grounds for believing that it was a foreign sauce, and it may have been nothing more than *soy*, which we import from India, and which is known to be an extract from fish fermented with mushrooms.

Certain races are reduced by their geographical position to living almost entirely on fish; they also give it to their draught animals, which are eventually inured by habit to this strange diet, and even use it as manure for their fields; yet the surrounding sea never fails to supply them with the same quantity.

It has been remarked that these peoples are less courageous than the flesh-eating races; they are pale in complexion, which is not at all surprising, because the component elements of fish are such as to augment the lymph rather than to strengthen the blood.

Many instances of longevity have also been observed among the ichthyphagous nations; either because their relatively light and unsubstantial diet saves them from the evils of plethora, or because the juices of fish, being designed by Nature solely for the formation of fish-bone and gristle destined to last a very short time, have the effect on human beings of retarding the solidification of all parts of the body which finally becomes the inevitable cause of natural death.

Be that as it may, fish, in the hands of a skilful cook, can become an inexhaustible source of gustatory delight; whether it is served up whole, chopped up, or in slices, boiled, fried in oil, cooked in wine, hot or cold, it is always well received; but it is never more welcome than when it appears in the form of a *matelote*.

Although this stew is imposed by necessity upon our bargees, and is only brought to perfection in riverside taverns, it is neverthless invested by them with unsurpassable virtues; and ichthyophiles never see it without going into raptures, some praising its wholesome taste, some its combination of several qualities, and others because it is possible to go on eating it almost indefinitely without fear of satiety or indigestion.

Analytical chemistry has been used to investigate the effects of a fish diet on the animal economy, and the results all go to show that it has a powerful effect on the sense of physical desire, and arouses the instinct of reproduction in both sexes.

Once the effect had been established, two immediate causes were ascertained, which anyone could appreciate, namely:

1. Certain ways of preparing fish, with seasoning of an obviously stimulating nature, such as caviare, red herring, soused tunny-fish, cod, stock-fish, and others;
2. The different juices contained in fish, which are highly inflammable and become oxygenated and rancid on digestion.

Closer analysis has revealed a third and even more potent cause, namely the presence of phosphorus, which is to be found already formed in the milt, and never fails to appear on decomposition.

These physical truths were doubtless unknown to the ecclesiastical authorities who imposed the quadragesimal fast on various religious communities, such as the Carthusians, the Recollects, the Trappists, and the Barefoot Carmelites of the reformed order of Saint Theresa; for it cannot be supposed that they wished to make the vow of chastity, which was already anti-social enough, even more difficult to keep.

No doubt under those conditions splendid victories were won, and rebellious senses quelled; but what falls occurred too, and what defeats! Tales of those defeats must have had a foundation in fact to invest a religious order with a reputation like that of Hercules among the daughters of Danaus, or Marshal de Saxe with Mademoiselle Lecouvreur.

For that matter, they might have found enlightenment in a tale which was already old in their day, since it has come down to us from the Crusades.

Sultan Saladin, wishing to find out to what lengths the dervishes could carry their continence, confined two within his palace, and for a given time had them fed on the most succulent meats.

Soon all trace of the severities they had practised on themselves was lost, and their bellies began to fill out again.

At this point two odalisques of surpassing beauty were given to them to be their companions; but their most skilful wiles failed to achieve their object, and the two saints emerged from this testing ordeal as pure as the diamond of Vizapoor.

The Sultan kept them in his palace, and to celebrate their triumph had them fed on a diet no less succulent than before, but consisting exclusively of fish.

After a few weeks they were exposed again to the twin powers of youth and beauty; but this time Nature prevailed, and the happy cenobites succumbed . . . magnificently.

In the present state of our knowledge it is probable that, if the course of events brought some monastic order back into being, the superiors in charge of the monks would adopt a diet more favourable to the accomplishment of their duties.

42. Philosophical Reflection

Fish, taken collectively in all their species, offer the philosopher an endless source of meditation and surprise.

The various forms of these strange creatures, the senses which they lack, the limited powers of those which they possess, the influence on their habits of the element in which they live and breathe and move, all combine to extend the range of our ideas, and our understanding of the infinite modifications which may arise from matter, movement, and life.

For my part, I look upon them with a feeling akin to respect, born of the conviction that they are antediluvian creatures; for the vast cataclysm which drowned our great-uncles about eight hundred years after the creation of the world was a time of joy, conquest, and festivity for the fishes.

43. On Truffles

Whoever says 'truffles' utters a great word which arouses erotic and gastronomic memories among the skirted sex, and memories gastronomic and erotic among the bearded sex.

This dual distinction is due to the fact that the noble tuber is not only considered delicious to the taste, but is also believed to foster powers the exercise of which is extremely pleasurable.

The origin of the truffle is unknown; it is found, but nobody knows anything of its birth or growth. The greatest minds have pondered over it; at one time it was thought that its seed had been discovered, and it was declared that truffles might be sown at will. Vain efforts and illusory promises! No harvest was ever reaped from that sowing; and perhaps that is no great misfortune; for since the price of truffles is partly a matter of caprice, they might well be held in less esteem if they were available in quantity and cheap.

'Rejoice, my dear,' I said one day to Madame de V—; 'a loom has just been shown to the Society for Encouragement on which it will be possible to manufacture superb lace for practically nothing.'

'Why,' the lady replied, with an air of supreme indifference, 'if lace were cheap, do you think anybody would want to wear such rubbish?'

44. Erotic Property of Truffles

Truffles were known to the Romans; but it does not appear that they ever tasted the French variety. Those which they enjoyed came from Greece, Africa, and above all Libya; their substance was white and reddish, and the Libyan truffles were the most sought after, as being at once more tender and more fragrant.

Gustus elementa per omnia quaerunt.[1] (Juvenal)

After the Romans a long interval occurred, and it was only recently that the truffle was rediscovered, for I have read several old cookery books in which no mention is made of it; its rediscovery may be said to have been witnessed by the generation which is passing away as I write.

About 1780, truffles were a rarity in Paris, being only obtainable, and then just in small quantities, at the Hôtel des Américains and the Hôtel de Provence; and a truffled turkey was a great luxury, only to be seen on the tables of great lords or courtesans.

We owe the increased supplies of the present day to the provision merchants, whose numbers have grown considerably, and who, seeing that truffles were finding favour, sent agents all over the kingdom. By paying good prices and using mail couriers and stage-coaches as means of transport, these agents made truffle-hunting a general activity; for since truffles cannot be planted, it is only by diligent searching that consumption can be increased.

It is safe to say that at the time of writing (1825), the fame of the truffle is at its zenith. Nobody dares to admit having been present at a meal which did not include a single truffled dish. However good in itself an entrée may be, it makes a poor show if it is not garnished with truffles. Who has not felt his mouth water at the very mention of truffles *à la provençale*?

A *sauté* of truffles is a dish of which the mistress of the house always does the honours herself; in short, the truffle is the jewel of cookery.

I set out to find the reason for this preference, for it seemed to me that several other substances had an equal claim to the honour; and I found that reason in the widespread belief that truffles are conducive to erotic pleasure; what is more, I became convinced that nearly all our tastes, predilections, and admirations are born of the same cause, so closely are we held in thrall by that most capricious and tyrannical of the senses.

1. 'They ransack all the elements for delicacies.' [Ed.]

The discovery prompted me to try to find out whether the popular belief was well founded and the property attributed to truffles a reality. An investigation of this sort is no doubt somewhat indelicate and likely to provoke cynical laughter. But *honni soit qui mal y pense*: the pursuit of truth is always praiseworthy.

I first of all approached the ladies, on account of their keen perception and sense of tact, but it was soon borne in on me that I should have embarked on my inquiries forty years earlier, for all the replies I received were ironical or evasive. Only one lady was frank with me, and I propose to quote here what she told me; she is a woman who is witty but unpretentious, virtuous but no prude, and for whom love is now only a pleasant memory.

'Monsieur,' she said to me, 'one day long ago when suppers were still the fashion, I supped at home *en trio* with my husband and a friend of his. Verseuil (that was the name of this friend) was a handsome fellow, not without wit, and a frequent visitor to my house; but he had never said anything to me to make me look on him in the light of a prospective lover, and if he occasionally paid me compliments, they were so discreet that only a fool could have taken offence at them. On the day in question he seemed destined to keep me company for the rest of the evening, for my husband had a business appointment and was due to leave us before long. The basis of our supper, which was a light meal, was a superb truffled fowl which the sub-delegate from Périgueux had sent us. In those days such a dish was a great luxury, and you can guess from its origin that in this case it was perfection itself. The truffles in particular were delicious, and you know how I love them. All the same, I restrained myself, and what is more, I drank only one glass of champagne; I had some sort of womanly premonition that something would happen before the evening was out.

'After a while my husband went off, leaving me alone with Verseuil, whom he regarded as completely harmless. At first we talked of matters of no consequence, but soon the conversation took a much narrower and more interesting turn. Verseuil was first complimentary, then expansive, affectionate, and tender, and finally, when he saw that I was simply amused by all his sweet nothings, so importunate that I could no longer have any doubts about his intentions. At that point I awoke as from a dream, and defended myself all the more sincerely in that my heart said nothing to me in his favour. He persisted, with an ardour which seemed likely to become dangerous; I was hard put to it to keep him at arm's length, and I admit to my shame that I only succeeded in doing so by persuading him that all hope was not denied to him in the future. Finally he took his leave; I went to bed and slept like a log. But the next day was the day of judgement; I examined my conduct of the previous evening, and found it reprehensible. I ought to have stopped Verseuil at his first words and not lent myself to a conversation which boded no good. My pride ought to have been aroused earlier, and my eyes armed with severity; I should have rung the bell, screamed, flown into a rage, in a word done everything I failed to do. What shall I say, Monsieur? I put it all down to the truffles; I am genuinely convinced that they had given me a dangerous predisposition; and if I have not abstained from them since (that would have been too drastic a step), at least I never eat them now without any pleasure they afford me being mingled with a little mistrust.'

A confession, however frank it may be, can never carry the weight of a doctrine. I therefore looked for further information; I searched my memory and consulted those men who by their profession are invested with special trust. I gathered them together in a committee, court, senate, sanhedrin, and areopagus; and we arrived at the following conclusion, which I offer for comment to the writers of the twenty-fifth century:

'The truffle is not a true aphrodisiac; but in certain circumstances it can make women more affectionate and men more attentive.'

White truffles are found in Piedmont which are highly esteemed; they have a faint taste of garlic, which does not

mar their perfection in the slightest, because it has no unpleasant after-effects.

The best truffles in France come from Périgord and Upper
Provence; they attain their full flavour about the month of
January.

Those which come from Bugey are also very choice; but
this kind has the defect of being difficult to preserve. I myself have made four attempts, for the benefit of those who
stroll on the banks of the Seine, and only one was successful;
but at least on that occasion my guests recognized both the
goodness of the thing and the merits of difficulty overcome.

Burgundy and Dauphiné truffles are of poor quality; they
are hard and lack substance; thus there are truffles and
truffles, just as there are degrees of merit in everything
else.

In order to find truffles, recourse is usually had to dogs
and pigs trained for the purpose; but there are also men with
so practised an eye that they have only to look at a field to
be able to say with some certainty whether it contains
truffles, and if so, what their size and quality will be.

Are Truffles Indigestible?

It only remains for us to discover whether the truffle is indigestible.

Our answer will be in the negative.

This official and final decision is founded:

1. On the nature of the actual subject of our inquiry (the
truffle is easy to masticate, weighs very little, and is neither
hard nor tough);

2. On our own observations, conducted over more than fifty
years, in the course of which we have never seen a single
truffle-eater suffering from indigestion;

3. On the evidence of the most famous practitioners in Paris,
which is a city of gourmands, and eminently trufflivorous;

4. And lastly, on the daily conduct of the legal fraternity,
who, all things being equal, consume more truffles than any

other class of citizens; witness, among others, Doctor Malouet, who used to eat enough of them to give an elephant indigestion, but who nevertheless lived to the age of eighty-six.

Hence it may be taken for certain that the truffle is a food as wholesome as it is agreeable, and that, eaten in moderation, it goes down as easily as a letter into a post-box.

That is not to say that indisposition may not be felt after a copious meal at which, among other things, truffles have been eaten; but such accidents only befall persons who after stuffing themselves at the first course, cram even more food into their mouths at the second, in their anxiety to miss none of the good things placed before them.

Then their indigestion is not the fault of the truffles; and it is certain that they would have suffered even greater agonies if instead of truffles they had in similar circumstances eaten the same quantity of potatoes.

Let us conclude with a true story, which shows how easily a mistake can arise from imperfect observation.

One day I had invited Monsieur S— to dine with me, a charming old gentleman, and a gourmand of the first rank. Either because I did not know his tastes, or in order to prove to all my guests that I had their happiness at heart, I had not been sparing with the truffles, which appeared under the aegis of a virgin turkey stuffed to advantage.

Monsieur S— fell upon them avidly, and as I knew that he had not died of them so far, I let him be, begging him not to go too fast, for no one had designs on his property.

All went well, and it was quite late when he took his leave; but on reaching home he was seized with violent stomach-ache, accompanied by retching, coughing and general sickness.

This disquieting state of affairs continued for some time: and had already been diagnosed as indigestion due to truffles, when Nature suddenly came to the patient's rescue. Monsieur S— opened his mouth wide, and shot out a single fragment of truffle, which hit the wall and rebounded with enough force to imperil the people attending to him.

All the distressing symptoms promptly ceased; calm was restored; the patient's digestion resumed its normal course, and he fell asleep to wake next morning in good fettle and completely unembittered by his experience.

The cause of the trouble was soon discovered. Monsieur S— has been eating for a great many years, and his teeth have proved unable to cope with the task he has imposed on them; some of the precious ivories have emigrated, and the rest no longer coincide as well as could be wished.

Under these conditions, one truffle had escaped mastication and gone down nearly whole; the action of digestion had carried it towards the pylorus, where it had temporarily lodged; this lodgement had been the cause of the evil, even as the expulsion of the truffle was the remedy.

Thus there was no indigestion, but only a blockage caused by the presence of a foreign body.

Such was the decision reached by the examining committee who saw the evidence and graciously invited me to report their findings.

Monsieur S— has none the less remained as fervently devoted to the truffle as ever, and still attacks it with all his old audacity; but he is careful to masticate it more thoroughly and swallow it more carefully; and he thanks God in the joy of his heart for enabling this sanitary precaution to prolong his earthly pleasures.

45. On Sugar

In our present state of scientific knowledge, we understand sugar to mean a sweet-tasting crystallizable substance, resoluble by fermentation into carbonic acid and alcohol.

Formerly the word implied the solidified and crystallized juice of the sugar-cane (*arundo saccharifera*).

This reed was originally found in the Indies; and it is certain that the Romans had no knowledge of sugar, either as a common article of food or as a crystal.

There are, it is true, a few pages in ancient literature

which seem to indicate knowledge of the art of extracting a sweet substance from certain reeds: Lucan says:

Quique bibunt tenera dulces ab arundine succos.[1]

But there is a considerable difference between water sweetened by a substance extracted from cane and sugar as we now know it; and the art had reached only a rudimentary stage among the Romans.

It was in the colonies of the New World that sugar really originated; the cane was imported there about two centuries ago, and flourished. Attempts were made to use its sweet juices, and after a series of experiments syrup, crude sugar, molasses, and refined sugar were successively extracted from them.

The cultivation of the sugar-cane has become an affair of prime importance; for it is a source of wealth not only to those who grow it, but also to those who process it, those who trade in its products, and those governments which tax it.

On Indigenous Sugar

For a long time it was believed that tropical heat was essential for the production of sugar, but about 1740 Margraff discovered its presence in certain plants in the temperate zone, including beetroot: and his discovery was confirmed by Professor Achard's experiments in Berlin.

At the beginning of the nineteenth century, when circumstances had made sugar scarce, and consequently dear in France, the Government appealed to scientists to make it an object of research.

This appeal was highly successful, and it was found that sugar was widely present in the vegetable kingdom; it was discovered in the grape, the chestnut, the potato, and above all the beetroot.

This last plant was made the object of widespread cultivation, and a host of experiments took place which showed

1. 'And who drink the sweet juice from the tender reed.' [Ed.]

that in this respect the Old World could dispense with the services of the New. Factories sprang up all over France and met with varying degrees of success; the new art of sac-charinification was naturalized, and the day may come when circumstances will force us to revive it.

The most important of these factories was the one which Monsieur Benjamin Delessert, a worthy citizen whose name is always associated with what is useful and good, established at Passy, near Paris.

A series of extensive operations enabled him to rid the process of its dubious elements; he made no secret of his discoveries, even to those who might have been tempted to become his rivals; the head of the Government visited him in person, and appointed him purveyor to the palace of the Tuileries.

When new circumstances, the Restoration and peace, brought back cheap sugar from the colonies, the beet-sugar factories lost a great part of their advantages. But several of them still flourish, and Monsieur Benjamin Delessert makes huge quantities every year at a fair profit, thus preserving methods which may well prove useful in the future.[1]

When beet sugar was first put on the market, prejudiced persons and ignorant masses declared that it tasted un-pleasant and was inefficient as a sweetener; some even main-tained that it was unwholesome.

The contrary has been proved by a series of exact experiments; and Monsieur le Comte Chaptal has embodied the result of these in his excellent work, *Chemistry Applied to Agriculture*, first edition, volume ii, page 12.

'The sugars extracted from these various plants,' says the famous chemist, 'are of exactly the same nature, and differ in

1. It may be added that the Society for the Encouragement of National Industry, at its general meeting, awarded a gold medal to Monsieur Crespel of Arras, who every year manufactures more than one hundred and fifty thousand pieces of beet sugar; and is able to make a profitable living, even when the price of cane sugar falls as low as 2 fr. 20 c. the kilogramme; this is because he has succeeded in utilizing the residue, from which he extracts spirits by distillation and which he then uses as cattle-fodder.

no respect from one another, when they have been refined to the same degree of purity. Taste, crystallization, colour, and specific gravity are absolutely identical, and the most experienced judge or consumer of these products may be defied to tell one from another.'

A striking example of the force of prejudice and the difficulty of establishing the truth is to be observed in Great Britain, where not ten persons in a hundred, chosen at random, believe that it is possible to make sugar out of beetroot.

Different Uses of Sugar

Sugar entered the world by way of the apothecary's laboratory. The importance of the part it proceeded to play in that laboratory may be judged from the old saying about anyone who lacked something essential, that he was 'like an apothecary without sugar'.

The fact that it came from such a source was enough to ensure that it obtained an unfavourable reception; some said that it heated the blood, some that it attacked the lungs, others that it was a cause of apoplexy; but calumny was forced to give way to truth, and more than eighty years have passed since someone coined that memorable aphorism: 'Sugar harms nothing but the purse.'

Under such an impenetrable aegis, sugar came every day into more general use, and there is no alimentary substance which has undergone more amalgamations and transformations.

Many people like eating pure sugar, and in some cases, most of them desperate, the doctors prescribe it in that form, as a remedy which can do no harm, and is at least pleasant to take.

Mixed with water, it is a refreshing, wholesome, and agreeable drink, which is sometimes effective as a medicine.

Mixed with a small proportion of water and subjected to heat, it produces syrups, to which any kind of flavour may be added; these drinks are always refreshing, and are so varied that they please every taste.

Mixed with water from which the calorie is then extracted it produces ices, which originated in Italy, and seem to have been introduced into France by Catherine de Médicis.

Mixed with wine, it produces a cordial, with such well-known restorative qualities that in some countries it is poured over cakes which are brought to newly married couples on their wedding night; just as in Persia the bride and groom are given sheep's trotters in vinegar.

Mixed with flour and eggs, it produces biscuits, macaroons, cracknels, sponge cakes, and all the many kinds of light pastry which constitute the fairly recent art of the confectioner.

Mixed with milk, it produces the various creams and blancmanges whose delicate and ethereal flavour makes such a welcome change after the substantial taste of meat.

Mixed with coffee, it brings out the full aroma of that beverage.

Mixed with coffee and milk, it makes a light, agreeable and easily procurable form of nourishment, most suitable for those persons who have to begin work immediately after breakfast. Coffee and milk is also a source of supreme pleasure to the ladies; but the perceptive eye of science has observed that excessive indulgence in it may prove harmful to that which they hold most dear.

Mixed with fruit and flowers, it produces jam, marmalade, preserves, jellies, pastes, and candies, enabling us to enjoy the fragrance of those fruits and flowers long after the period fixed by Nature for their duration. In this connexion, sugar might also be used to advantage in the art of embalming, which is still in a rudimentary stage in our civilization.

Finally, sugar mixed with alcohol produces spirituous liqueurs, which as everyone knows were invented to put new ardour into the aged Louis XIV, and which, by their forceful effect on the palate and their fragrant fumes, form the *nec plus ultra* of gastronomic delight.

These are not all the uses of sugar. It may be said to be the universal condiment, which never spoils anything. There are people who use it with meat, sometimes with vegetables, and often with fresh fruit. It is essential to the mixed drinks which are so fashionable today, such as punch, negus, syllabub, and others of exotic origin; and its applications are of infinite variety, since they can be modified to suit the tastes of peoples and individuals.

Such is this substance, the very name of which was almost unknown to the Frenchmen of the time of Louis XIII, yet which has become a prime necessity to those of the nineteenth century; for there is scarcely a woman, especially a woman of means, who does not spend more on sugar than on bread.

Monsieur Delacroix, that charming and prolific author, was once heard at Versailles to complain of the price of sugar, which at that time was over five francs a pound. 'Ah,' he said in melting tones, 'if ever sugar comes down to thirty sous again, then as long as I live I shall never drink water without sugar in it.'

His hopes were fulfilled; he is still alive, and I trust that he has kept his word.

46. *Origin of Coffee*

The first coffee-tree was found in Arabia, and in spite of the various transplantations which that shrub has since undergone, Arabia still remains the source of the best coffee.

According to an old tradition coffee was discovered by a goat-herd, who noticed a strange restlessness and hilarity in his flock whenever they had browsed on coffee-berries.

Even if that legend is true, however, only half the honour of the discovery would belong to the observant goat-herd; the other half must be allowed to the first man who thought of applying heat to the beans. For the decoction of crude coffee is a mediocre beverage; but carbonization develops the aroma and oil which are the characteristic of coffee as we drink it today; and these qualities would never have been known without the application of heat.

The Turks, who are our masters in this matter, never use a mill to grind their coffee beans; they pound them in mortars with wooden pestles; and when those instruments have been used for a long time, they become valuable and are sold at a high price.

I felt it incumbent on me, for several reasons, to find out whether there was any difference between the results obtained by the two methods, and if so, which was to be preferred. Accordingly I carefully roasted a pound of pure Mocha, and divided it into two equal parts, one of which was then ground in a mill, and the other pounded after the Turkish fashion.

I made coffee with each of the two powders; I took an equal quantity of each; and on each I poured an equal quantity of boiling water, conducting the whole operation with absolute impartiality.

I tasted the two coffees, and also submitted them to the most eminent connoisseurs. The unanimous verdict was that the coffee made with the pounded powder was clearly superior to that made from the ground beans.

Anyone is at liberty to repeat the experiment. Meanwhile I can cite a curious example of the different effects obtained from different methods of manipulation.

'Monsieur,' Napoleon said one day to Senator Laplace, 'why is it that a glass of water in which I dissolve a lump of sugar seems so much better than one in which I place a like quantity of powdered sugar?'

'Sire,' replied the scientist, 'there are three substances whose elements are identical, namely, sugar, gum and starch; they only differ in certain conditions, the secret of which Nature keeps to herself; and I think it possible that under the action of the pestle, a few portions of the powdered sugar assume the character of gum or starch, and cause the difference which occurs in that case.'

This anecdote received some publicity at the time, and

subsequent investigations have confirmed the accuracy of the Senator's observation.

Different Ways of Making Coffee

A few years ago all minds were simultaneously turned to the problem of finding the best way of making coffee, a phenomenon which, though no one suspected it, was probably due to the fact that the head of the Government was extremely partial to that beverage.

It was suggested that it should be made without roasting it, without reducing it to powder, by infusing it cold, by boiling it for three quarters of an hour, by placing it in a sealed boiler, and so on.

In my time I have tried every one of these methods and all the others which have been put forward down to the present day, and my considered opinion is that the best of all is the method called *à la Dubelloy,* which consists in placing the coffee in a porcelain or silver receptacle pierced with very small holes, and pouring boiling water over it. This first decoction is brought to boiling-point again, and again passed through the strainer, after which the coffee will be as clear and as good as possible.

In one of my experiments I tried to make coffee in a high-pressure boiler; but the result was a mixture of extractive matter and bitterness, fit for nothing but a Cossack's gullet.

Effects of Coffee

Learned doctors have expressed a variety of opinions concerning the sanitary properties of coffee, and have not always seen eye to eye; we will steer clear of the fray, and turn our attention only to the most important of them all, namely its influence on the organs of thought.

It is beyond doubt that coffee causes considerable excitement in the brain; and anyone drinking it for the first time is certain to be robbed of some of his sleep.

Sometimes this effect is softened or modified by habit; but there are many individuals who always remain subject to this excitement, and are consequently obliged to give up drinking coffee altogether.

I have said that the effect may be modified by habit, but this does not prevent it from occurring in another form; for I have observed that those persons who are not prevented by coffee from sleeping at night need it to keep awake by day, and never fail to fall asleep during the evening when they have not taken any coffee after dinner.

There are many others, moreover, who are sleepy all day long when they have not drunk their cup of coffee in the morning. Voltaire and Buffon were great coffee-drinkers and perhaps derived from that practice, one, the admirable clarity which is in all his works, and the other, the fervent harmony of his style. It is evident that several passages in the *Essays on Man*, about the dog, the tiger, the lion, and the horse, were written in a state of extreme cerebral exaltation.

The insomnia caused by coffee is not distressing; one's perceptions are sharper and one has no wish to sleep; that is all. There is none of the agitation and unhappiness which accompany insomnia brought on by any other cause; nevertheless, this untimely excitement may prove very dangerous in the long run.

In the old days, only people of mature years drank coffee; now everyone drinks it, and it may be the sting of its mental lash which drives such a huge crowd to take the roads leading to Olympus and the Temple of Memory. The cobbler author of the tragedy of *The Queen of Palmyra*, which all Paris heard read a few years ago, was greatly addicted to coffee; he therefore rose higher than the joiner of Nevers, who was nothing but a drunkard.

Coffee is a far more powerful liquor than is commonly believed. A man of sound constitution can drink two bottles of wine a day, and live to a great age; the same man could not stand a like quantity of coffee for the same period; he would go out of his mind or die of consumption.

I once saw a man in London, in Leicester Square, who had been crippled by immoderate indulgence in coffee; he was no longer in any pain, having grown accustomed to his condition, and had cut himself down to five or six cups a day.

It is the duty of all papas and mammas to forbid their children to drink coffee, unless they wish to have little dried-up machines, stunted and old at the age of twenty. This warning is particularly directed to Parisians, whose children are not always as strong and healthy as if they had been born in other parts of the country, such as the Department of the Ain.

I myself am one of those who have been forced to give up coffee, and I will end this chapter by relating how one day I fell completely beneath its spell.

The Duc de Massa, at that time Minister of Justice, had asked me to undertake a piece of work which called for the closest application; he had given me very short notice, for he wanted it the following day.

I therefore resigned myself to a night's work; and in order to guard against the risk of falling asleep, I fortified my dinner with two large cups of strong aromatic coffee.

I came home at seven o'clock, having been told to expect the relevant papers about that time; but instead I found a letter informing me that, owing to some official formality, I would not receive them until the following morning.

Thus disappointed, in the full meaning of the term, I returned to the house at which I had dined, and played a game of piquet without experiencing any of the distractions to which I am usually subject.

For this I praised the coffee; but while enjoying the advantage it had given me, I was not without anxiety as to how I was to pass the night. However, I went to bed at the usual time, thinking that even if my slumbers were not as sound as they might be, I would at least sleep four or five hours, which would carry me gently through to the following morning.

I was mistaken; after two hours in bed I was wider awake than ever, and in a state of lively mental activity. My brain was like a mill with all its wheels revolving, but nothing for them to grind.

I felt that I must make some use of this disposition or the need for sleep would never come; and so I spent the time by turning a short story, which I had recently read in an English book, into verse.

I soon finished it, and as I was still as wide awake as before, I started on a second, but in vain. My poetic ardour cooled at the end of a dozen lines, and I was forced to give up.

In the end I spent the whole night without sleeping a wink, or even dozing for a single moment; I got up, and spent the day in the same condition, which remained unchanged by either the food I ate or the work I had to do. Finally, when I lay down the next night at my accustomed hour, I calculated that I had not closed my eyes for forty hours.

47. *Origin of Chocolate*

The first men who landed in America were driven there by the thirst for gold. At that time mines were almost the only known source of wealth; agriculture and trade were in their infancy, and political economy was as yet unborn. The Spaniards, then, found precious metals; but this discovery was in a sense a barren one, because metal falls in value in proportion to the quantity discovered, and we have many more active methods of increasing the wealth of the world.

But those lands, where the heat of the sun brings the fields to a state of extreme fertility, were found to be ideally suited to the cultivation of sugar and coffee; moreover, the potato, the indigo plant, vanilla, quinine, and cacao were discovered there, and these were real treasures.

If these discoveries took place despite the obstacles put in the way of curiosity by a jealous nation, it is reasonable to hope that they will be multiplied tenfold in the future, and that the researches of the scientists of old Europe in so many unexplored countries will enrich the three kingdoms, animal, vegetable, and mineral, with a host of new substances, some of which, like vanilla, will provide us with new sensations, and others, like cacao, with new alimentary resources.

What we call *chocolate* is made by cooking the kernel of the cacao bean with sugar and cinnamon; such is the classic definition of chocolate. Sugar is an integral part of it; for from the kernels alone only cacao-paste or cocoa is obtained, and not chocolate. When the delicious flavour of vanilla is added to the sugar, cinnamon, and cacao, the *nec plus ultra* is attained of the perfection to which this preparation can be brought.

It is to this small number of substances that taste and experience have reduced the numerous ingredients which had been successively tried as adjuncts to cocoa, such as pepper, pimento, aniseed, ginger, aciola, and others.

The cacao tree is indigenous in both the islands and mainland of South America; but it is now generally agreed that the trees which yield the best fruit are those growing on the banks of the Maracaibo, in the valleys of Caracas, and the rich province of Sokomusco. There the kernel of the bean is larger, and the flavour sweeter and more concentrated. Since these regions became more accessible, it has been possible to make daily comparisons, and trained palates are now unerring in their choice.

The Spanish ladies of the New World love chocolate to the point of madness; not content with drinking it several times a day, they sometimes order it to be brought to them in church. This sensual indulgence often attracted the censure of the bishops, but they eventually closed their eyes to it, and the Reverend Father Escobar, whose metaphysics were as subtle as his morality was accommodating, formally declared that liquid chocolate was not a breach of fasting, thus stretching for the benefit of his fair penitents the ancient proverb: *Liquidum non frangit jejunum.*[1]

Chocolate was introduced into Spain about the beginning

1. 'Liquid does not break a fast.' [Ed.]

of the seventeenth century, and its use rapidly became popular, owing to the predilection which women and monks, especially the latter, showed for this aromatic drink. Life in Spain has not changed in this respect and to this day chocolate is the principal refreshment on social occasions throughout the Peninsula.

Chocolate crossed the mountains with Anne of Austria, the daughter of Philip II and wife of Louis XIII. The Spanish monks also made it known by making presents of it to their French brethren, and successive Spanish ambassadors helped to bring it into fashion too. At the beginning of the Regency it was in more general use than coffee, because in those days it was taken as an agreeable form of nourishment, while coffee was still regarded as a rare and costly drink.

It is well known that Linnaeus called cacao *cacao theobroma*, the drink of the gods. Attempts have been made to find a reason for this emphatic qualification; some attribute it to his passionate predilection for chocolate; others to his desire to please his confessor; still others a wish to flatter the queen who had first introduced the custom. (*Incertum*)

Properties of Chocolate

The nature and properties of chocolate, and its place in the category of foods hot, cold, or cool, have been the occasion of solemn dissertations; but it must be admitted that these learned studies have contributed very little to the manifestation of truth.

However, time and experience, those two great teachers, have conclusively proved that chocolate, when carefully prepared, is a wholesome and agreeable form of food; that it is nourishing and easily digestible; that unlike coffee, of which indeed it is the antidote, it holds no terrors for the fair sex; that it is very suitable for persons faced with great mental exertion, preachers, lawyers, and above all travellers; and finally that it agrees with the feeblest stomachs, has proved beneficial in cases of chronic illness, and remains the last resource in diseases of the pylorus.

Chocolate owes these various properties to the fact that as it is just an *eleosaccharum,* few substances contain such a high proportion of alimentary particles, so that it is almost entirely animalizable.

During the war[1] cacao was difficult to obtain and very expensive; efforts were made to find a substitute, but all in vain; and one of the blessings of peace has been the disappearance of the various brews which we had to drink out of politeness, but which were no more chocolate than an infusion of chicory is Mocha coffee.

There are some people who complain of being unable to digest chocolate, and others who, on the contrary, declare that it contains too little nourishment, and passes too quickly through the system.

It is extremely likely that the former have only themselves to blame, and that the chocolate they drink is of poor quality or badly prepared; for good chocolate well made should agree with any stomach in which there remains the smallest vestige of digestive power.

As for the others, there is a simple remedy; let them reinforce their breakfast with a small meat pasty, a cutlet, or a broiled kidney, wash it all down with a good bowl of *Sokomusco,* and thank God for providing them with an active stomach.

This gives me an opportunity to insert an observation which can be relied on as absolutely exact.

When you have breakfasted well and copiously, if you swallow a generous cup of good chocolate at the end of the meal, you will have digested everything perfectly three hours later, and you will be able to dine in comfort. . . . Out of zeal for science, and by dint of eloquence, I have persuaded a good many ladies to try this experiment, although they protested that it would kill them; in every case they were delighted with the result, and none of them failed to pay due tribute to the Professor.

Persons who drink chocolate regularly are conspicuous for unfailing health and immunity from the host of minor

1. The Napoleonic Wars. [Translator.]

ailments which mar the enjoyment of life; they are also less inclined to lose weight; these are two advantages which any-one may verify in his own circle of acquaintances and among people whose diet can be ascertained.

This is the right place to speak of the properties of choco-late flavoured with amber; properties which I have verified in a great many experiments, the result of which I am proud to lay before my readers.

So let any man who has drunk too deeply of the cup of pleasure, or given to work a notable portion of the time which should belong to sleep; who finds his wit temporarily losing its edge, the atmosphere humid, time dragging, and the air hard to breathe, or who is tortured by a fixed idea which robs him of all freedom of thought; let such a man, we say, administer to himself a good pint of ambered choco-late, allowing between sixty and seventy-two grains of amber to a pound, and he will see wonders.

In my own peculiar way of specifying things, I call am-bered chocolate 'the chocolate of the afflicted', because in each of the various conditions listed above there is a feeling hard to define but *common to them all,* which resembles affliction.

Difficulty of Making Good Chocolate

Very good chocolate is made in Spain; but we have stopped importing it from that country, because the Spanish makers are not all equally skilful, and the customer is forced to drink what he receives, whether it is good or bad.

Italian chocolate is not much to the French taste; gen-erally speaking, the cacao is over-roasted, which makes the chocolate bitter and insufficiently nutritious, because part of the kernel has been burnt up.

Now that drinking chocolate has become universally popular in France, everyone has tried his hand at making it, but few have attained perfection, because the process is very far from being easy.

First of all, you must be able to tell good cacao from bad,

and be determined to use only the best; for not even the finest quality cacao is entirely free from blemish, and misguided self-interest often overlooks damaged kernels, which should be thrown out to obtain the best results. The roasting of cacao is another delicate operation, and demands a certain tact not far removed from inspiration. There are some workers who are born with this skill and who never make mistakes.

A special talent is also needed for the proper regulation of the quantity of sugar which must go into the composition; no invariable rule can be laid down, for the amount must be varied according to the flavour of the kernels, and the degree of heat to which the cacao has been brought.

The grinding and mixing demands no less care, for it is on their absolute perfection that the digestibility of the chocolate partly depends.

Other considerations must govern the choice and quantity of the flavouring, which cannot be the same for chocolate intended to be taken as food, and for chocolate intended to be eaten as a sweet. It will also depend on whether or not vanilla is to be added to the mixture; so that, in order to make exquisite chocolate, a number of very subtle equations must be solved, which we profit by without even being aware of their existence.

For some time now, machines have been used for making chocolate; we do not believe that this method adds anything to its perfection, but it achieves a great saving of labour, and those who have adopted this method should be able to sell their chocolate cheaper. The contrary, however, seems to be the case; and this shows all too clearly that the real spirit of commerce is not yet naturalized in France, for in all fairness the advantage obtained by the use of machines should be equally profitable to the merchant and the consumer.

Being ourselves very fond of chocolate, we have run the gamut of nearly all the dealers, and we have now settled upon Monsieur Debauve, of No. 26 Rue des Saints-Pères; he is a purveyor of chocolate to the King, and we rejoice to see that the sun's rays have lighted on the worthiest of all. There is nothing surprising about that; Monsieur Debauve is a distinguished pharmacist, and brings to his chocolate-making all the learning he had acquired for use in a wider sphere.

Those who have never used their hands can have no idea of the difficulties which must be overcome before perfection can be attained in any material, nor of how much care, skill, and experience are needed to produce chocolate which is sweet but not insipid, strong but not bitter, aromatic but not sickly, and thick but free from sediment.

Such are the qualities of Monsieur Debauve's chocolate; it owes its supremacy to a sound choice of materials, a firm determination to allow nothing inferior to leave his factory, and the keen eye of the proprietor which watches over every detail of the work.

Following the guidance of sound doctrine, Monsieur Debauve has also endeavoured to supply his numerous customers with palatable antidotes against certain minor ailments.

Thus, to persons lacking in flesh he offers a body-building chocolate, flavoured with salep; to those whose nerves are weak, anti-spasmodic chocolate, flavoured with orange-blossom; to irritable persons, almond-milk chocolate; and to this list he will doubtless add 'chocolate for the afflicted' prepared with amber *secundum artem*.

But his supreme merit consists in his offering, at a modest price, an excellent everyday chocolate, which is enough in itself for our morning breakfast, delights us at dinner with our creams, and enchants us yet again at the end of the evening with our ices, and sweets, and other drawing-room dainties, not to mention the amusing distraction of crackers with or without mottoes.

Our only acquaintance with Monsieur Debauve is through his wares; we have never set eyes on him; but we know that he is helping considerably to free France from the tribute she used to pay to Spain, by providing Paris and the provinces with a chocolate whose reputation is constantly increasing. We also know that every day he receives new orders from abroad; and it is on these grounds, and as a founder member of the Society for the Encouragement of National Industry, that we here accord him a form of honourable mention of which the reader will discover that we are anything but prodigal.

Official Method of Preparing Chocolate

The Americans prepare their cacao in the form of an unsweetened paste without sugar; when they wish to make chocolate they send for boiling water; each person scrapes into his cup as much cacao as he requires, pours the hot water over it, and adds sugar and flavouring to suit his taste.

This method is contrary to both our habits and our tastes; we prefer the chocolate to reach us ready prepared. Transcendental chemistry informs us that in this condition it must neither be scraped with a knife nor crushed with a pestle, because the collision which takes place in these two cases starches certain portions of the sugar and makes the drink insipid.

So, to make chocolate, that is to say, to prepare it for immediate consumption, take about one and a half ounces for each cup of water, and let it dissolve slowly while the water comes to the boil, stirring it with a wooden spatula; let it boil for a quarter of an hour, to give the solution consistency, and serve piping hot.

Over fifty years ago Madame d'Arestrel, Superior of the Convent of the Visitation at Belley, said to me: 'Monsieur, when you wish to drink good chocolate, have it made the day before in a porcelain coffee-pot, and left overnight. The night's rest concentrates it, and God cannot frown on this little refinement, for He is himself all excellence.'

7. The Theory of Frying

48. Introduction

It was a fine day in the month of May; the sun was shedding its gentlest rays on the smoke-begrimed roofs of the city of pleasures, and for once there was neither dust nor mud in the streets.

The great mail-coaches had long since ceased to rumble over the cobblestones; the heavy carts were still at rest, and the only vehicles at large were those open carriages from which fair ladies, both indigenous and exotic, sheltered beneath the most elegant of hats, are accustomed to glance disdainfully at the ugly and coquettishly at the handsome.

In short, it was three o'clock in the afternoon when the Professor settled down in his chair of meditation.

His right leg rested vertically on the floor; his left was stretched out diagonally; his back was suitably supported, and his hands lay on the lion's-head extremities of the arms of that venerable chair.

His lofty brow revealed a love of serious study, his mouth a taste for pleasant distractions. His demeanour was calm and his bearing such that no one seeing him could have failed to say: 'This old man must surely be a sage.'

Thus seated, the Professor summoned his chief cook; and soon the servant appeared, ready to receive advice, instruction, or commands.

Address

'Maître la Planche,' said the Professor in those grave tones which go straight to the heart, 'all who sit at my table proclaim you a soup-maker of the highest order, and that is well, for soup is the first consolation of a hungry stomach;

but I note with sorrow that in the art of frying you have still a lot to learn.

'Yesterday I heard you groaning over that triumphal sole which you served up all pale, flabby, and discoloured. My friend R—[1] looked at you disapprovingly; Monsieur H. R. pointed his gnomonic nose to the west, and President Sibuet wept over the dish as if it were a national disaster.

'This misfortune befell you because you disregarded theory, failing to appreciate its importance. You are a little stubborn, and I find it hard to convince you that the phenomena which occur in your laboratory are simply the fulfilment of the eternal laws of nature, and that certain things which you do carelessly, and only because you have seen others do them, none the less possess the loftiest scientific origins.

'Listen carefully then, and learn, so that you may never again have cause to blush over your handiwork.'

Chemistry

'Not all the liquids which you expose to the action of fire can be charged with an equal quantity of heat; Nature has made them unequally receptive; she alone knows the secret of this order of things, which we call *caloric capacity*.

'Thus, you could dip your finger into boiling spirits of wine with impunity; but you would withdraw it hastily from boiling brandy, and more quickly still from boiling water; while a brief immersion in boiling oil would cause you serious injury, for oil has at least three times the heating capacity of water.

'It is due to this state of affairs that hot liquids act differently on the sapid substances immersed in them. Those which are immersed in water grow soft, disintegrate, and finally turn to pulp: that is how broth or extracts are made.

1. Monsieur R—, born in Seysell, a district of Belley, about 1757. An elector of the *grand collège*, he may be cited as a striking example of the happy outcome of prudent behaviour combined with the most inflexible probity.

On the other hand, those which are immersed in oil shrink, take on varying degrees of colour, and in the end become entirely carbonized.

'In the first case, the water dissolves and absorbs the internal juices of the foodstuffs immersed in it; and in the second, those juices are preserved, because the oil cannot dissolve them; and if the substance dries up, it is because its humid parts have finally evaporated under the continued influence of heat.

'These two different processes also have different names: the process of boiling foodstuffs in oil or fat is called *frying*. I have said already, I believe, that for culinary purposes *oil* and *fat* are nearly synonymous, since fat is simply solidified oil, and oil is liquid fat.'

Applications of the Theory

'Fried foods are welcome at any banquet; they introduce an appetizing variety into the meal, and are pleasant to the eye; they retain their original flavour, and can be eaten with the fingers, a quality which is always appreciated by the ladies.

'Frying also provides cooks with countless means of disguising food which has already been served up the day before and stands them in good stead in unforeseen emergencies; for it takes no longer to fry a four-pound carp than to boil an egg.

'The whole merit of frying consists in the *surprise*; for such is the name given to the sudden action of the boiling liquid which carbonizes or scorches the surface of the substance in question, at the very moment of its immersion.

'By means of this *surprise* a sort of ceiling is formed over the object, which prevents the fat from penetrating it, and concentrates the juices inside, so that they undergo an internal cooking process which gives the dish all the flavour of which it is capable.

'The *surprise* will only occur when the liquid is so hot that its action is sudden and instantaneous; but it only reaches this point after fairly prolonged exposure to the heat of a blazing fire.

'The following method will show whether the fat has attained the required degree of heat: Cut a piece of bread into the form of a sippet and dip it in the frying-pan for five or six seconds; if it comes out crisp and brown, proceed immediately with the immersion; if not, you must stoke the fire and start the experiment all over again.

'Once the *surprise* has been effected, damp the fire down so that the cooking is not too rapid, and so that the juices you have imprisoned may undergo the influence of a sustained heat which draws them together and enhances their flavour.

'You have doubtless observed that the surface of wellfried foodstuffs will no longer dissolve salt or sugar, even though they need one or other of those substances. Therefore you will not fail to reduce the salt or sugar to a fine powder, so that it acquires an extreme adhesive quality, and, when sprinkled on fried food, seasons it by means of juxtaposition.

'I say nothing of the choice of oils and fats; you have already received sufficient enlightenment on that point from the various cookery books I have placed at your disposal.

'But do not forget that when you are given a few trout, each scarcely a quarter of a pound in weight, straight from some freshwater stream that murmurs far from the capital, do not forget, I say, to fry them in the finest olive oil at your command; this simple dish, salted, peppered, and adorned with slices of lemon, is worthy to be laid before an Eminence.[1]

'Give the same treatment to smelts, which are a special joy

1. Monsieur Aulissin, a learned Neapolitan advocate and no mean performer on the cello, was dining with me one day when, eating something which pleased him greatly, he said: '*Questo è un vero boccone di cardinale!*' 'Why,' I replied, in the same tongue, 'don't you say, as we do, *a dish fit for a king?*' 'Monsieur,' he answered, 'we Italians consider that kings cannot be gourmands, because their meals are too short and solemn; but cardinals are a different matter!' And he gave that peculiar whooping chuckle of his: hou, hou, hou, hou, hou, hou!

to connoisseurs. The smelt is the warbler of the sea; fish and bird are alike in being small, delicate, and altogether superior.

'These two prescriptions are founded on the nature of things. Experience has taught us that olive oil should only be used in operations which can be performed within a short space of time, or which require no great heat, because prolonged boiling invests it with an empyreumatic and unpleasant taste, due to the presence of certain particles of parenchyma, which are very difficult to get rid of, and which become carbonized.

'You have ventured into my infernal regions, and you have known the glory of being the first man to offer to an astounded world a huge fried turbot; that day was a day of jubilation among the elect.

'Go then: continue to take care over all you do, and never forget that from the moment guests set foot in my diningroom, it is *we* who are responsible for their well-being.'

8. On Thirst

49. An Introduction

Thirst is the inner consciousness of the need to drink.

The various fluids in our bodies which sustain life are constantly evaporating at a heat of 104°; and the wastage which ensues would soon render those fluids unfit to fulfil their appointed task if they were not frequently replenished and renewed; their needs are the cause of the sensation of thirst.

We believe that the seat of thirst is situated throughout the digestive system. When a man is thirsty (and as a sportsman we have often been in that predicament) he can feel that all the absorbent parts of his mouth, throat, and stomach are parched, and if thirst is sometimes allayed by the application of liquids to parts of the body other than these organs, as, for example, by means of a bath, it is because as soon as those liquids are introduced into the system, they are rapidly carried towards the seat of the trouble, and so effect a cure.

Various Kinds of Thirst

A careful examination of this need for liquid refreshment reveals the existence of three kinds of thirst: latent thirst, factitious thirst, and burning thirst.

Latent or habitual thirst is the equilibrium imperceptibly maintained between transpiratory evaporation and the necessity of supplying its wants; it is this form of thirst which invites us to drink during meals, although we feel no pain, and enables us to drink at almost any time of the day. This thirst is always with us, and is, as it were, a part of our existence.

Factitious thirst is peculiar to the human race, and springs from that innate instinct which leads us to seek in liquids a power not invested in them by Nature, and only produced by fermentation. It is rather an artificial luxury than a natural need; and thirst of this kind is really unquenchable, because the drinks consumed with the object of appeasing it invariably give it new life. In the end it becomes a habit, and it is this thirst which afflicts every drunkard in the world; in most cases imbibing only stops when the drink runs out or when it has overcome the drinker and put him out of action.

When, on the contrary, we slake our thirst with pure water, which seems to be its natural antidote, we never drink a mouthful beyond our needs.

Burning thirst is induced by an increased need to drink and the impossibility of satisfying latent thirst.

It is called *burning* because it is accompanied by a burning of the tongue, dryness of the palate, and consuming heat throughout the body.

The sensation of thirst is so acute that the word is synonymous, in nearly all languages, with extreme longing and imperious desire; thus we speak of a thirst for gold, riches, power, vengeance, etc., expressions which would not have become current if it were not enough to have been thirsty only once in a lifetime in order to recognize their appropriateness.

Appetite is accompanied by an agreeable sensation, as long as it stops short of hunger; thirst has no twilight zone, but is no sooner felt than it causes distress and anxiety; and the anxiety becomes excruciating when there is no hope of alleviating it.

By a just compensation, the act of drinking may in certain circumstances provide us with the keenest pleasure; and when a terrible thirst is quenched, or a moderate thirst allayed by some delicious drink, the whole papillary apparatus is titillated, from the tip of the tongue to the depths of the stomach.

Death is caused much more rapidly by thirst than by

hunger. There are examples of men who, having some water, have lived more than a week without food, whereas those who are completely deprived of anything to drink never survive beyond five days.

The reason for this difference is that the hungry man dies simply from exhaustion and weakness, whereas the thirsty man is assailed by a burning fever which grows more acute from hour to hour.

Not everyone can stand thirst so long; witness a certain soldier of the Swiss Guard of Louis XVI, who died in 1787 after being only twenty-four hours without drink.

He was at an inn with some of his comrades, one of whom, when he held out his glass for more wine, accused him of drinking more often than the others, and of being unable to go without for a single moment. In reply he wagered that he would go twenty-four hours without a drink; and his bet was accepted, the stakes being ten bottles of wine.

From that moment the soldier drank no more, although he had to sit and watch his comrades drinking for over two hours before they left the inn.

The night, as you may imagine, passed well enough, but at dawn he found it very hard to do without the tot of brandy he always drank on rising.

All morning he was restless and ill at ease; he came and went, got up and sat down without any reason, and seemed not to know what to do with himself.

At one o'clock he took to his bed, hoping to find peace there; he was in pain and positively ill; but it was in vain that his comrades urged him to have a drink. He declared that he would hold out till evening; he was intent on winning the wager; and doubtless he was also sustained by a certain military pride which prevented him from giving in to pain.

He held out like this until seven o'clock; but at half past seven he lost consciousness, entered into a death-agony, and expired, unable even to taste the glass of wine which was held to his lips.

I obtained all these details that same evening from

Monsieur Schneider, a worthy man and a piper in the Company of Swiss Guards, in whose house at Versailles I was lodging at the time.

50. *Causes of Thirst*

Various circumstances, together or apart, can contribute to provoke thirst. We are about to indicate some of these which have not been without a certain influence on our way of life.

Heat provokes thirst; hence man's age-old tendency to take up his quarters beside a stream.

Bodily toil provokes thirst; for this reason employers never fail to revive the strength of their workmen with drinks; hence the saying that he gets the best price for wine who gives it to his employees.

Dancing provokes thirst; hence the numerous stimulating or refreshing drinks which have always been served at balls.

Declamation provokes thirst; hence the glass of water which all orators sip with studied elegance, and which will soon be seen on the ledge of every pulpit, next to the white handkerchief.[1]

The pleasures of the flesh provoke thirst; hence those poetical descriptions of Cyprus, Amathontes, Cnidos, and other haunts of Venus, in which there is never any lack of cool groves and streams that murmur as they meander along.

Singing provokes thirst; hence the universal reputation singers have of being indefatigable drinkers. Being a singer myself, I rise to protest against the slander, which no longer has any truth in it.

The singers who frequent our drawing-rooms today drink with discretion and sagacity; but what they have lost on the

---

1. Canon Délestra, a most agreeable preacher, always used to swallow a preserved nut during the interval he allowed his congregation between each point in his sermon for coughing, spitting, and blowing their noses.

one hand they regain on the other, for they are no longer topers, they are gourmands, and it is said that the fanatical celebration of the Feast of St Cecilia by the Transcendental Harmony Society has been known to last more than twenty-four hours.

51. An Example

Exposure to a high wind is a very active cause of thirst; and I believe that the following anecdote will be read with pleasure, especially by sportsmen.

It is well known that quails have a great liking for mountainous districts, where they are more certain of success in hatching their eggs, because harvesting is done there much later than in the lowlands.

When the rye is cut, they retreat into the oats and barley; when the mowing of the last two begins, they withdraw into those parts where the grain is not ripe.

Then is the time to shoot them, for all the quails which a month earlier were scattered over the countryside can be found within the space of a few acres; and as the season is nearly over they are as large and fat as anyone could wish.

It was in order to shoot quails that I found myself one day with a few friends on the slopes of a mountain in the district of Nantua, in the canton called Plan d'Hotonne. We were about to begin shooting, on one of those beautiful September mornings when the sun shines with a brilliance unknown to *cockneys*.[1]

But while we were breakfasting, a violent and most unwelcome wind blew up from the north; which did not prevent us, however, from taking the field.

We had not been shooting for more than a quarter of an hour when the softest member of the party began to complain of thirst; and no doubt he would have been teased about this if the rest of us had not felt thirsty too.

We all drank, for the donkey carrying our canteen was

1. This is the name given to Londoners who have never left their city; it is equivalent to the Parisian *badaud*.

following us; but the relief was of short duration. Our thirst soon returned, and with such intensity that some of us thought that they were ill, and others that they were going to be; there was even talk of returning home, which would have meant a tramp of twenty-five miles for nothing.

I had had time to collect my ideas, and I had discovered the reason for this extraordinary thirst. I called my friends together, and told them that we were under the influence of four circumstances which were combining to make us thirsty: the marked decrease in the pressure of the atmosphere on our bodies, which was bound to make our blood circulate more rapidly; the force of the sun's direct rays; the long walk, which was making us all breathe heavily; and, above all else, the force of the wind, which, piercing us through and through, was drying up our perspiration and depriving our skin of its natural moisture.

I added that there was no danger in all this; but that, the enemy being known, we had to fight him; and it was resolved that we should drink at regular intervals of half an hour.

This precaution proved inadequate, however, and our thirst remained invincible; neither wine, nor brandy, nor wine-and-water, nor brandy-and-water were of any avail. We were thirsty even while we drank, and thoroughly wretched all day long.

However, the day came to an end, like any other; the proprietor of the Latour farm offered us hospitality, and supplemented our provisions with his own. We had a wonderful dinner, and soon afterwards went out and buried ourselves in the hay, where we enjoyed the most delicious sleep.

Next day my theory received the sanction of experience. The wind had died down completely during the night; and although the sun was just as bright as the day before, and even hotter, we none the less shot for several hours without feeling very thirsty.

But the harm was already done; our flasks, although we had been careful to fill them before setting out, were unable to stand up to the frequent attacks we made on them; they were left like bodies without souls, and we fell into the snares of the local innkeepers.

There was no other course open to us, but we did not give in without a murmur, and I hurled a speech full of invective at that desiccating wind, when I saw that a dish worthy of a king's table, a dish of spinach in quails' fat, was going to be washed down with a wine hardly better than Suresnes.[1]

1. Suresnes, a pretty village ten miles from Paris. It is famous for its bad wines. There is a saying that to drink a glass of Suresnes, three persons are required: the one who drinks it, and two acolytes to hold him up and prevent him from losing heart. The same is said of the wine of Périeux; but people drink it all the same.

9. On Drinks[1]

52. Introduction

The word drink is used of any liquid which can be used to accompany our food.

Water seems to be the most natural drink. It is found wherever there are animals, takes the place of milk among adults, and is no less necessary to us than air.

Water

Water is the only drink which really quenches thirst, and that is the reason why it can only be drunk in comparatively small quantities. Most of the other liquors which man imbibes are only palliatives, and if he had confined himself to water, it would never have been said of him that one of his privileges was to drink without being thirsty.

The Prompt Effect of Drinks

Drinks are absorbed into the animal economy with extreme ease; their effect is prompt, and the relief which they give almost instantaneous. Lay a substantial meal before a tired man, and he will eat with difficulty and be little the better for it at first. Give him a glass of wine or brandy, and immediately he feels better: you see him come to life again before you.

A curious occurrence, of which my nephew, Colonel Guigard, told me, lends support to this theory. My nephew is no storyteller by nature, but the truth of his tale is beyond question.

1. This chapter is purely philosophical; a detailed account of the various known drinks could not be included in my work as planned; there would have been no end to it.

He was at the head of a detachment returning from the siege of Jaffa, and they had reached a point only a few hundred paces from the place where they were due to make a halt and find some water when they noticed some dead bodies on the road; they were the corpses of some soldiers belonging to a detachment a day's march ahead of my nephew's, who had died of the heat.

Among the victims of that burning climate was a carabineer who was known to several of my nephew's men. He had presumably been dead for over twenty-four hours, and the sun, beating down on him all day, had turned his face as black as a crow.

Some of his comrades came over to the body, either to look at him one last time, or to collect their inheritance, if there was anything to inherit; and they were astonished to find his limbs still flexible; and even a little warmth in the neighbourhood of the heart.

'Give him a drop of *sacré-chien*,' said the wag of the detachment; 'I'll bet that unless he's gone a long way into the next world, he'll come back for a taste of that.'

Sure enough, at the first spoonful of spirits the dead man opened his eyes; everyone cried out in amazement; and after his temples had been rubbed with the spirits and he had been given a little more to drink, he was able, with some assistance, to keep his seat on a donkey.

They led him like this to the well; during the night he was looked after carefully, and given a few dates to eat, with some other light food; and the following day, again mounted on the donkey, he reached Cairo with the rest.

53. Strong Drinks

A thing of enormous interest is that sort of instinct, as general as it is imperious, which leads us in search of strong drinks.

Wine, the most delightful of drinks, whether we owe it to Noah, who planted the vine, or to Bacchus, who pressed juice from the grape, dates from the childhood of the world;

and beer, which is attributed to Osiris, goes back to a period beyond which nothing certain is known.

All men, even those it is customary to call savages, have been so tormented by this craving for strong drinks, that they have always managed to obtain them, however limited the extent of their knowledge.

They have turned the milk of their domestic animals sour, or extracted juice from various fruits and roots which they suspected of containing the elements of fermentation; and wherever human society has existed, we find that men were provided with strong liquors, which they used at their feasts, sacrifices, marriages, or funerals, in short on all occasions of merry-making or solemnity.

Wine was drunk and its praises sung for many centuries before men guessed at the possibility of extracting the spirituous part which makes its strength; but when the Arabs taught us the art of distillation, which they had invented for the purpose of extracting the scent of flowers, and above all that of the rose which occupies such an important place in their writings, then men began to believe that it was possible to discover in wine the cause of that special savour which has such a stimulating influence on the organ of taste; and so, step by step, alcohol, spirits of wine, and brandy were discovered.

Alcohol is the prince of liquids, and carries the palate to its highest pitch of exaltation; its various preparations have opened up a new source of pleasure;[1] it invests certain medicaments[2] with a power which they could not otherwise have attained; and it has even become a formidable weapon in our hands, for the nations of the New World have been subdued and destroyed almost as much by brandy as by firearms.

The method by which alcohol was discovered has led to other important results; for consisting as it does in the separation and exposure of the parts which make up a body, and distinguish that body from all others, it has served as a model to scholars pursuing analogous researches; and they

1. Liqueurs.   2. Elixirs.

have made known to us entirely new substances, such as strychnine, quinine, morphine, and others, both discovered and to be discovered in the future.

Be that as it may, this thirst for a kind of liquid which Nature has enveloped in veils, this strange desire that assails all the races of mankind, in every climate and temperature, is most worthy to attract the attention of the philosophic observer.

I, among others, have pondered it, and I am tempted to place the craving for fermented liquors, which is unknown to animals, with anxiety regarding the future, which is likewise unknown to animals, and to regard both as distinctive attributes of the masterpiece of the last sublunary revolution.

10. On the End of the World

54. Philosophic Reflection

I said 'the last sublunary revolution', and that thought, expressed in those terms, has carried me a long, long way.

Incontrovertible evidence informs us that our globe has already suffered several absolute changes, each one nothing less than an *end of the world*; and an indefinable instinct warns us that more revolutions are to come.

Many times already it has been thought that such revolutions were close at hand, and there are still people alive whom the watery comet foretold by the worthy Jérôme Lalande sent hurrying to the confessional.

Judging by what has been said on the subject, men are prone to invest this catastrophe with vengeance and destroying angels, trumpets and other no less terrifying accessories.

Alas, there is need of no such fuss for our destruction; we are not worthy of so much pomp; and if the Lord so wills, He can change the face of the globe without the help of ceremonial apparatus.

Let us suppose, for example, that one of those wandering stars, whose course and mission are alike unknown, and whose appearance has always been accompanied by a display of terror; let us suppose, I say, that some comet passes close enough to the sun to be charged with superabundant heat, and comes close enough to the earth to cause for the space of six months a temperature of 168° (twice as high as that which marked the appearance of the comet of 1811).

At the end of that fatal season, all living things, both animal and vegetable, will have perished; every sound will have died away; the earth will revolve in silence, until new circumstances develop new germs; and the cause of disaster will remain lost in the endless fields of the air, and will never have been closer to us than several million miles away.

This course of events, which is just as likely as any other, has always seemed to me an admirable subject for speculation; and I have no hesitation in dwelling on it now.

It is interesting to follow in imagination that ascensional heat, to foresee its gradual action and effects, and to ask:

Quid during the first day, and the second, and so on to the last?

Quid on air, earth, and water, on the formation, mixture, and explosion of gases?

Quid on man, in relation to age, sex, strength, and weakness?

Quid on obedience to the law, submission to authority, respect for persons and property?

Quid on the means we might look for, or the attempts we might make, to avoid the danger?

Quid on the bonds of love, friendship, and kinship, on selfishness and devotion?

Quid on religious sentiment, faith, resignation, hope, etc.?

History may be able to throw some light on the moral influences involved; for the end of the world has already been foretold several times, even to a day.

I genuinely feel some regret at not telling my readers how I settled all these problems in my wisdom, but I would not like to deprive them of the pleasure of reaching their own conclusions: an occupation which can shorten the hours of a sleepless night, or provide material for daytime siestas.

Great danger looses all bonds. When the yellow fever was raging in Philadelphia about 1792, husbands were seen to refuse their wives entry to their homes, children deserted their parents, and many other similar phenomena took place.

Quod a nobis Deus avertat![1]

1. 'May God avert this from us!' [Ed.]

11. On Gourmandism

55. *Introduction*

I have consulted all the dictionaries about the word *Gourmandism*, and am far from satisfied with what I have found. There is endless confusion between *gourmandism*, properly so called, and *gluttony* or *voracity*; whence I conclude that lexicographers, excellent fellows though they may be in other respects, are not to be numbered among those charming scholars who eat a partridge wing with easy grace, and wash it down, little finger in the air, with a glass of Lafite or Clos Vougeot.

They have forgotten, utterly forgotten, social gourmandism, which combines the elegance of Athens, the luxury of Rome, and the delicacy of France, and which unites careful planning with skilled performance, gustatory zeal with wise discrimination; a precious quality, which might well be called a virtue, and is at least the source of our purest pleasures.

Definitions

Let us then define our terms and make ourselves clear.

Gourmandism is an impassioned, reasoned, and habitual preference for everything which gratifies the organ of taste.

Gourmandism is the enemy of excess; indigestion and drunkenness are offences which render the offender liable to be struck off the rolls.

Gourmandism includes *friandise*, which is simply the same preference applied to light, delicate, and insubstantial food, such as preserves and pastry. It is a modification introduced in favour of the ladies and those gentlemen who resemble them.

From whatever point of view gourmandism is considered, it deserves nothing but praise and encouragement.

From the physical point of view, it is the result and proof of the sound and perfect condition of the organs of nourishment.

From the moral point of view, it shows implicit obedience to the commands of the Creator, who, when He ordered us to eat in order to live, gave us the inducement of appetite, the encouragement of savour, and the reward of pleasure.

Advantages of Gourmandism

From the point of view of political economy, gourmandism is the common bond which unites the nations of the world, through the reciprocal exchange of objects serving for daily consumption.

It is gourmandism which sends wines, spirits, sugar, spices, pickles, salted foods, and provisions of every kind, down to eggs and melons, across the earth from pole to pole.

It is gourmandism which determines the relative price of things mediocre, good, and excellent, whether their qualities are the effect of art or the gift of nature.

It is gourmandism which sustains the hopes and the spirit of rivalry of the host of fishermen, huntsmen, farmers, and others who every day fill the richest larders with the result of their labours and discoveries.

And lastly, it is gourmandism which forms the livelihood of the industrious throng of cooks, confectioners, bakers, and others of all descriptions concerned with the preparation of food, who in their turn employ other works of every kind for their needs, thus giving rise at all times to a circulation of funds incalculable in respect to mobility and magnitude by even the most expert brains.

Let it be remembered too that the industry which has gourmandism as its object enjoys the special advantage that it depends on the one hand on the greatest fortunes and on the other on the recurring needs of everyday life.

In the present state of society it is difficult to imagine a

race which could live on bread and vegetables alone. Such a
race, if it existed, would infallibly be subjugated by any carnivorous army, like the Hindus, who have successively fallen
prey to all their assailants; or else it would be converted by
the skill in cookery of its neighbours, like the Boeotians of
old, who became gourmands after the battle of Leuctra.

56. *More Advantages*

Gourmandism also has considerable fiscal importance;
toll dues, customs duties, and indirect taxes thrive on it.
Everything we consume pays tribute, and gourmands are the
chief mainstay of every nation's wealth.

What shall we say of the swarm of cooks who for centuries
past have left France to exploit the gourmandism of other
lands? Most of them succeed in their endeavours, and obeying an instinct which never dies in a Frenchman's heart,
bring back to their native soil the fruits of their economy.
This access of wealth is more important than might be imagined, and these men, like the others, will have their genea-
logical tree.

If nations were grateful, none would have better reason
than France to raise altars and a temple to Gourmandism.

57. *The Power of Gourmandism*

In 1815, under the November Treaty,[1] France was required
to pay seven hundred and fifty millions[2] to the Allies in
three years.

A further condition required her to meet the individual
claims of the inhabitants of the various Allied countries,
which, with the interest fixed by the sovereigns of those
countries, amounted to over three hundred millions.[3]

1. This was the Second Treaty of Paris (the first had been signed in
1814), the final settlement of the Napoleonic Wars. [Translator.]
2. It is difficult to estimate equivalent values, but this sum represents
approximately £180 m. in 1970. [Translator.]
3. Approximately £72 m. in 1970. [Translator.]

Finally, to this must be added the requisitions of all kinds made by the enemy generals, which they sent off in cartloads to the frontiers, and which later had to be paid for out of the public purse; in all, over fifteen hundred millions.[4]

There was every reason to fear that such considerable payments, which were made day after day *in cash*, might put an intolerable strain on the exchequer, and cause a depreciation of all fictitious values, followed by all the misfortunes which overwhelm a penniless country deprived of the means of obtaining money.

'Alas,' said men of property, as they watched the fatal tumbril going to be loaded up in the Rue Vivienne, 'alas, there goes our money on its way out of the country; next year, we shall go down on our knees before a crown piece; we shall be ruined and reduced to beggary, all enterprises will fail; borrowing will be impossible; and we shall be faced with decline, stagnation, and civil death.'

Events gave the lie to these fears, and to the amazement of all students of finance, the payments were made with ease, credit improved, loans were oversubscribed, and during the whole period of this superpurgation the rate of exchange, that infallible index of the circulation of money, remained in our favour; in other words, there was mathematical proof that more money was coming into France than going out of it.

What was the power which came to our aid? What divinity performed this miracle?

Gourmandism.

When the Britons, the Germans, the Teutons, the Cimmerians, and the Scythians poured into France, they brought with them a rare voracity and stomachs of uncommon capacity.

They were not content for long with the official cheer forthcoming from forced hospitality; they aspired to more delicate pleasures; and before long the queen of cities had become a vast refectory. These intruders ate in restaurants, in hotels, in taverns, at street-stalls, and even in the streets.

4. Approximately £360 m. in 1970. [Translator.]

They stuffed themselves with meat, fish, game, truffles, pastry, and above all with our fruit.

Their thirst was as insatiable as their appetite; and they always asked for the most expensive wines, in the hope of discovering unheard-of joys, which they were subsequently astonished not to experience.

Superficial observers did not know what to think of this endless feasting for no reason; but the true Frenchman laughed and rubbed his hands, saying: 'They are under a spell, and by tonight they will have paid us back more crowns than the Treasury handed over to them this morning.'

It was a golden time for all who ministered to the pleasures of taste. Véry finished making his fortune; Achard laid the foundations of his; Beauvilliers amassed his third, and Madame Sulot, whose shop in the Palais-Royal was only a few feet square, sold up to twelve thousands tarts a day.[1]

The influence of that period has continued to this day; foreigners come pouring in from every part of Europe to resume in peacetime the pleasant habits which they acquired during the war; they must come to Paris; and when they are there they must indulge their tastes, no matter what the cost. And if our public bonds are in favour, it is due not so much to the high rate of interest they carry, as to the instinctive confidence everyone inevitably feels in a people in whose midst gourmands are happy.[2]

58. *Portrait of a Pretty Gourmand*

Gourmandism is by no means unbecoming in women; it suits the delicacy of their organs, and compensates in some degree

1. When the army of invasion passed through Champagne, it took six hundred thousand bottles of wine from Monsieur Moët's cellars at Épernay, a town famed for the beauty of its cellars. He soon found consolation for this enormous loss; for the looters acquired a taste for his wines, and the orders which he receives from the North have more than doubled since that time.

2. The calculations on which this chapter is based were furnished by Monsieur M.B., an aspirant to gastronomical distinction, who is not without qualifications, being a financier and a music-lover.

for the pleasures they must forgo, and the ills to which Nature seems to have condemned them.

There is no more charming sight than a pretty gourmand in action: her napkin is daintily tucked in; one hand rests on the table; the other conveys to her mouth elegantly cut morsels, or a wing of partridge for her teeth to bite; her eyes are bright, her lips glistening, and all her movements full of grace; and she does not lack that touch of coquetry which women show in everything they do. With such advantages she is irresistible, and even Cato the Censor could not look at her unmoved.

Anecdote

But here a bitter memory comes to mind.

One day, being placed next to pretty Madame M—d at table, I was inwardly rejoicing at my good fortune, when she suddenly turned to me and said: 'Your health!' I promptly began a neat reply, but I never finished, for the coquette turned towards her other neighbour, and asked him to drink with her. They touched glasses; and that left a wound in my heart which many years have failed to heal.

Women are Gourmands

There is something instinctive in the penchant for gourmandism which prevails among the fair sex, for gourmandism is favourable to beauty.

A series of exact and rigorous observations has shown that a succulent, delicate, and well-chosen diet delays the outward signs of old age for a long time.

It lends new brilliance to the eyes, new bloom to the skin, and new strength to the muscles; and as it is certain, physiologically, that slackening of the muscles is the cause of wrinkles, those dread enemies of beauty, it is no less true to say that, all things being equal, those who know how to eat look ten years younger than those to whom that science is a mystery.

Painters and sculptors are well aware of this truth, for they never depict a person who fasts out of choice or duty, such as a miser or an anchorite, without giving him the pallor of sickness, the thinness of poverty, and the wrinkles of decrepitude.

59. *Effects of Gourmandism on Sociability*

Gourmandism is one of the principal bonds of society; for it is gourmandism that gradually draws out that convivial spirit which every day brings all sorts together, moulds them into a single whole, sets them talking, and rounds off the sharp corners of conventional inequality.

It is gourmandism too which inspires the efforts every good host must make to entertain his guests, and the gratitude of his guests when they see what pains have been taken on their behalf; and this is the place to cry eternal shame on those stupid eaters who swallow the choicest dainties with culpable indifference, or breathe in with sacrilegious insouciance the fragrance of a limpid nectar.

General Law

Any display of ingenious hospitality calls for an explicit eulogy; and wherever the desire to please is evident, a word of praise is customary.

60. *Influence of Gourmandism on Conjugal Happiness*

Finally, gourmandism, when it is shared, has the most marked influence on the happiness which may be found in the married state.

Two married gourmands have a pleasant opportunity to meet at least once a day; for even those who sleep apart (and there are many such) eat at the same table; they have a subject of conversation which never grows stale, for they talk not only about what they are eating, but also of what they have eaten, what they are about to eat, what they have observed at other houses, fashionable dishes, new culinary inventions, etc., etc.; and such chit-chat is full of charm.

No doubt music too has strong attractions for those who love it; but it must be played, and that requires an effort. Besides, a cold, a lost music-book, an instrument out of tune, or even a headache, and there is no music.

But a common need calls man and wife to table, and a common inclination keeps them there; they naturally show each other those little courtesies which reveal a desire to please; and the manner in which meals are conducted is an important ingredient in the happiness of life.

This last piece of wisdom, which is new to France, did not escape the English moralist, Richardson; he enlarges on it in his novel *Pamela*, where he depicts the different ways in which two married couples spend their day.

The two husbands are brothers; the elder is a peer in full possession of the family estate; the younger is Pamela's husband, disinherited on account of this marriage, and living on the proceeds of his half-pay in straitened circumstances not far removed from poverty.

The peer and his lady enter their dining-room from opposite directions, and greet each other coldly, although it is their first meeting of the day. They sit down at a lavishly spread table, surrounded by lackeys gleaming with gold; they help themselves in silence and eat without zest. However, when the servants have withdrawn, a kind of conversation begins between them; but sharp words are exchanged, a quarrel ensues, and the pair rise from table in a fury, to seek their separate rooms, where each thinks of the sweetness of the widowed state.

The younger brother, on the other hand, on reaching his humble lodging, is welcomed with tender effusion and the sweetest of caresses. He sits down at a frugal board; but the excellence of his meal is assured, for Pamela herself has cooked it. They eat with delight, chatting about their affairs, their projects, and their love. A half-bottle of Madeira serves to prolong both meal and conversation; then the same bed receives them both, and after the transports of mutual love, sweet slumber brings them forgetfulness of the present and dreams of better days to come.

All honour to gourmandism, such as we describe it to our readers, as long as it does not make a man lazy or extravagant! For just as the vices of Sardanapalus have not turned men against women, so the excesses of Vitellius should make no man turn his back on a well-chosen, ordered feast.

When gourmandism becomes gluttony, greed, and debauchery, it loses both its name and its advantages; it then falls outside our province and enters that of the moralist, who will treat it with his counsel, or of the doctor, who will cure it with his drugs.

La gourmandise as the Professor has described it in this chapter, has no name except in French; it cannot be rendered by the Latin *gula*, nor the English *gluttony*, nor the German *Lüsternheit*; and we therefore advise anyone who might be tempted to translate this instructive work to retain the word unchanged; that is what all other nations have done with *la coquetterie* and the words derived from it.

Note by a Patriotic Gourmand

I note with pride that coquetry and gourmandism, those two great modifications which extreme sociability have made to our most pressing needs, are both of French origin.

12. On Gourmands

61. Not Everyone can be a Gourmand

There are some individuals to whom Nature has denied either the organic delicacy or the power of concentration without which the tastiest dishes go unappreciated.

Physiology has already recognized the first of these two classes, and has shown that certain tongues are ill equipped with the papillae whose function it is to absorb and appreciate savours. They can convey to their unfortunate owners nothing but a dull sensation, and are to savours what blind eyes are to light.

The second class is made up of the absent-minded, the garrulous, the busybodies, the ambitious, and others who try to do two things at once, and only eat to fill their bellies.

Napoleon

Such a man was Napoleon; he was irregular in his meals, and a quick and careless eater. But this was an instance of that absolute will-power which he applied to everything. As soon as his appetite made itself felt, it had to be satisfied immediately; and his kitchen services were so arranged that anywhere and at any time he had only to say the word, and a fowl, cutlets, and coffee could immediately be placed before him.

Born Gourmands

But there is a privileged class of persons who are physically and organically predestined to enjoy the pleasures of taste.

I have always been a good Lavaterian and Gallist, and I believe in innate tendencies.

There are individuals who have evidently come into the world destined to see badly, to walk badly, or to hear badly, because they are born short-sighted, lame, or deaf, so why should there not be others who are predisposed to an unusually acute perception of certain sensations?

Again, no one with the smallest gift of observation can have failed to notice every day physiognomies which bear the unmistakable imprint of some dominant characteristic, such as contemptuous indifference, self-satisfaction, misanthropy, sensuality, etc., etc. It is true that these qualities may exist together with an insignificant face, but when the physiognomy is strongly marked, it rarely lies.

The passions act on the muscles; and very often, though a man remains silent, the various thoughts preoccupying him may be read in his face. This muscular tension, if it becomes at all habitual, will in the end leave visible traces, and so give a permanent and recognizable character to the physiognomy.

62. Sensual Predestination

Individuals predestined to gourmandism are generally of medium height; they have round or square faces, bright eyes, small foreheads, short noses, full lips, and well-rounded chins. The women are buxom, pretty rather than beautiful, with a tendency to run to fat. Those women whose gourmandism consists chiefly of a love of sweet things have finer features, a more delicate air, neater figures, and above all, a very special way with their tongues.

Such is the exterior beneath which to look for the most agreeable company; for these are the guests who accept everything they are offered, eat slowly, and savour each morsel thoughtfully. They are never in a hurry to leave the place where they have found true hospitality; and they are invited to stay all evening, because they know the games and pastimes appropriate to gastronomical gatherings.

Those, on the contrary, to whom Nature has refused an aptitude for the pleasures of taste, have long faces, noses, and eyes; whatever their height, there is something elongated in their proportions. Their hair is dark and flat, and they are never plump; it was they who invented trousers.

The women whom Nature has afflicted with the same misfortune are angular in body, are easily bored at table, and only live for cards and scandal.

This physiological theory will, I hope, find few opponents, because everyone can verify it among his own acquaintances; all the same, I am going to give it further support by means of examples.

One day I was a guest at an important dinner, and seated opposite me was a very pretty girl whose face was thoroughly sensual. I turned to my neighbour and whispered to him that with such features it was impossible for that young person not to be a great gourmand.

'What nonsense!' he replied; 'she cannot be more than fifteen, and that is not the age of gourmandism. . . . Still, let us watch her . . .'

The first signs were unfavourable, and I began to fear for my reputation; for during the first two courses the young lady showed a discretion which amazed me, and I was afraid that I had come across one of those exceptions which exist for every rule. But at last came dessert, a copious and varied dessert which revived my hopes. Those hopes were not disappointed; for not only did she sample every dish which was offered to her, but she even asked for dishes to be brought from the farthest ends of the table. In short she tried everything; and my neighbour marvelled that that little stomach could hold so many things. Thus my diagnosis was justified and science triumphed once again.

Two years later I met the same person again; it was a week after her marriage, and she had developed very pleasingly; she had begun to use a little coquetry, and, displaying all the charms that fashion allows to be revealed, she was ravishing. Her husband was a picture; he was like a certain ventriloquist who could laugh on one side of his face and weep on the other; that is to say, he seemed glad that his wife was so much admired, but no sooner did some admirer show too ardent an interest than he was afflicted by the pangs of obvious jealousy. The latter sentiment prevailed; he carried off his wife to a distant region, and that, for me, was the end of her biography.

On another occasion, I made a similar remark about the Duc Decrès, who was Minister of the Navy for so many years.

It will be remembered that he was a fat, short, swarthy, curly-haired, square-built man, with a round face, a prominent chin, thick lips, and the mouth of a giant; so I pronounced him on the spot a predestined lover of good cheer and beautiful women.

Very gently and very softly, I breathed this physiognomic verdict into a pretty, and, so I believed, discreet woman's ear. Alas, I was mistaken. She was a daughter of Eve, and if she had kept my secret it would have choked her. And so, that same evening, his Excellency was informed of the scientific inference which I had drawn from his face and person.

This I learned next day, when I received a very charming letter from the Duke, modestly disclaiming the two qualities – estimable though they are – which I had discovered in him. I did not admit defeat. I replied that Nature does nothing in vain; that she had clearly marked him out for certain missions; that if he failed to carry them out, he would be disobeying her wishes; that I was of course not entitled to any such confidences, etc., etc.

There the correspondence closed; but not long afterwards all Paris learned from the newspapers of the memorable battle which took place between the Minister and his cook, a prolonged and hard-fought battle, in which his Excellency did not always have the upper hand. Now, if after such an exploit the cook was not dismissed (and he was not), I may, I think, draw the conclusion that the Duke was absolutely dominated by the talents of that artist, and that he despaired of finding another who could gratify his taste so perfectly; otherwise he could never have overcome the repugnance which he must have felt, at being served by so bellicose a domestic.

I was writing these lines, one fine winter evening, when Monsieur Cartier, a former first violin at the Opera, and a skilful performer, came into my room and sat down by my fireside. I was full of my subject, and gazing at him intently, I said:

'Dear Professor, how is it that you are no gourmand, when you have all the appearance of one?'

'I was a great gourmand once,' he replied, 'but now I abstain.'

'Is that out of wisdom?' I asked.

He made no answer, but heaved a Walter Scott sigh which was very like a groan.

63. Gourmands by Calling

If some men are predestined gourmands, others are gourmands by virtue of their calling; and mention must here be made of four great strongholds of gourmandism: finance, medicine, letters, and religion.

Finance

The financiers are the heroes of gourmandism. Heroes is the proper word, for there was a fight, and the nobility would have crushed the financiers under the weight of their titles and escutcheons, if the financiers had not countered with their strong-boxes and sumptuous tables. Cooks did battle with genealogists, and although the dukes did not wait to take their leave before they made fun of their hosts, they had come as guests, and their presence was proof of their defeat.

Moreover, all those who amass large fortunes easily are almost bound to become gourmands.

Unequal conditions produce unequal wealth, but unequal wealth does not produce unequal needs: and a man who every day could afford a dinner large enough for a hundred people is often more than satisfied after eating a leg of chicken. Gourmandism must therefore use all its resources to revive that shadowy appetite with new dishes which sustain it without damaging it, and soothe it without surfeiting it. It was thus that Mondor became a gourmand, and that countless others have followed his example.

In all the lists of recipes to be found in elementary cookery books, there are always several bearing the designation *à la financière*. And it is well known that in the past it was not the king, but the farmers-general,[1] who ate the first green peas of the season, which always cost eight hundred francs for the dish.

Things are not otherwise in our own day; the tables of finance still offer the most perfect products of nature, the most precocious fruits of the hot-house, the choicest creations of art; and the most distinguished personages are not too proud to sit down at these banquets.

64. Medicine

Causes no less powerful, although of a different nature, influence the medical profession; they are gourmands by seduction, and would need to be made of bronze in order to resist the force of circumstances.

Our dear doctors are the more welcome wherever they go, in that health, which is under their patronage, is the most precious thing in the world; so they become spoilt children in every sense.

Always anxiously awaited, they are sure to be greeted eagerly. A pretty patient summons them; a young girl embraces them; a father, a husband confides his loved one to their care. Hope turns their right flank, gratitude their left; they are fed like pigeons and must needs submit; within six months the habit has taken hold of them, and they are gourmands past redemption.

I ventured to expound these views one day when I was

1. A farmer-general was a person authorized in France under the *ancien régime* to buy the right to collect taxes. [Translator.]

one of nine guests at a dinner presided over by Doctor Corvisart. This was about 1806.

'You are,' I cried in the inspired tones of a puritan preacher, 'all that is left of a host which once spread all over France. Alas, the members of that host are all scattered or laid low; there are no more farmers-general, no more abbés, no more chevaliers, no more white monks. You alone now form the entire gustative body. Bear your mighty burden with fortitude, even if you should meet the fate of the three hundred Spartans at Thermopylae!'

I spoke, and there was no murmur of dissent; we acted accordingly, and the truth remains.

At dinner I made an observation worthy to be set down.

Doctor Corvisart, the most amiable of men when he chose, drank no wine but iced champagne. Consequently, in the early stages of the meal, while we others were occupied with eating, he was loquacious and full of tales and anecdotes. At dessert, on the other hand, when everyone began to talk more freely, he became serious, taciturn, and sometimes morose.

From this observation, and others of a similar nature, I have drawn the following conclusion: The Wine of Champagne, which is stimulating in its first effects (*ab initio*), is stupefying in those which follow after (*in recessu*) and this, moreover, is well known to be an effect of the carbonic acid gas which champagne contains.

65. A Reproach

Since I am on the subject of doctors, I wish before I die to reprove them for the barbarous severity they show towards their patients.

Once anyone falls into their hands, he must suffer a whole string of prohibitions, and give up all the pleasant habits of life.

I rise to protest against the majority of these vetoes, as being useless.

I say useless, because the sick almost never want to eat what would do them harm.

A rational doctor ought never to lose sight of the natural tendencies of his patients, nor to forget that if distressing sensations are by nature injurious, pleasant ones are beneficial. A little wine, a spoonful of coffee, a few drops of liqueur, have been known to bring back a smile to the most hippocratic countenances.

What is more, let me assure these bedside tyrants that their prescriptions are almost always ineffectual; the patient tries to avoid complying with them, his friends never fail to come up with reasons to support him in his resolve, and he gets neither better nor worse as a result.

The ration of a sick Russian, in 1815, would have made a Paris market porter drunk, and the English ration would have laid a Limousin low. Yet there was no escaping the full dose, for military inspectors constantly patrolled our hospitals, and supervised both issue and consumption.

I state my opinion with all the more confidence in that it is founded on numerous proved facts, and the best practitioners are coming round to my system.

Canon Rollet, who died about fifty years ago, was a heavy drinker, following the custom of those ancient days; he fell sick, and the doctor's first word laid a ban on all use of wine. Nevertheless, on his next visit, he found his patient in bed, and beside him an almost complete *corpus delicti*, to wit, a table covered with a snow-white cloth, a crystal goblet, a noble bottle, and a napkin with which to wipe the lips.

At the sight of these things he flew into a violent rage and was talking of withdrawing from the case, when the poor canon cried in doleful tones: 'Ah, but Doctor, remember that when you forbade me the use of wine, you did not forbid me the pleasure of seeing the bottle.'

The doctor who attended Monsieur de Montlucin of Pont-de-Veyle was even more cruel; he not only laid a ban on wine, but even ordered his patient to drink water in large doses.

Soon after the physician's departure, Madame de Montlucin, eager to enforce the prescription and ensure her husband's return to health, brought him a large glass of the purest and most limpid water.

The sick man took it meekly enough, and began drinking it with a resigned air; but after one mouthful he stopped, and handed the glass back to his wife saying: 'Take it my dear, and keep it for another time; I have always heard it said that medicine must not be wasted.'

66. Letters

In the empire of gastronomy, the territory of literature is very close to that of medicine.

In the reign of Louis XIV men of letters were drunkards; they conformed with fashion, and the memoirs of the time are highly edifying on this subject. Nowadays they are gourmands, a fact which represents a considerable change for the better.

I am far from sharing the opinion of the cynic Geoffroy, who declared that if modern works are lacking in force, it is because authors drink nothing but sugar-and-water.

I consider, on the contrary, that he was mistaken in two respects, and was wrong as to both the fact and the consequence.

The present period is rich in talents; it may be, indeed, that their very multitude is harmful to them; but posterity, passing judgement more calmly, will find much to admire in them, just as we ourselves have done justice to Racine and Molière, who were coldly received by their contemporaries.

Never has the position of writers in society been more agreeable. They no longer live in those lofty regions which were once a subject of reproach, the fields of literature have grown more fertile, and the springs of Hippocrene now run with gold; an author is the equal of any man, and no longer hears the voice of patronage; and to crown his happiness, gourmandism heaps him with her dearest favours.

Writers are invited everywhere on account of the esteem

felt for their talents; because their talk usually has a piquant flavour; and also because it has become the fashion for each social set to have its man of letters.

These gentlemen always arrive a little late, when they are all the more welcome because they have been missed; they are plied with dainties to make them come again, and wined and dined to make them sparkle; and they find all that perfectly natural, they grow accustomed to it, and become gourmands for life.

Things have even gone so far as to cause a certain amount of scandal. Some inquisitive persons have alleged that certain authors had been seduced at the luncheon table, that certain promotions had been decided at the dinner-table, and that the temple of immortality had been opened with a fork. But these were malicious rumours, and they died like so many; what is done is well done, and I only mention it here to show that I am conversant with every aspect of my subject.

67. Religion

Finally, the ranks of the devout contain many of the most faithful votaries of gourmandism.

By the *devout* we mean what Louis XIV and Molière meant, that is to say, those whose whole religion consists in outward practices; we are not concerned here with pious and charitable people.

Let us see how the vocation comes to them. Among those who seek salvation, the greater number choose the smoothest path; those who shun the company of men, sleep on bare boards, and wear hair shirts, have always been exceptions and always must be.

Now there are some things which are unequivocally damnable and never to be indulged in, such as dancing, the theatre, gambling and other similar pastimes.

While these pastimes and those who indulge in them are held in abomination, gourmandism steals on to the scene, wearing the most theological features.

By divine right man is king of nature, and everything the earth produces was created for him. It is for him that the quail grows fat, for him that Mocha coffee is fragrant, for him that sugar benefits health.

Why then should the good things Providence offers not be used, at least in moderation, especially if we continue to look on them as perishable things, and above all if they increase our gratitude towards the Author of all things?

These reasons are supported by others no less cogent. Can those who guide our souls and keep us in the way of salvation be too well received? Should not meetings with such an excellent purpose be made pleasurable and thus more frequent?

Sometimes, too, the gifts of Comus come unsought; it may be a memory of schooldays, or the gift of an old friendship, a pentitent wishing to humble himself, a relative paying a visit, or a protégé repaying a debt. How can such offerings be refused? And how can the recipient fail to match them in his turn? That is the least one can do.

Moreover, it has always been so.

The old monasteries were very storehouses of delicious food; and this is the reason why certain gourmands mourn their dissolution so bitterly.[1]

Several monastic orders, notably that of Saint Bernard, made a special practice of good cheer. The cooks of the clergy have extended the boundaries of their art; and when Monsieur de Pressigny, who died Archbishop of Besançon, came back from the conclave which had nominated Pius VI, he said that the best dinner which he had eaten in Rome had been given by the General of the Capuchins.

68. *The Chevaliers and the Abbés*

We cannot bring this chapter to a more fitting close than by

1. The best liqueurs in France were made at La Côte, by the Visitandines; the Sisters of Niort invented angelica preserves; the orange-flower cakes of the Sisters of Château Thierry were widely praised; and the Ursulines of Belley possessed a recipe for incredibly delicious comfits.

making honourable mention of two orders which the Revolution made an end of, but which we have seen in all their glory: the chevaliers and the abbés.

What gourmands they were, the dear fellows! It was impossible to mistake those flared nostrils, wide-open eyes, glistening lips, and flickering tongues; yet each class had its special way of eating.

There was something military about the method of the chevaliers; they took every mouthful with dignity, worked on it calmly, and darted glances of approval first at the master of the house, and then at the mistress.

The abbés, on the contrary, nestled up to their plates; their right hand curled like a cat's paw snatching chestnuts from the fire; their physiognomy was a picture of pleasure, and their gaze concentrated in a manner easier to imagine than to describe.

As three quarters of the present generation have never seen anything like the chevaliers and abbés we have just mentioned; and as some knowledge of them is indispensable in order to understand many books written in the eighteenth century, we shall borrow from the author of the *Historical Essay on the Duel* a few passages which leave nothing to be desired on this subject. (See *Miscellanea* No. 20.)

69. Gourmands and Longevity

On the basis of my recent reading, I am more than happy to be able to give to my readers a piece of good news, namely that good cheer is far from being harmful to health, and that, all things being equal, gourmands live longer than other men.

This was arithmetically proved in an excellent paper lately read by Doctor Villermet at the Academy of Science.

He compared the various classes of society in which good cheer is habitual with those which are poorly fed, covering the entire social scale. He also compared the various quarters of Paris with one another according to their wealth, for it is well known that wide divergencies exist in this respect, as, for example, between the Faubourg Saint-Marceau and the Chaussée-d'Antin.

Finally, the Doctor carried his researches into the regions of France, and compared them in respect to the fertility of the soil; everywhere he obtained the same result, that mortality diminishes in proportion to the increased ability to eat well, and hence that those whose unhappy fate it is to be poorly nourished may at least be sure that death will free them from that fate the sooner.

The two extremes are so widely separated that in the most favourable conditions only one individual in fifty dies in one year, whereas in the most poverty-stricken communities one in four dies in the same space of time.

That is not to say that those who enjoy good cheer never fall sick; alas, no, they too sometimes fall into the clutches of the medical fraternity, who are accustomed to refer to them as *good patients*; but as they have received a stronger dose of vitality, and every part of their constitution is in better condition, Nature has more resources to fall back on, and the body offers an incomparably stronger resistance to the process of destruction.

This physiological truth is likewise borne out by history, which informs us that on every occasion when imperious circumstances, such as war, sieges, or unseasonable weather, have produced a shortage of food, the consequent distress has always been accompanied by contagious disease and a great increase in mortality.

The Lafarge insurance scheme, which all Parisians will remember, would doubtless have prospered, if its promoters had taken into account the facts revealed by Doctor Villermet.

They calculated the rate of mortality according to the tables of Buffon, Parcieux, and others, which are all based on figures taken from all classes and all ages of a population. But as those who invest capital against future needs have generally escaped the dangers of childhood, and are accustomed to a wholesome, well-regulated, and sometimes tasty diet, *death did not come up to expectations*, and the speculation proved a failure. There were doubtless other causes, but none so fundamental.

For this final observation we are indebted to Professor Pardessus.

Monsieur du Belloy, Archbishop of Paris, who lived to be nearly a hundred, possessed a splendid appetite; he loved good cheer, and on several occasions I have seen his patri-archal countenance light up on the appearance of some noteworthy dish. Napoleon invariably treated him with deference and respect.

13. On Gastronomical Tests

70. Introduction

We have seen in the preceding chapter that the distinctive character of those whose claim to the honours of gourmandism is more insistent than justified consists in their dull-eyed and phlegmatic appearance when surrounded by good cheer.

They do not deserve to have treasures lavished on them, the worth of which they cannot appreciate; and it struck us as essential to be able to know them for what they are. Accordingly, we looked for means of acquiring information of such importance for the gauging of men and the assessing of guests.

We devoted ourselves to this inquiry with that diligence which knows no failure, and it is thanks to our perseverance that we are now able to present the honourable brotherhood of hosts with our discovery of *gastronomical tests*, a discovery which will do honour to the nineteenth century.

By *gastronomical tests*, we mean dishes of recognized savour and such indisputable excellence that the mere sight of them must arouse all the gustative powers of a properly constituted man; from which it follows that in such a case all those whose face shows no kindling of desire or glow of ecstasy can justly be marked down as unworthy of the honours of the occasion and the pleasures involved.

The method of the tests, duly examined and discussed in supreme council, was inscribed in the golden book in the following terms, taken from a language which never changes:

Utcumque ferculum, eximii et bene noti saporis, appositum fuerit, fiat autopsia convivae; et nisi facies ejus ac oculi vertantur ad ecstasim, notetur ut indignus.

Which was translated by the accredited translator of the supreme council as follows:

'Whenever a dish of well-known and very special savour is served, the guests shall be closely scrutinized, and all those whose physiognomy shows no rapture shall be marked down as unworthy.'

The power of the tests is relative, and they must be suited to the faculties and habits of the various classes of society. Every circumstance must be taken into account, and every test calculated to cause admiration and surprise; it is a sort of dynamometer, increasing in force as one goes up into the higher regions of society. Thus the test prepared for a man of humble means living in the Rue Coquenard, for example, would operate imperfectly on a head clerk, and would have no effect at all at a dinner given to a chosen few by a financier or a minister.

In the enumeration we are about to make of dishes which have been raised to the dignity of tests, we shall begin with those adjusted to the lowest pressure; we shall then gradually ascend, to illustrate our theory, in such a way that not only may our readers use our tests to their own advantage, but each may invent new tests on the same principle, give his name to them, and make use of them in that sphere of society to which chance has called him.

At one time it was our intention to append, as a matter of interest, recipes for composing the various preparations we have suggested as tests; but in the end we refrained, for we considered that we would be doing an injustice to the various books which have appeared on the subject, including that of Beauvilliers and the recently published *Cook of Cooks*. We shall therefore content ourselves with referring our readers to these books, as well as to those of Viard and Appert, pointing out that the latter contains certain scientific views hitherto absent from works of this nature.

It is greatly to be regretted that the public may not enjoy the tachygraphical account of what was said in the council, when it deliberated on the tests. The proceedings must remain wrapped in mystery; but there is at least one circumstance which I have been given permission to disclose.

A member[1] spoke in favour of negative tests, or tests by privation.

For example, an accident destroys some admirable dish, or a hamper of game, which should have arrived by the mail, is delayed, whether in fact or by supposition; on receipt of this distressing news, the guests would be watched and the gradual clouding of their brows carefully observed; by which means a reliable scale of gastric sensibility would be obtained.

But this proposal, attractive though it seemed at first sight, broke down under closer examination. The president observed, and with good reason, that such an occurrence, while acting only superficially on the ill-favoured organs of the indifferent, might exercise a baneful influence on the true believer, and even cause a fatal seizure. And so, despite some insistence on the part of its author, the motion was unanimously rejected.

We shall now proceed to enumerate the dishes we have judged suitable to be used as tests; we have divided them into three series, in a gradually ascending scale, according to the order and method indicated above.

FIRST SERIES

Presumed Income: 5,000 francs (competency)
A choice fillet of veal, larded with fat bacon and cooked in its own gravy;
A farm turkey, stuffed with Lyons chestnuts;
Fat caged pigeons, barded and suitably cooked;
Eggs *à la neige*;
A dish of *Sauerkraut,* garnished with sausages, and crowned with smoked Strasbourg bacon.
Expression: 'Ah! This looks good; come on, we must do it justice.'

SECOND SERIES

Presumed Income: 15,000 francs (affluence)
A rosy-hearted fillet of beef, larded and cooked in its own gravy;

1. Monsieur F.S., whose classic features, refined taste, and administrative talents well qualify him to become the perfect financier.

A haunch of venison with gherkin sauce;
A boiled turbot;
A leg of pré-salé mutton *à la provençale;*
A truffled turkey;
Early green peas.
Expression: 'My dear fellow, what a splendid sight! This is indeed a feast of feasts.'

THIRD SERIES

Presumed Income: 30,000 francs and upwards (wealth)
A seven-pound fowl, stuffed with Périgord truffles until it is made spherical;
A huge Strasbourg *pâté de foie gras*, in the shape of a bastion;
A big Rhine carp *à la Chambard*, richly adorned and garnished;
Truffled quails *à la moelle*, served on buttered toast flavoured with basil;
A stuffed and larded pike, bathed in creamy crayfish sauce *secundum artem;*
A well-hung roast pheasant, larded *en toupet*, served on toast dressed *à la Sainte Alliance*;
A hundred early asparagus, five or six threads in diameter, with osmazome sauce;
Two dozen ortolans *à la provençale,* as described in *The Secretary and the Cook.*
Expression: 'Ah, Monsieur (or Your Grace), what an admirable man your cook must be! One never comes across such marvels anywhere but here!'

General Observation

If a test is to produce its full effect, it must be applied on a comparatively large scale; experience, founded on knowledge of mankind, has taught us that the rarest and tastiest dish loses its influence when it is not served in lavish proportions; for the first reaction of the guests is checked by the fear that he is going to be served a tiny helping, or even, in certain situations, that he is going to be obliged to refuse the dish altogether, out of politeness; a predicament which often arises at the tables of pretentious misers.

I have had several opportunities of gauging the effect of gastronomical tests; but a single example will suffice.

I once attended a dinner of gourmands of the fourth degree, at which only two of the profane were present, my friend R— and myself.

Following an admirable first course, there appeared, among other dishes, a huge Barbezieux cockerel,[1] truffled fit to burst, and a Gibraltar-rock of Strasbourg *foie gras*.

This sight produced a marked but almost indescribable effect on the company, something akin to the 'silent laughter' mentioned by Cooper; I felt certain that here was a subject for observation.

Sure enough, all conversation ceased, for hearts were full to overflowing; the skilful movements of the carvers held every eye; and when the loaded plates had been handed round, I saw successively imprinted on every face the glow of desire, the ecstasy of enjoyment, and the perfect calm of utter bliss.

1. Men of authority have assured me that the flesh of the cockerel, if not tenderer, is at least more succulent than the flesh of the capon. My many activities have prevented me from testing the truth of this assertion, and I must ask my readers to do so for themselves. But I believe we may assume it to be well founded, for there is an element of sapidity in the first which is wanting in the second.

A witty woman once said to me that she was able to tell gourmands by their pronunciation of the word *good*, in such phrases as 'That's good, that's very good,' etc.; she declared that adepts instil into that one short monosyllable an accent of truth, tenderness, and enthusiasm such as ill-favoured palates can never attain.

14. On the Pleasures of the Table

71. Introduction

It is certain that more pain is felt by man than by all the other sentient creatures which inhabit our globe.

Nature condemned him to suffering from the start through the nakedness of his skin, the shape of his feet, and the instinct of war and destruction which has everywhere been found implanted in the human race.

The animals have not been stricken with this curse; and if it were not for such fighting as is caused by the instinct of reproduction, pain would be unknown to most species: whereas man, who can only experience pleasure intermittently, and through a small number of organs, may at all times, and through every part of his body, be subjected to appalling pain.

This decree of fate has been aggravated in its execution by a host of ills caused by the habits of social life, so that the keenest and most satisfying pleasures imaginable can never, either in intensity *or* duration, compensate for the atrocious pain caused by certain maladies, such as gout, toothache, acute rheumatism, and strangury, or the terrible tortures practised in certain lands.

It is this fear of pain which causes man, without even knowing it, to seek opposite extremes, and to cling desperately to the few pleasures which Nature has placed within his reach.

For the same reason he adds to their number, improves, perfects, and even worships them; for in pagan times, for many centuries, all the pleasures were secondary divinities, under the patronage of superior gods.

The severity of the new religions put an end to those personages; Bacchus, Diana, Cupid, and Comus are now nothing more than poetic memories; but the thing survives, and under the strictest of all faiths there is still merriment and feasting at marriages, baptisms, and even funerals.

72. Origin of the Pleasures of the Table

Meals, in the sense in which we understand the word, began with the second age of man; that is to say, as soon as he stopped living wholly on fruits. The dressing and distribution of meat necessarily brought each family together, as the father shared out the produce of his hunting among his children, and later, the grown-up children performed the same service for their aged parents.

These gatherings were at first confined to the closest relatives, but gradually came to include friends and neighbours.

Later, when the human race had spread far and wide, the weary traveller would sit down at these primitive meals, and tell what was happening in distant lands. Thus hospitality was born, with rites held sacred by every nation; for even the most savage tribe undertook to respect the life of him who had eaten its own bread and salt.

It was the meal which was responsible for the birth, or at least the elaboration of languages, not only because it was a continually recurring occasion for meetings, but also because the leisure which accompanies and succeeds the meal is naturally conducive to confidence and loquacity.

73. Difference between the Pleasures of Eating and the Pleasures of the Table

Such, in the nature of things, must have been the origin of the pleasures of the table, which must be carefully distinguished from their necessary antecedent, the pleasure of eating.

The pleasure of eating is the actual and direct sensation of a need being satisfied.

The pleasures of the table are considered sensations born

of the various circumstances of fact, things, and persons accompanying the meal.

The pleasure of eating is common to ourselves and the animals, and depends on nothing but hunger and the means to satisfy it.

The pleasures of the table are peculiar to mankind, and depend on preliminary care over the preparation of the meal, the choice of the place, and the selection of the guests.

The pleasure of eating requires, if not hunger, at least appetite; the pleasures of the table, more often than not, are independent of the one and the other.

Both of these two conditions may be observed at any dinner.

At the beginning of the meal, and throughout the first course, each guest eats steadily, without speaking or paying attention to anything which may be said; whatever his position in society, he forgets everything to become nothing but a worker in the great factory of Nature. But when the need for food begins to be satisfied, then the intellect awakes, talk becomes general, a new order of things is initiated, and he who until then was a mere consumer of food, becomes a table companion of more or less charm, according to the qualities bestowed on him by the Master of all things.

74. Effects

There are neither raptures, nor ecstasies, nor transports of bliss in the pleasures of the table; but they make up in duration what they lose in intensity, and are distinguished above all by the merit of inclining us towards all the other pleasures of life, or at least of consoling us for the loss of them.

In short, at the end of a good dinner, body and soul both enjoy a remarkable sense of well-being.

The physical effect is that the brain is refreshed, the face brightens up, the colouring is heightened, the eyes grow brighter, and a pleasant warmth pervades the limbs.

The mental effect is that wits are sharpened, the imagin-ation is fired, and jokes are made and exchanged; and if La Fare and Saint-Aulaire go down to posterity as witty authors, it will be chiefly owing to the fact that they were good table companions.

Again, one may often find round a single table all the modifications which extreme sociability has introduced into our midst: love, friendship, business, speculation, influence, solicitation, patronage, ambition, intrigue; that is why conviviality affects every aspect of human life, and bears fruits of every flavour.

75. Industrial Accessories

As a direct consequence of these circumstances, all the re-sources of human industry were employed to add to the dur-ation and intensity of the pleasures of the table.

Poets complained that the neck, being too short, curtailed the pleasure of degustation; others deplored the small ca-pacity of the stomach; and some even went so far as to re-lieve that organ of the necessity of digesting a first meal, in order to obtain the pleasure of swallowing the second.

This last was man's supreme effort to increase the pleasures of taste; and when it was found impossible to go beyond the limits set by Nature, he turned to the accessories, which offered him wider scope.

Vases and bowls were filled with flowers; the guests were crowned with wreaths; and meals were served beneath the vault of heaven, in gardens and groves, amid all the marvels of nature.

To the pleasures of the table the charms of music and the sound of instruments were added, as when the court of the king of the Phaecians sat feasting, and the singer Phemius sang to them of the deeds and warriors of old.

Often dancers, tumblers, and mimes of both sexes and every kind of costume gave occupation to the eyes without detracting from the pleasures of taste; exquisite perfumes floated in the air; and sometimes beauty was called upon to serve at table wearing no veils, so that all the senses were regaled together.

I could fill several pages with evidence in support of what I say. The Greek and Roman authors, and our own old chronicles, are there ready to be transcribed; but this research has been done already, and my facile erudition would make a poor show in comparison; I therefore state as fact what others have proved; a right which I often use, and which the reader should be glad to allow me.

76. Eighteenth and Nineteenth Centuries

Man used these various means more or less according to circumstances, to increase his pleasure; and to them we have added others which new discoveries have revealed to us.

It is true that we are too particular, these days, to tolerate the Roman vomitory; but we have done better, and the same end is now attained in a way that does not offend good taste.

New dishes have been devised, so seductive that they continually renew the appetite, and yet so light that they flatter the palate without surfeiting the stomach. Seneca would have said: *Nubes esculentas.*

We have in fact progressed so far in alimentary skill that if the need to go about our business did not compel us to leave the table, and if the need for sleep did not demand satisfaction, meals could be prolonged indefinitely, and there would be no certain means of deciding the period which might elapse between the first sip of Madeira and the last glass of punch.

It must not be supposed, however, that all these accessories are indispensable to the pleasures of the table. Those pleasures may be tested almost to the full whenever the four following conditions are combined: passable food, good wine, pleasant companions, and sufficient time.

Thus I have often thought how I would have loved to be present at the frugal meal which Horace offered to his neighbour, or to the guest driven by bad weather to seek shelter beneath his roof: a plump chicken, a kid (probably well fattened), and for dessert, grapes, figs, and nuts. On this meal, accompanied by wine harvested when Manlius was consul (*nata mecum consule Manlio*) and by the talk of that sweet poet, it seems to me that I could have supped magnificently.

> *Ac mihi seu longum post tempus venerat hospes*
> *Sive operum vacuo gratus conviva per imbrem*
> *Vicinus, bene erat non piscibus urbe petitis,*
> *Sed pullo atque haedo; tum*[1] *pensilis uva secundas*
> *Et nux ornabat mensas, cum duplice ficu.*[2]

In the same way, today or tomorrow, three pairs of friends will feast on a leg of boiled mutton and Pontoise kidneys washed down with Orléans wine and limpid Médoc; and after rounding off the evening with delightful unfettered talk, they will completely forget that finer dishes and more skilful cooks exist.

On the other hand, however exquisite the food, and however sumptuous the accessories, there will be no pleasures of the table if the wine is bad, the guests collected haphazardly, their faces gloomy, and the meal eaten in haste.

Anecdote

But the impatient reader may ask, how, in this year of grace 1825, must a meal be contrived in order to combine the conditions which procure the pleasures of the table in the highest degree?

That question I am about to answer. Compose yourselves, readers, and pay attention; Gasterea inspires me, the prettiest of all the Muses; I shall be clearer than an oracle, and my precepts will go down the ages.

1. Dessert is here clearly indicated and distinguished by the adverb *tum* and the words *secundas mensas*.
2. And if after a long interval a friend came to see me, or a neighbour was a welcome guest on a rainy day when I couldn't work, we fared well not on fish sent from town but on a pullet and a kid, then a string of grapes for dessert.

'Let the number of guests be not more than twelve, so that the talk may be constantly general;

'Let them be chosen with different occupations but similar tastes, and with such points of contact that the odious formalities of introduction can be dispensed with;

'Let the dining-room be well lighted, the cloth impeccably white, and the atmosphere maintained at a temperature of from sixty to seventy degrees;

'Let the men be witty without being too pretentious, and the women charming without being too coquettish;[1]

'Let the dishes be few in number, but exquisitely choice, and the wines of the first quality, each in its class;

'Let the service of the former proceed from the most substantial to the lightest, and of the latter, from the mildest to the most perfumed;

'Let the progress of the meal be slow, for dinner is the last business of the day; and let the guests conduct themselves like travellers due to reach their destination together;

'Let the coffee be piping hot, and the liqueurs chosen by a connoisseur;

'Let the drawing-room be large enough to allow a game at cards to be arranged for those who cannot do without, yet still leave space for postprandial conversations;

'Let the guests be detained by the charms of the company and sustained by the hope that the evening will not pass without some further pleasure;

'Let the tea be not too strong, the toast artistically buttered, and the punch mixed with proper care;

'Let retirement begin not earlier than eleven o'clock, but by midnight let everyone be in bed.'

Whoever has been present at a meal fulfilling all these conditions may claim to have witnessed his own apotheosis; and for each of them which is forgotten or ignored, the guests will suffer a proportionate decrease of pleasure.

I have said that the pleasures of the table, such as I have described them, can be of quite lengthy duration; I am go-

---

1. I am writing this in Paris, between the Palais-Royal and the Chaussée-d'Antin.

ing to prove this by giving the true and detailed history of the longest meal I have ever eaten; this is a sweet I am putting in the reader's mouth, as a reward for his kindness in reading my book.

At the lower end of the Rue du Bac there used to live a certain family composed as follows: the doctor, aged seventy-eight; the captain, aged seventy-six; and their sister Jeannette, aged seventy-four. They were relatives of mine, and always welcomed me very kindly when I went to see them.

'Dammit!' Doctor Dubois said to me one day, raising himself on tip-toe to slap me on the back, 'you are always boasting of your *fondues* (scrambled eggs with cheese), till our mouths water at the thought of them; we cannot stand it any longer. One of these days we are coming to breakfast with you, the captain and I, to find out what they are like.' (It was about 1801, I think, that he teased me like this.)

'By all means,' I replied; 'and you shall have one in all its glory, for I'll make it myself. Your proposal fills me with joy. Come round tomorrow, at ten o'clock, military time.'[1]

At the appointed hour my two guests appeared, newly shaved and carefully combed and powdered; two little old men, still hale and hearty.

They smiled with pleasure when they saw the table ready, a white cloth, three places laid, and in each place two dozen oysters, with a bright golden lemon in their midst.

A tall bottle of Sauterne stood at each end of the table, carefully wiped except for the corks, which indicated in no uncertain manner that a long time had passed since it had been drawn.

Alas for the countless gay breakfasts of old, when oysters were swallowed by the thousand! I saw the end of those breakfasts, for they went out with the abbés, who always ate at least a gross of oysters, and the chevaliers, who went on eating them for ever. I regret them, but philosophically;

1. Whenever a rendezvous is announced in this way, the first dish must be served up as the clock strikes, and all late comers are regarded as deserters.

if time can change governments, what powers it must have over mere customs!

After the oysters, which proved admirably fresh, came broiled kidneys, a jar of truffled *foie gras*, and the *fondue*.

The ingredients were all ready in the saucepan which was placed on the table over a spirits-of-wine burner. I officiated on the field of battle, and none of my movements escaped my cousins' notice.

They went into raptures over the dish, and asked me for the recipe, which I promised to give them, meanwhile telling them two anecdotes on the subject which the reader may perhaps encounter elsewhere.

After the *fondue* came fresh fruit and preserves, a cup of real Mocha made *à la Dubelloy* (a method which was then beginning to be known), and finally two different kinds of liqueur, a detergent spirit and a soothing oil.

When breakfast was well and truly over, I proposed a little exercise, in the form of a tour of my apartment, which, though far from elegant, is both vast and comfortable, and where my friends felt all the more at home in that the ceilings and gilding date from the middle of the reign of Louis XV.

I showed them the clay original of the bust of my pretty cousin, Madame Récamier, by Chinard, and her portrait in miniature by Augustin; they were both so impressed that the doctor pressed his thick lips to the portrait, while the captain made so free with the bust that I was obliged to chastise him; for if all the admirers of the original were to do likewise, that voluptuously rounded bosom would soon be reduced to the condition of Saint Peter's toe at Rome, which the faithful have worn away with their kisses.

Next I showed them a few casts after the best sculptors of antiquity, some pictures which are not without merit, my guns and musical instruments, and some fine editions of French and foreign authors.

In the course of this polymathical excursion, they did not forget my kitchen. There I showed them my economical stock-pot, my Dutch oven, my clockwork turn-spit, and my steamer. They examined everything with minute attention, all the more astonished in that their own kitchen had remained unaltered since the days of the Regency.

We had just returned to the drawing-room when the clock struck two. 'Botheration!' exclaimed the doctor, 'it is dinner-time, and my sister Jeannette will be waiting for us. We must go home at once. Not that I feel at all hungry, but I must have my soup for all that. It is such an old habit of mine that whenever I let a day go by without taking it, I say with Titus: *Diem perdidi.*'[1]

'My dear doctor,' I replied, 'why go so far in search of what is close at hand? I will send word to your sister that you are staying with me, and that you are going to give me the pleasure of your company at dinner; though I must ask for your indulgence towards the meal which will not have all the merit of an *impromptu* composed at leisure.'

The two brothers held an ocular deliberation over my invitation, and then formally accepted it. I promptly dispatched a *volante* to the Faubourg Saint-Germain, and had a word with my master cook; and within a very short space of time, drawing on his own resources and those of neighbouring restaurateurs, he served us up a very neat and appetizing little dinner.

I was filled with satisfaction when I saw the alacrity with which my two friends sat down, pulled their chairs up to the table, spread out their napkins, and prepared for action.

They met with two surprises which I had not realized would be novelties to them; for I gave them Parmesan with their soup, and a glass of dry Madeira after it. Both had been recently imported by Monsieur le Prince de Talleyrand, the greatest of diplomats, to whom we are indebted for so many profound and witty sayings, and who, whether in power or in retirement, has always commanded the interest of the nation.

The dinner went very well, with respect to both its essential substance and its necessary accessories, and my friends contributed as much indulgence as gaiety to the meal.

1. 'I have lost a day.' [Ed.]

After dinner, I proposed a game of piquet; but the captain said they preferred the *far niente* of the Italians, so we drew our chairs up to the fire.

Despite the charms of the *far niente*, I have always thought that nothing makes conversation easier than some occupation of a trivial kind, so I suggested we should take tea.

Tea was something quite novel to Frenchmen of the old school; nevertheless, they agreed to try it. I made it in their presence, and they drank a few cups of it, with all the more pleasure in that till then they had never regarded it as anything but a form of medicine.

Long experience had taught me that one surrender leads to another, and that he who once sets out on the path of acceptance soon forgets how to refuse. So it was in an almost dictatorial tone that I talked of ending up with a bowl of punch.

'But you will kill us!' said the doctor.

'But you will make us drunk!' said the captain.

My only reply was to call for sugar, lemons, and rum.

I mixed the punch, and in the meantime toast was made, thin, delicately buttered, and salted to perfection.

This time I met with some opposition. My cousins declared that they had eaten quite enough, and that they would not touch the toast. But knowing the charm of that simple preparation, I replied that my only anxiety was that there might not be sufficient. Sure enough, it was not long before the captain took the last slice, and I caught him looking to see if any was left, or if more was being made; so I ordered more straight away.

Meanwhile time had not stood still, and the hands of my clock had passed the eighth hour.

'We must fly,' said my guests; 'we really must go and eat a little salad with our poor sister, who hasn't set eyes on us all day.'

This time I made no objection; and, mindful of the courtesy due to two such charming old men, I saw them to their carriage and watched them drive away.

The reader may ask whether so long a sitting was not marred by a few tedious moments.

I shall answer in the negative; my guests' interest was maintained by the making of the *fondue*, the tour of my apartment, a few novelties at dinner, the tea, and above all the punch, which they had never tasted before.

Moreover, the doctor was acquainted with the genealogy and reputation of everyone in Paris; the captain had spent part of his life in Italy, both in the army and as an envoy to the court of Parma; and I have travelled a great deal myself; we conversed without pretension, and listened when it was our turn. This was more than enough to make the time pass smoothly and swiftly.

Next morning I received a letter from the doctor, in which he was kind enough to inform me that the little debauch of the day before had had no evil after-effects; on the contrary, he said, after a good night's rest they had risen wonderfully refreshed and ready to begin all over again.

15. On Shooting-Luncheons

77. Introduction

Of all the circumstances of life in which eating counts for something, one of the most agreeable is undoubtedly the shooting-luncheon; and of all known interludes, none can be prolonged to so great a length with so little risk of boredom.

After a few hours of exercise, the most energetic sportsman feels the need for rest; his face has been caressed by the morning breeze; skill has not failed him in the hour of need; and the sun is nearing the highest point in its course. The sportsman accordingly decides to rest for an hour or so, not because of an excess of weariness, but in response to that instinct which warns us that our energy is not inexhaustible.

A shady spot takes his fancy; soft grass welcomes him, and the murmur of the nearby spring invites him to deposit in its cool waters the flask of wine destined to refresh him.[1]

Then, with calm contentment, he takes out of his knapsack the cold chicken and golden-crusted rolls packed for him by loving hands, and places them beside the wedge of Gruyère or Roquefort which is to serve as his dessert.

He is not alone during these preparations; with him is the faithful animal which Heaven created to serve him; squatting beside him, the dog looks up with loving eyes at his master; cooperation has brought them closer; they are two friends, and the servant is proud and happy to share his master's meal.

Theirs is an appetite unknown alike to the worldly, who

1. I commend white wine to my fellow-sportsmen; it is less affected by movement and heat than red wine, and quenches the thirst more agreeably.

never give hunger time to arrive, and the devout, who never take the exercise which arouses it.

At length the delicious meal comes to an end; each has had his share, and all has gone peacefully and in an orderly manner. Now, since the midday hour is also an hour of rest for all creation, why not give a few moments to sleep?

These pleasures are increased tenfold when several friends enjoy them together; for in that case a more copious meal will have been brought along in military canteens, now turned to the gentler uses of peace. Then there will be gay talk about the prowess of the one, the blunders of another, and the prospects of the afternoon!

And what if attentive servants now arrive, bearing those vessels dedicated to Bacchus in which an artificial chill keeps strawberry juice, pineapple juice, and Madeira cold as ice: delicious liqueurs, divine concoctions, which send a delightful freshness coursing through the veins, and fill the senses with a bliss unknown to the profane?[1]

Yet even now we have not reached the end of this enchanted progress.

78. The Ladies

There are days when our wives and sisters, our cousins and their pretty friends, are invited to join in our pastimes.

At the appointed hour light carriages arrive and prancing steeds, bearing beautiful ladies, plumes and flowers. There is

1. It was my friend, Alexandre Delessert, who first made use of this charming device. We were shooting at Villeneuve, under a blazing sun, with the thermometer at 90° in the shade. Thus situated in the torrid zone, he had had the foresight to instruct *potophorus** servants to follow us, who bore, in leather buckets lined with ice, all that could be desired in the way of comfort and refreshment. Each made his choice and felt a new man. I am tempted to think that the application of so cold a liquid to arid tongues and parched throats causes the most delicious sensation that may be tasted with a clear conscience.

* Monsieur Hoffman condemns this expression on account of its resemblance to the phrase *pot-au-feu*; he is in favour of the better-known alternative *oenophorus*.

something military and coquettish about the ladies' toilette;
and now and then the Professor's eye catches glimpses which
cannot be the result of chance alone.

Soon the flank of each carriage opens to reveal treasures
from Périgord, marvels from Strasbourg, sweets from
Achard's, and all the portable products of the most cunning
laboratories.

Nor has champagne been forgotten; that potent elixir
sparkles merrily in beauty's hand; everyone sits down on the
grass and falls to; corks fly, and there is such laughing, talking, and merry joking as befits a meal with the universe for
dining-room and the sun for illumination. And appetite, that
heavenly emanation, lends the meal a vivacity unknown indoors, however lavish the embellishments.

However, all things must come to an end; and at last the
host gives the signal; everyone rises, the men picking up
their guns and the ladies their hats. Farewells are made, the
carriages drive off, and beauty vanishes, to be seen no more
until the close of day.

This is what I have seen in the higher regions of society,
by the waters of Pactolus; but such luxury is far from indispensable.

I have shot in the centre of France and in the remotest
regions; I have seen charming women and girls radiant with
youth come gaily to the rendezvous in gigs or simple country
carts, or mounted on the humble ass which is the glory and
fortune of the inhabitants of Montmorency; I have seen
them the first to laugh at the discomfort of their con-
veyances; I have seen them spread out on the grass turkey in
transparent jelly, home-made pâté, and salad ready for mixing; I have seen them dance light-footed round the camp
fire; I have taken part in the games and frolics which follow
such gypsy meals, and I am convinced that they are not less
gay, less charming, nor less pleasurable for want of luxury.

And when the time comes to separate, why should not a
few kisses be exchanged – first with the king of the chase,
because he is in his glory; then with the duffer of the party,
because he is out of luck; and after that with the others, to

avoid all risk of jealousy? At parting custom authorizes, allows, and even enjoins us to profit by it.

But prudent sportsmen with an eye to the main chance should shoot straight and fill their bags before the arrival of the ladies. For experience has proved that after their departure the sport is rarely fruitful.

Countless conjectures have been made in an attempt to explain this curious effect. Some attribute it to the digestive process, which always makes the body a little cumbersome; some to the wandering of a mind which can no longer concentrate; and some to the influence of whispered colloquies, which fill a man with a longing to return home.

As for ourselves, whose glance has read the very depths of hearts, we believe that, if the sportsmen are of inflammable material, and the ladies of tender years, it is inevitable that, when the sexes come together, some spark of desire should escape to scandalize the chaste Diana, and cause her to withdraw her favour from the delinquents for the rest of the day.

We say 'for the rest of the day', because the story of Endymion teaches us that the goddess is anything but severe after the setting of the sun. (See the picture by Girodet.)

We have only touched on this matter of shooting-luncheons which might well form the subject of an amusing and instructive treatise. As such we bequeath it to whichever of our intelligent readers may be willing to investigate it further.

16. On Digestion

79. Introduction

'Man lives not on what he eats, but on what he digests,' says an old proverb. We must therefore digest to live: rich and poor, king and shepherd are equal in the face of this ineluctable law.

Yet how few are those who know what they are doing when they digest! Nearly all are like Monsieur Jourdain, who spoke prose without knowing it; and for their benefit I am about to give a simple account of the digestive process, being convinced that Monsieur Jourdain was a far happier man when the philosopher had shown him that what he was speaking was prose.

80. Ingestion

Appetite, hunger, and thirst are warning signs that the body needs new strength; and pain, that universal monitor, loses no time in tormenting us if we are unwilling or unable to obey those signs.

We accordingly indulge in eating and drinking, which together constitute ingestion, an operation which begins when the food enters the mouth, and ends when it enters the oesophagus.[1]

The whole journey is only a few inches long, but a great deal takes place before it is completed.

The solid foodstuffs are divided by the teeth; the different glands with which the mouth is lined moisten them; the tongue pounds them and mixes them together, pressing

1. The oesophagus is the canal which, beginning at the back of the wind-pipe, connects the gullet with the stomach; its upper end is called the *pharynx*.

them against the palate to squeeze out the juice and taste their savour, and binding them into a solid mass in the middle of the mouth; after which, pushing against the lower jaw, it rises in the middle so that the mass is drawn down the slope towards the back of the mouth and received by the pharynx, which contracts in its turn, forcing it into the oesophagus, which by a peristaltic movement conveys it into the stomach.

When one mouthful has been dealt with like this, a second follows in the same fashion; the drinks swallowed in the intervals take the same road, the process of deglutition continuing until the same instinct which had initiated ingestion warns that it is time to finish. The first injunction, however, is seldom obeyed; for it is one of the privileges of man to drink when he is not thirsty, and the present-day cook knows how to make us eat when we are not hungry.

Before each morsel of food can reach the stomach, it has to avoid two dangers; and the way it does this is a remarkable *tour de force*.

The first is the danger of being pushed back to the rear of the nostrils; but fortunately the lowering of the veil of the palate and the construction of the pharynx prevent this from happening.

The second is the danger of falling into the trachea or windpipe, across which all our food must pass; and this is a far more serious risk, for as soon as any foreign body enters the trachea, a convulsive cough begins which continues until the substance is expelled.

However, by means of an admirable mechanism, the glottis contracts during the act of swallowing; it is also shielded by the epiglottis, which covers it, and we instinctively hold our breath during deglutition, so that it may be said that generally speaking, despite this strange conformation, food reaches the stomach without much difficulty; and there the empire of the will comes to an end, and digestion, properly so called, begins.

81. *Function of the Stomach*

Digestion is a purely mechanical operation, and the digestive apparatus may be likened to a mill furnished with sifters, which extract the nutritious elements from food and reject the non-animalizable residue.

The manner in which digestion operates in the stomach, whether by coction, maturation, fermentation, or gastric, chemical, or vital dissolution, has been the subject of prolonged and heated discussion.

In fact, something of all these enters into the process; and the mistake lies in seeking to attribute to a single agent the result of several causes which necessarily operate together.

Thus the foodstuffs, impregnated with all the fluids furnished by the mouth and the oesophagus, are further soaked, when they reach the stomach, in the gastric juices with which it is always filled; they are then subjected for several hours to a heat of over one hundred degrees; they are sifted and mixed by the organic movements of the stomach, which their presence excites; they act on one another as a result of this juxtaposition; and it is impossible for fermentation not to take place, since almost every alimentary substance is fermentescible.

In consequence of all these operations, the chyle begins to form; the alimentary layer immediately above it is the first to be appropriated, and, passing through the pylorus, falls into the intestines; the next follows, and the next again, until nothing is left in the stomach, which may be said to be emptied by mouthfuls, in the same way as it was filled.

The pylorus is a sort of fleshy funnel, communicating between the stomach and the intestines; it is so constructed that food cannot return up it without great difficulty. This important passage is liable to be blocked up, and then death by starvation follows, after prolonged and terrible pain.

The intestine which receives the food as it emerges from the pylorus is the duodenum, so called because it is twelve fingers long.

The chyle, on reaching the duodenum, enters on a new phase, through mixture with the bile and the pancreatic juices; it loses the greyish-white colour which it had before, turns yellow, and begins to acquire the stercoral odour, which grows stronger as it approaches the rectum. The various elements of which the mixture is composed act on one another reciprocally; the chyle is in process of formation, and analogous gases are necessarily formed at the same time.

As the organic impulse which forces the chyle from the stomach continues, it pushes it towards the small intestines; there the chyle is separated, absorbed by the organs destined for that purpose, and carried on towards the liver, there to mingle with the blood and repair the losses caused by the absorption of the vital organs and transpiratory exhalation.

It is difficult to explain how the chyle, which is a white liquid and more or less insipid and odourless, comes to be extracted from a mass whose colour, smell, and flavour must be extremely pronounced.

Be that as it may, this extraction of the chyle appears to be the specific end of digestion, and as soon as it mingles with the circulation, the individual is made aware of the fact by an increase in vitality, and an intimate conviction that his losses have been repaired.

The digestion of liquids is much less complicated than the digestion of solids, and can be explained in a few words.

The alimentary part is separated and taken into the chyle, and goes through all the vicissitudes described above.

The purely liquid part is absorbed by the stomach's suckers and thrown into circulation; it is then taken through the emulgent arteries to the loins, which filter and elaborate it, and by means of the ureters[1] send it into the bladder in the form of urine.

In this last receptacle the urine, although retained by a sphincter, does not remain for long; its irritant action creates a need, and soon voluntary constriction brings it to the light

1. The ureters are two ducts, of the thickness of a quill pen, which start from each of the loins and end at the neck at the back of the bladder.

of day, causing it to gush out through those irrigation channels which we all know, but never mention by name.

Digestion occupies a longer or shorter time according to the particular disposition of individuals. But it may be given an average term of seven hours, or rather more than three hours for the stomach, and the rest for the journey to the rectum.

By means of this explanation, which I have taken from the best authors and duly purged of anatomical dryness and scientific abstractions, my readers will henceforth be able to estimate the exact point at which the last meal they have eaten is to be found; namely, during the first three hours in the stomach; later, between the stomach and the intestines; and at the end of seven or eight hours, in the rectum, awaiting its turn to be expelled.

82. *Influence of Digestion*

Of all corporeal operations, digestion is the one which has the most powerful influence on the mental state of the individual.

Nobody should be surprised by this assertion, for it could not possibly be otherwise.

The most elementary rules of psychology teach us that the mind can only be impressed by means of its subject organs, which keep it in touch with external things; whence it follows that, when those organs are in poor condition, weak or inflamed, the deterioration inevitably influences the sensations, which are the intermediary and occasional means of intellectual activity.

Thus our accustomed manner of digesting, and particularly the latter part of the process, makes us habitually sad or gay, silent or talkative, morose or melancholy, without our being aware of it, and above all without our being able to avoid it.

In this respect it would be possible to separate the civilized portion of mankind into three great divisions, namely, the regular, the constipated, and the lax.

It can be demonstrated not only that all persons falling within one of these three categories have similar natural dispositions and certain propensities in common, but also that there is something analogous in the manner in which they carry out the various missions which chance has allotted to them in the course of life.

In order to make my meaning clear, I will take an example from the vast field of literature. I believe that men of letters, for the most part, owe their choice of genre to their stomach.

According to my theory, comic poets will be found among the regular, tragic poets among the constipated, and pastoral and elegiac poets among the lax; whence it follows that the most lachrymose of poets is only removed from the most comic of poets by a degree of digestionary coction.

It was by applying this principle to courage that a member of the court of Louis XIV at the time when France was suffering from the onslaughts of Prince Eugene of Savoy, exclaimed: 'If only I could give him diarrhoea for a week! I'd soon make him the biggest coward in all Europe.'

'Let us make haste,' said an English general, 'and throw our men into battle while they still have some beef left in their bellies.'

Among the young, digestion is often accompanied by a slight shivering, and among the old, by a strong desire for sleep.

In the former case, Nature is withdrawing the heat from the surface to make use of it in her laboratory; in the latter, the same motive power, weakened by age, is unable to cope with the labour of digestion and the stimulation of the senses at one and the same time.

In the initial stages of digestion, it is dangerous to engage in mental activity, and more dangerous still to indulge the cravings of the flesh. Hundreds of men are carried away every year down the stream which flows to the graveyards of the capital, because, after dining well, and sometimes by reason of dining too well, they have not been able to shut their eyes and stop up their ears.

The above observation contains a warning, even for reckless youth; a piece of advice for grown men, who forget that time never stands still; and a penal law for all on the wrong side of fifty.

Some people become and remain ill-humoured throughout the period of digestion; that is not the time either to lay plans before them, or to ask favours of them.

Notable among these people was Marshal Augereau; during the hour immediately following his dinner, he was ready to kill anyone, friend or foe.

I once heard him say that there were two individuals in the army whom the commander-in-chief was always at liberty to have shot, namely his chief of staff and his orderly officer. Both were present at the time: General Chérin made an obsequious but witty reply; the orderly officer said nothing, but probably thought no less for all that.

At that time I myself was attached to the Marshal's staff, and a place was always laid for me at his table; but I rarely showed my face there, for fear of these periodic squalls; I was afraid that at a word he might send me to do my digesting in the cells.

I have often met him since in Paris; and when on one occasion he courteously expressed his regret at not having seen more of me, I made no secret of my reasons. We laughed over them together; but he virtually admitted that I had not been entirely unjustified.

We were then at Offenberg, and the staff one day complained of the absence of fish and game in the mess. This complaint was well-founded, for it is a recognized maxim that the victor should enjoy good cheer at the expense of the vanquished. The same day I accordingly wrote a very polite letter to the keeper of the forests, drawing his attention to the trouble and prescribing the remedy.

This keeper was a tall, swarthy, dried-up old fellow, who detested the sight of us, and probably kept us as badly supplied as possible for fear that we might take root in his territory. His reply, accordingly, was full of evasions, and to all intents and purposes a refusal. The gamekeepers had been frightened away by our soldiers; the fishermen were out of hand; the waters were too full, etc., etc. To which good reasons I made no answer, but instead sent ten grenadiers to be lodged and boarded by him until further orders.

The ruse had its effect; two days later, very early in the morning, a large cart drew up outside our quarters, loaded with good things; the gamekeepers had presumably come back, the fishermen returned to duty, for it contained enough game and fish to last us more than a week: venison, woodcock, carp, pike . . . it was a gift from heaven.

On receipt of this peace-offering, I delivered the poor keeper from his unwelcome guests. He came to see us; I made him see reason; and for the rest of our stay we had only to congratulate ourselves on his good behaviour.

17. On Rest

83. Introduction

Man was not made to enjoy endless activity; Nature destined him for an interrupted existence, and his perceptions are bound to cease after a certain period. He may extend that period of activity by varying the style and nature of his sensations, but this continuity of existence leads him to desire rest. Rest leads to sleep, and sleep brings dreams.

Here we find ourselves at the uttermost bounds of humanity; for a man asleep is no longer a social being; the law still protects him, but no longer commands his obedience.

I may here appropriately insert a curious tale told to me by Dom Duhaget, formerly Prior of the Carthusian Monastery at Pierre-Châtel.

Dom Duhaget came of a very good Gascon family, and had served with distinction in the army; for twenty years he had been an infantry captain, and he was a Chevalier of the Order of Saint Louis. I have never known a man of more genuine piety or more engaging conversation.

'At —,' (so his story began) 'where I was Prior before I came to Pierre-Châtel, we had a certain brother of a very melancholy humour; a sombre character, who was known to walk in his sleep.

'Sometimes, in one of his attacks, he would leave his cell and return to it alone; at other times he lost his way and had to be led back. Doctors were called in, and prescribed various remedies; by the time of which I am speaking his lapses had become less frequent, and we had stopped worrying about him.

'One evening, having stayed up beyond my ordinary hour, I was at my desk working on some papers, when I heard the door of my room, from which I scarcely ever removed the key, being opened; and a little later I saw this brother enter, in a complete somnambulistic trance.

'His eyes were wide open, but fixed in a stare; he wore nothing but the tunic in which he had presumably gone to bed, and in one of his hands he held a large knife.

'He walked straight to my bed, the position of which he knew, and seemed to make sure, by groping with his hands, that I was in it; after which he struck three blows so hard that the blade pierced the bed-clothes and penetrated far into the mattress, or rather the straw which served me as one.

'When he passed me on his way to the bed, his features were contracted and his brows furrowed; when he had struck the blows, he turned round, and I saw that his face had cleared and that he wore an air of satisfaction.

'The glare of the two lamps which stood on my desk made no impression on his eyes; he went back the way he had come, quietly opening and closing the two doors which led to my cell; and a little later I made sure that he was returning peacefully to his own.

'You can imagine,' continued the Prior, 'the state I was in during this terrible apparition. I shuddered when I thought of the danger I had just escaped, and I gave thanks to Providence; but I was so overwrought that I was unable to close my eyes once that night.

'Next morning I sent for the somnambulist, and asked him outright what he had dreamed of the night before.

'He was visibly troubled by my question. "Father," he replied, "I dreamed such a strange dream that I find it hard to tell it to you. It may be the work of the Devil, and . . ." "I order you to tell it to me," I said; "a dream is always involuntary: it is just an illusion. Speak frankly."

' "Father," he then said, "I had scarcely gone to bed when I dreamed that you had killed my mother; that her ghost had appeared to me, still bleeding, to demand vengeance; and that I had been filled with such fury at the sight that I had rushed to your room like one possessed, found you in your bed, and stabbed you where you lay. Soon afterwards I awoke, bathed in sweat, full of loathing for my sinful deed; and then I blessed God that so foul a crime had not been committed : .."

' "It was more nearly committed than you think," I said, gravely and quietly.

'Then I told him what had happened, and showed him the marks left by the blows which he had intended for me.

'At the sight of those marks he threw himself at my feet, weeping and groaning over the involuntary crime which he might have committed, and imploring me to impose whatever penance I thought suitable.

' "No," I cried; "I shall not punish you for an involuntary deed; but in future I give you dispensation from attending the night offices, and I warn you that your cell will be locked from the outside after the evening meal, and opened only to allow you to attend low mass at daybreak." '

If, in the circumstances from which he had escaped only by a miracle, the Prior had been killed, the somnambulistic monk would not have been punished, because the murder would not have been deliberate.

84. *Time for Rest*

The general laws governing the globe which we inhabit have inevitably influenced the mode of existence of mankind. The alternation of night and day, which takes place all over the world, with certain variations, but always in such a way that in the long run one balances the other, has naturally determined the time for action and the time for rest; and it seems probable that our life would have been quite different if we had had an endless day.

Be that as it may, when a man has enjoyed for a certain period of time the fullness of his life, there comes a moment when he can stand no more; his impressionability gradually diminishes; the best-directed attacks made on his senses have no effect, his organs refuse what they had previously clamoured for, his soul is saturated with sensations. The time for rest has arrived.

It goes without saying that here we are speaking of social man, surrounded with all the comforts and resources of advanced civilization; for this need for rest comes far more rapidly and regularly to those who labour strenuously in study or workshop, travelling, fighting, shooting, or in any other sphere of activity.

With rest, as with all restorative processes, Nature, our excellent Mother, has combined considerable pleasure.

The man who rests experiences a feeling of well-being as general as it is indefinable; he feels his arms fall to his sides of their own accord, his fibres loosened, and his brain refreshed; his senses are at peace, his sensations dulled; he desires nothing and ceases to reflect; a veil of gauze stretches before his eyes. A few moments more and he will be asleep.

18. On Sleep

85. Introduction

Althought there exist men so constituted that they may almost be said never to sleep, it is nevertheless generally true that the need for sleep is as imperious as hunger or thirst.

The forward sentries of an army often fall asleep, even in the act of throwing snuff into their eyes to keep them open; and Pichegru, when Bonaparte's police were hunting him, paid 30,000 francs for a single night's sleep, during which he was betrayed and handed over to them.

86. Definition

Sleep is that state of torpor in which man, cut off by the forced inactivity of his senses from external things, is only alive in a mechanical respect.

Sleep, like night, is preceded and followed by twilight stages, the first of which leads to absolute inertia, the second to renewed activity.

Let us examine these two phenomena.

At the beginning of sleep, the organs of the senses gradually sink into inactivity; first taste, then sight and smell; hearing holds out a little longer, and touch remains perpetually on guard, for it is there to warn us, through pain, of the dangers which may befall the body.

Sleep is always preceded by a feeling of voluptuousness: the body yields to it gladly, in the certain expectation of obtaining fresh strength, and the mind gives way to it trustfully, in the hope that its means of activity will be revived.

It is from a failure to appreciate this sensation, although it is positive enough, that men of great learning have likened sleep to death, which all living creatures resist with all their might, and which is marked by unmistakable symptoms which fill even animals with horror.

Like all other forms of pleasure, sleep may become a passion, for persons have been known to spend three quarters of their life asleep; and like all passions, it then produces only baneful effects, namely slothfulness, indolence, debility, stupidity, and death.

The school of Salerno allotted only seven hours to sleep without distinction of age or sex. This is too strict a doctrine; some allowance should be made for children out of necessity and for women out of consideration; but it may be taken for certain that more than ten hours passed in bed will constitute excess.

In the initial stages of twilight sleep the individual retains his will-power, and could, if he wished, rouse himself; the eye too has not yet lost all its power. *Non omnibus dormio,* said Maecenas; and in this condition painful truths have dawned on many a husband. A few ideas continue to obtrude, but incoherently; faint glimmerings of light linger on, and half-formed objects seem to pass before the eyes. But this stage is of short duration; soon everything disappears, all sensation ceases, and absolute sleep supervenes.

What of the mind in the meantime? It lives its separate life; it is like the pilot of a ship becalmed, a mirror in the night, a lute which no one touches; it awaits some new stimulation.

However, certain psychologists, including Monsieur le Comte de Redern, maintain that the mind is never inactive; and the Count cites as proof the fact that whenever a man is roused suddenly from his first sleep, he experiences the sensation of someone disturbed in the midst of an important undertaking.

This observation is not unfounded, and calls for close investigation.

For the rest, this state of absolute unconsciousness is not of long duration; scarcely ever exceeding five or six hours; little by little the losses are made good; an obscure feeling of existence begins to come back, and the sleeper enters into the kingdom of dreams.

19. On Dreams

Dreams are unilateral impressions which enter the mind without the help of external things. They are commonplace phenomena, but nevertheless extraordinary, and as yet we know little about them.

The fault lies with the scientists, who have not yet provided us with a sufficient body of evidence from which to draw conclusions. When they have given us this indispensable information, the dual nature of man will be better understood.

In the present state of our knowledge, it is believed that a subtle and powerful fluid exists in our bodies, which transmits to the brain whatever impressions are received by the senses; and that ideas are born of the excitement caused by those impressions.

Absolute sleep is due to the wastage and inertia of this fluid.

It is to be assumed that the work of digestion and assimilation, which continues unceasingly during sleep, makes good this loss, so that a time comes when the individual, though once more in possession of all the faculties required for action, is not yet subject to stimulation by external objects.

Then the nervous fluid, which is mobile by nature, flows along the nerve-channels to the brain; it makes its way through the same places, following the same course as when the individual is awake, since it arrives by the same route; and thus it produces the same effects, although with less intensity.

The reason for this difference in intensity seems to me to be easy to grasp. When a man who is awake is impressed by an external object, the sensation is precise, sudden, and inevitable; the entire organ is in motion. But when the same impression is conveyed to him in his sleep, only the posterior part of his nerves is in motion; the sensation must necessarily be less acute and less positive; to make ourselves more clearly understood, let us say that in the case of the waking man a shock is felt by the whole organ, while in the case of the sleeping man there is only a tremor in the part nearest to the brain.

It is true that in voluptuous dreams Nature attains her end almost as completely as when we are awake; but this difference is due to the difference in the organs concerned; for any sort of excitement is enough to rouse the instinct of generation, and each sex possesses all the requisite material for the consummation of the act for which Nature has destined it.

87. Research to be Undertaken

When the nervous fluid flows to the brain, it always passes through the channels destined for the exercise of one or other of our senses; and that is why it arouses certain sensations or series of ideas in preference to others. Thus, we imagine that we can see when the optic nerve is affected, that we can hear when the auditive nerves are affected, etc.; and it may here be noted as a curious circumstance that the sensations experienced in dreaming are very rarely connected with taste or smell. When we dream of a flower-bed or a meadow, we see the flowers without smelling them; when we dream of eating a meal, we see the dishes without tasting them.

It would be a task worthy of the greatest scientist to try to find out why two of our senses have no effect on the mind during sleep, while the other four enjoy almost all their ordinary powers. I know of no psychologist who has tackled this problem.

Let us also remark that the more internal the feelings we experience in sleep, the greater their effect. Thus the most sensual ideas are nothing compared to the anguish we feel if we dream of having lost a beloved child, or of being sentenced to be hanged. In such cases it is possible to wake up soaked in sweat or bathed in tears.

88. Nature of Dreams

However fantastic the ideas may be which occur to us in our sleep, they will be found on closer examination to be recollections or combinations of recollections. Indeed I am tempted to say that dreams are simply the memory of the senses.

Their strangeness, then, consists only in that the association of these ideas is unusual, being outside the laws of chronology, convention, and time; so that, in the last analysis, no one has ever dreamed of what was previously quite unknown to him.

We shall not be surprised by the singularity of our dreams, if we reflect that in the waking man four faculties are constantly watching over and correcting one another, namely sight, hearing, touch, and memory; whereas in the sleeping man each sense is left to its own resources.

I am tempted to compare these two states of the brain with a piano at which a musician sits, idly running his fingers over the keys and evoking some remembered melody, to which, if he used all his powers, he could fit a complete harmony. This analogy may be carried much further, if we add that reflection is to ideas what harmony is to sounds; and that certain ideas contain other ideas, just as a primary sound contains secondary sounds, etc., etc.

89. Dr Gall's System

But here, carried away by a subject which is not without its charm, I find myself on the confines of Dr Gall's system, which teaches the multiformity of the organs of the brain.

I ought to go no further, nor transgress the limits I have laid down for myself; yet out of love for science (to which it can be seen that I am no stranger), I cannot resist inserting here two examples which are the result of careful observation on my part, and which can be the more confidently relied on, in that there are several persons among my readers who can corroborate them.

First Observation

About 1790, in a village called Gevrin, a district of Belley, there lived an extremely cunning merchant; his name was Landot, and he had made a sizeable fortune.

One day he was suddenly afflicted with such a serious stroke that he was thought to be dead. The medical fraternity came to his assistance, and he recovered; but not without loss, for he left behind him almost all his intellectual faculties, including memory. However, as he was able to get round fairly well, and had regained his appetite, he was left in control of his affairs.

When they saw him in this condition, those who had had dealings with him before imagined that the time had come to take their revenge, and under the pretext of keeping him company, came to see him from all sides, with proposals for purchases, sales, exchanges, and other deals of the sort which had hitherto made up his staple business. But his assailants met with a rude shock, and soon found that things were very different from what they had expected.

The old fox had lost none of his commercial cunning, and the same man who sometimes failed to recognize his servants, and even forgot his own name, was still aware of the price of every commodity, and the value of every acre of meadow, vineyard, or woodland for three leagues around.

On these matters his judgement remained intact; and as they had no suspicion of this, most of those who tried to catch the sick merchant off his guard were caught themselves in the very traps they had set for him.

Second Observation

There lived at Belley a certain Monsieur Chirol, who had served for a long time in the royal bodyguard, under both Louis XV and Louis XVI.

His intellect was just equal to the services he had been called on to perform all his life; but he had in a supreme degree a talent for gaming, and not only played all the old games, such as ombre, piquet and whist, with considerable skill, but also, when fashion introduced a new one, mastered all its subtleties after playing three hands.

Now this Monsieur Chirol was afflicted with paralysis, and the stroke was so severe that he fell into a state of almost complete insensibility. Two things, however, were spared in him; his digestive faculties and his talent for gaming.

Every day he came to the house where for more than twenty years it had been his habit to play, sat down in a corner, and stayed there motionless and somnolent, without paying attention to what was going on around him.

When the time came to make up a game, he would be invited to take a hand; he always accepted and dragged himself over to the table; and there it was soon apparent that the disease which had paralysed the greater part of his faculties had left his gaming skill completely intact.

Shortly before his death, Monsieur Chirol gave a striking proof of the integrity of his existence as a card-player.

There descended upon us at Belley a Parisian banker, whose name, I think, was Monsieur Delins; he carried letters of introduction; he was a stranger, he was a Parisian; all this was more than enough, in a little country town, to make everyone do everything in their power to make his visit a pleasant one.

Monsieur Delins was both a gourmand and a gambler. In the former respect he was given ample occupation, being kept five or six hours at table every day; in the latter he was more difficult to amuse; he had a great fondness for piquet, and spoke of playing at six francs a counter, which far exceeded our dearest rate of play.

To overcome this difficulty, a club was formed, which some joined, while others refrained, according to their estimate of the chances; one party maintained that Parisians are far more knowing in such matters than provincials, while the other declared, on the contrary, that every inhabitant of that great city had a grain or two of bluff in his make-up. Whatever the truth of the matter the club was formed; and to whom was the duty of defending the common purse entrusted? To Monsieur Chirol . . .

When the Parisian banker saw that great, pale, cadaverous figure sidle up to the table and sit down opposite him, he thought at first that it was a joke; but when the spectre picked up the cards, and proceeded to shuffle them with masterly skill, he began to think that here was an opponent who might once have been worthy of him.

He was not long in discovering that what he had thought of the past was true of the present; for not only in this first game, but in many of the succeeding games too, Monsieur Delins was beaten, thrashed, and so thoroughly plucked, that on his departure he had to pay out more than six hundred francs, which were scrupulously distributed among the members of the club.

Before he left, Monsieur Delins came to thank us for the hospitality we had shown him; but he protested mildly about the moribund condition of his opponent, and assured us that he would never be able to hold up his head again, after being so soundly beaten by a corpse.

Conclusion

The conclusion to be drawn from these two observations is simple: it seems obvious to me that the stroke which in each case damaged the victim's brain respected that part which had been so long employed in the intricacies of commerce in the one case, and cards in the other; and no doubt that part was better able to resist the stroke because continual exercise had strengthened it, or because the same impressions, constantly repeated, had left deeper traces on it than elsewhere.

90. *Influence of Age*

Age has a marked influence on the nature of our dreams.

In childhood we dream of games, gardens, flowers, trees, and other cheerful things; later, of pleasures, love, fighting, and marriage; later still, of business, travel, and the favour of princes or their representatives; and even later, of our affairs, worries, money, past pleasures, and friends long since dead.

91. *Dream Phenomena*

Sleep and dreams are sometimes accompanied by certain strange phenomena, an investigation of which may be of service to the science of anthropology; and with that end in view I propose to record here three observations of my own, chosen from among those which, in the course of a long life, I have made in the silence of the night.

First Observation

One night I dreamed that I had discovered the secret of freeing myself from the law of gravity, so that it was all one to me whether my body went up or down, and I was able to do either with equal facility, just as I wished.

I found this sensation delightful; and perhaps many people have had the same dream, or one like it; but what is specially noteworthy is that I can remember understanding perfectly (or so at least it seems to me) the means which had led to this condition, and that they appeared so simple that I wondered why no one had discovered them earlier.

When I woke up, this explanatory part of the dream escaped me completely, but the conclusion remained; and since that time it has been my firm belief that sooner or later some intellect more enlightened than mine will make this discovery and I look forward to that day.

92. Second Observation

Only a few months ago I experienced during my sleep an altogether extraordinary sensation of pleasure. It consisted of a sort of delightful agitation of every particle of my being; a delicious tingling, which began in the epidermis, all the way from head to foot, and thence penetrated to my very marrow. I seemed to see a violet flame playing around my forehead.

Lambere flamma comas et circum tempora pasci.[1]

I calculate that this sensation, which was definitely physical, lasted at least thirty seconds, and I awoke filled with an amazement not unmixed with awe.

From this sensation, which is still vividly present in my memory, and from a few observations made in the cases of ecstatic and highly-strung persons, I have drawn the following inference, that the limits of pleasure are as yet neither known nor fixed, and that we have no idea what degree of bodily bliss we are capable of attaining. I hope that in a few centuries the physiologist will be able to control these extraordinary sensations, and procure them at will, just as opium is used to produce sleep, and that posterity will thereby obtain compensation for the terrible sufferings we are sometimes forced to undergo.

The proposition I have just enunciated finds some support in analogy; for, as I have already remarked, the art of harmony, which today procures such acute, pure and eagerly-sought-after pleasures, was entirely unknown to the Romans: the discovery was made not more than five hundred years ago.

93. Third Observation

One night in the year VIII (1800), having gone to bed after an uneventful day, I woke up about one o'clock in the morning, an hour when I am usually in my first sleep, and

1. 'Flame licked his hair and played around his temples.' [Ed.]

found myself in a quite extraordinary state of mental excitement; my conceptions were vivid, my thoughts profound; the sphere of my intelligence seemed to have expanded, I was sitting up and my eyes were affected by a sensation of pale, vaporous, indeterminate light, which in no way served to make objects visible.

To judge by the host of ideas which passed rapidly through my brain, I might have thought that I had spent several hours in this condition; but my clock convinced me that it had lasted just over half an hour. I was roused from it by an external incident independent of my will, and so brought back to the things of this world.

At once the luminous sensation was dispelled, and I felt my powers diminish; the limits of my intelligence contracted, and in short, I became once more what I had been the day before. But as I was wide awake, my memory still retained, though in faded colours, some of the ideas which had crossed my mind.

The first concerned time. It seemed to me that past, present, and future were identical and reduced to a single point, so that it was equally simple to foresee the future and to recall the past. That is all that remained to me of my first intuition, which was partly affected by those which followed.

My attention was next directed towards the senses; I classified them in order of perfection, and coming to believe that we must possess internal as well as external senses, I began to investigate the nature of the former.

I had already discovered three, and almost four, when I came back to earth. Here they are:

1. *Compassion,* which is a precordial sensation, felt on seeing a fellow creature's suffering;
2. *Predilection,* which is a feeling of preference, not simply for an object, but also for everything connected with that object or reminiscent of it;
3. *Sympathy,* which is likewise a feeling of preference, attracting two objects to each other.

It might at first sight be thought that these last two feelings are one and the same; but what sets them apart is the fact that *predilection* is not always reciprocal, while *sympathy* is necessarily so.

Finally, while dwelling on *compassion*, I reached a conclusion which struck me as irrefutable, but which I might not have perceived at another time, namely that compassion is the source of that beautiful principle which is the original basis of all laws:

Alteri ne facias quod tibi fieri non vis. [Do not do to others what you would not have them do to you.]

I might add that so marvellous is my recollection of the condition in which I was on this occasion, and of what I then experienced, that I would gladly, if it were possible, give all the remaining years of my life for one month of such an existence.

Men of letters will understand me more easily than other people, for there are few of them to whom something similar has not occurred, though doubtless to an inferior degree.

The author is warm in bed, lying in a horizontal position, with his nightcap on; he thinks of the work on which he is engaged; his imagination grows excited, ideas abound, expressions follow hard on their heels; and since to write he must get up, he gets dressed, removes his night-cap, and sits down at his desk.

Then, suddenly, he finds that everything has changed; the ardour of his imagination has cooled, the thread of his ideas has snapped, the expressions he needs are lacking; he is forced to search laboriously for what he had found so easily before, and all too often he is forced to put off the work to some more propitious day.

All this is easily explained by the effect which the change of position and temperature must produce on the brain; this is another instance of the influence of the physical on the mental.

In studying the above experience I have perhaps been led too far; but in the end I arrived at the belief that the excitable behaviour of the Orientals was in part due to the fact that, being of the Mohammedan faith, they always keep their heads warmly covered; and that it was in order to obtain the contrary effect that those who laid down laws for our own monks imposed on them the necessity of having that part of their person shaven and uncovered.

20. On the Influence of Diet on Rest, Sleep, and Dreams

94. Introduction

Let a man rest or sleep or dream; he still remains subject to the laws of nourishment, and does not leave the empire of gastronomy.

Theory and experience are united in proving that the quality and quantity of food consumed exerts a powerful influence on work, rest, sleep, and dreams.

95. Effect of Diet on Work

The ill-nourished man cannot stand up for long to the strain of continuous toil; his body sweats all over, his strength soon abandons him, and for him rest is nothing but the impossibility of action.

If his work is of the mental variety, his ideas lack vigour and precision; reflection fails to knit them together, and judgement to analyse them; his brain is soon worn out with vain endeavour, and he falls asleep on the field of battle.

I have always thought that the famous suppers at Auteuil, like those at the houses of Rambouillet and Soissons, did a great deal of good to the authors of the time of Louis XIV; and the cynic Geoffroy (if the fact were true) could not have been far wrong when he taunted the poets of the late eighteenth century with the sugar-and-water he believed to be their favourite drink.

Following up this theory, I examined the works of certain authors known to have lived in poverty and distress; and sure enough I found no force in them, except when they were obviously stirred by consciousness of their woes, or an envy which was often none too well disguised.

He, on the contrary, who eats well, and repairs his losses

with prudence and discretion, is capable of performing almost incredible feats.

The Emperor Napoleon, on the eve of his departure for Boulogne, worked continuously for more than thirty hours with his Council of State and the heads of his various departments, taking no refreshment apart from two very short meals and a few cups of coffee.

Brown mentions an English Admiralty clerk who, having accidentally lost certain documents which he alone was qualified to work on, spent fifty-two hours on end rewriting them. He could never have survived such an enormous loss of energy without a special diet; he sustained himself in the following manner: first on water, then light food, then wine, then beef tea and finally opium.

I remember one day meeting a courier whom I had known in the army, and who had just returned from Spain, where he had been sent post-haste by the government (*correo ganando horas*); he had completed the journey in twelve days, spending only four hours in Madrid. A few glasses of wine, with an occasional bowl of broth were all that he had consumed throughout this whole period of hard riding and sleepless nights; and he added that more solid fare would infallibly have left him incapable of proceeding on his way.

96. *Effect of Diet on Dreams*

The influence of diet upon dreams is no less marked.

A hungry man cannot sleep; the anguished cravings of his stomach keep him painfully awake, and if weakness and exhaustion force him to fall asleep, his slumber will be light, restless, and broken.

He, on the contrary, who has exceeded the bounds of discretion in his eating, falls fast asleep at once; if he has dreams, no recollection of them will remain, because the nervous fluid has passed in all directions along the sensitive ducts. For the same reason his awakening is sudden and abrupt; he returns painfully to social life; and when the effects of sleep have completely worn off, he continues for a long time to feel the fatigue of digestion.

It may be laid down as a general maxim that coffee drives away sleep. Habit weakens and may completely overcome this disadvantage; but it infallibly afflicts all Europeans when they drink it for the first time. Some foods, on the other hand, gently induce sleep; such are those in which milk predominates, the entire family of lettuces, and, above all, a rennet apple eaten immediately before going to bed.

97. Continued

Experience, based on millions of observations, has proved that diet determines the nature of dreams.

Generally speaking, all foods of a slightly stimulating kind cause dreaming: such are red meat, pigeon, duck, game, and above all hare.

The same property has been discovered in asparagus, celery, truffles, spices, and particularly vanilla.

But it would be a mistake to think that these somniferous substances ought to be banished from our tables, for the dreams they induce are for the most part light and agreeable, and prolong our existence, even while it seems suspended.

There are those to whom sleep is a life apart, a sort of novel in serial form; each of their dreams has a sequel, and they continue in one night's dream what they had begun the night before, seeing in their sleep familiar faces they have never met in the real world.

98. Conclusion

The man who has reflected on his physical existence and conducts it according to the principles we are laying down, prepares his rest, his sleep, and his dreams carefully and wisely.

He shares out his work so as to avoid exhaustion; he lightens it by varying it carefully; and he refreshes his faculties by short intervals of rest, which relieve them without destroying that continuity which is sometimes essential.

If, in the day-time, he needs a longer rest, he never yields to it except in a sitting position; he spurns sleep, unless it comes upon him irresistibly, and above all he avoids making a habit of it.

When night brings the hour of diurnal rest, he retires to a well-ventilated room, takes care not to surround himself with curtains which would force him to breathe the same air a hundred times over, and avoids closing the shutters, so that whenever his eyes open, they may be soothed by whatever light lingers on.

He stretches himself out on a bed slightly raised at the head; his pillow is stuffed with horsehair; his night-cap is made of linen; his chest is not weighed down with blankets, but he is careful to keep his feet warmly covered.

He has eaten wisely, though refusing neither good nor excellent cheer; he has drunk the best wines, and, albeit cautiously, even the most famous. At dessert his talk has been gallant rather than political, and he has made more madrigals than epigrams; he has drunk a cup of coffee, if it agrees with his constitution, and accepted a few moments later a spoonful of excellent liqueur, simply to sweeten his mouth. In all things he has shown himself a charming guest, a distinguished connoisseur; and yet he has only barely exceeded the limits of necessity.

Under these circumstances he goes to bed content with himself and the rest of the world; his eyes close; he passes through the twilight zone, and then falls fast asleep for a few hours.

Soon Nature has levied her tribute, and his losses are repaired by assimilation. Then sweet dreams provide him with a mysterious existence; he sees those he loves, resumes his favourite occupations, and is wafted to those places where he has known happiness.

At last, he feels sleep gradually dispelled, and returns to social life with no reason to regret wasted time, because even in sleep he has enjoyed activity without fatigue and pleasure unalloyed.

21. On Obesity

99. Introduction

If I had been a qualified doctor, I would in the first place have written a monograph on obesity; then I would have established my empire in that sphere of the profession. I would thus have enjoyed the dual advantage of having the healthiest of people as my patients, and being daily besieged by the prettier half of the human race; for to acquire a perfect degree of plumpness, neither too much nor too little, is the life-study of every woman in the world.

What I have not done, another doctor will do: and if he is at once learned, discreet, and a handsome fellow, I guarantee that he will obtain miraculous successes.

Exoriare aliquis nostris ex ossibus haeres![1]

Meanwhile, I am going to lead the way; for a chapter on obesity is essential in a work which has man and his meals as its subject.

By *obesity* I mean that state of fatty congestion in which, without the individual being ill, his limbs gradually increase in volume and lose their original shape and harmony.

There is a type of obesity which is confined to the belly; I have never known an example to occur among women; for they are generally made of softer stuff than men, and obesity, when it attacks them, spares no part of their person. I call this variety *gastrophory,* and those affected by it *gastrophors.* I myself am one of them; but although I am the bearer of a fairly prominent paunch, the lower part of my legs is still hard, and the sinews as loosely knit as those of an Arab horse.

For all that, I have always regarded my paunch as a re-

1. 'From my dead bones may some heir arise!' [Ed.]

doubtable enemy; I have beaten it and reduced it to majestic proportions; but in order to beat it I had to fight it, and whatever merit this work contains, I owe to a struggle of thirty years duration.

I will begin with an extract from more than five hundred dialogues I have had at table with such of my neighbours as were either threatened or afflicted with obesity.

STOUT PARTY: Heavens! What delicious bread! Where do you get it?

MYSELF: From Monsieur Limet, in the Rue de Richelieu: he is baker to their Royal Highnesses the Duc d'Orléans and the Prince de Condé; I first went to him because his shop is nearby, and I am faithful to him because I have proclaimed him the best panificator in the world.

STOUT PARTY: I must remember that; I eat a great deal of bread, and for rolls such as these I would willingly do without all the rest.

ANOTHER STOUT PARTY: But what on earth are you doing, swallowing the liquid part of your soup, and leaving that delicious Carolina rice?

MYSELF: I am following a special diet.

STOUT PARTY: That's a poor diet, I can tell you! Rice is the joy of my life, together with flour, noodles, and things of that sort; there's nothing more nutritious, cheaper, or more easily digestible.

A VERY STOUT PARTY: Monsieur, be so good as to pass me those potatoes in front of you. At the rate they're disappearing I am afraid of being too late.

MYSELF: Monsieur, they are within your reach.

VERY STOUT PARTY: But aren't you going to help yourself? There are enough for both of us, and after us the deluge.

MYSELF: No thank you; to my mind the only value of potatoes is as a safeguard against starvation; apart from that, I know of nothing more utterly insipid.

VERY STOUT PARTY: What gastronomical heresy! There's nothing better than potatoes; I eat them in every conceivable form, and if any appear in the second course, whether *à la*

Lyonnaise or *au soufflé* I here and now stake my claim to them.

STOUT LADY: You would be kindness itself if you would get them to pass me those Soissons haricot beans I see at the end of the table.

MYSELF [*after complying with her request while singing softly to a well-known tune*]:

> Happy the Soissons folk who grow
> That king of beans the haricot!

STOUT PARTY: You mustn't joke about them; they are a real source of wealth for the region. Paris pays large sums of money for them. And I beg leave also to praise those little marsh beans they call English beans; when they are young and fresh, they are food for the gods.

MYSELF: Anathema on all beans, both haricot and English!

STOUT PARTY [*with a resolute air*]: That for your anathema! Anyone would think you were a whole council in yourself!

MYSELF [*to another stout lady*]: Allow me to congratulate you on your excellent health, Madame: it seems to me you have grown a little plumper since I last had the honour of seeing you.

STOUT LADY: That is doubtless due to my new diet.

MYSELF: How so?

STOUT LADY: For some time now I have taken to breakfasting off a very good rich soup, a bowlful big enough for two; and what soup! The spoon stands upright in it.

MYSELF [*to another*]: Madame, if your eyes don't deceive me, you will accept a little of this charlotte? Let me attack it for you.

STOUT LADY: Well, Monsieur, my eyes do deceive you; there are only two things here I really like, and they are both of the masculine gender: one is that rice-cake with the golden stripes, and the other that gigantic sponge-cake; for you must know that I adore all sweet cakes.

MYSELF [*to another*]: While they are talking politics over

there, Madame, may I interrogate this frangipane tart on your behalf?

STOUT LADY: Please do: nothing agrees with me so well as pastry. We have a pastry-cook lodging with us at home, and I do believe my daughter and myself between us absorb the whole of the rent he pays us, and more besides.

MYSELF [*after looking at the young person*]: The diet obviously suits you to perfection: your daughter is a very beautiful person, with every advantage.

STOUT LADY: Yet, believe it or not, her girl friends sometimes tell her she is too fat.

MYSELF: Perhaps they say that out of envy . . .

STOUT LADY: Quite possibly. In any case, I am marrying her off soon, and the first baby will put everything to rights.

Through conversations such as these I elucidated a theory whose elements I had first elucidated outside mankind, namely that the chief cause of corpulence is a diet with starchy and farinaceous elements; and in this way I satisfied myself that the same diet is always followed by the same effect.

Sure enough, carnivorous animals never grow fat (consider wolves, jackals, birds of prey, crows, etc.).

Herbivorous animals do not grow fat easily, at least until age has reduced them to a state of inactivity; but they fatten very quickly as soon as they begin to be fed on potatoes, grain, or any kind of flour.

Obesity is never found either among the savages, or in those classes of society in which men work to eat, and eat only to live.

100. Causes of Obesity

From the observations noted above, the accuracy of which anyone can verify, it is easy to discover the principal causes of obesity.

The first is the natural constitution of the individual. Nearly all men are born with certain predispositions, of which their physiognomy bears the stamp. Out of a hundred persons who die of consumption, ninety have brown hair, long faces, and pointed noses. Out of a hundred obese persons, on the other hand, ninety have short faces, round eyes, and snub noses.

It is certain therefore that there are persons virtually doomed as it were to corpulence, persons whose digestive activities, all things being equal, create more fat than those of their fellows.

This physical truth, of which I am firmly convinced, sometimes influences my way of looking at things in a most unfortunate manner.

When there appears in society a vivacious, pink-cheeked young person, with a pert nose, rounded contours, and short plump hands and feet, everybody is entranced and finds her charming; everyone, that is, but I. For, taught by experience, I look at her with eyes of twelve years hence, see the ravages which obesity will have wrought on those fresh young charms, and groan inwardly over ills so far non-existent. This anticipatory compassion is a painful sensation and furnishes one proof, among a thousand others, that man would be unhappier than he already is, if he could foresee the future.

The second of the chief causes of obesity is the floury and starchy substances which man makes the prime ingredients of his daily nourishment. As we have said already, all animals that live on farinaceous food grow fat willy-nilly; and man is no exception to the universal law.

Starch produces its effect sooner and more surely in conjunction with sugar; sugar and fat both contain hydrogen as a common element; both are inflammable. With this addition, it is the more active in that it pleases the palate more, and because sweet dishes are seldom eaten until the natural appetite has already been satisfied, when only that luxury appetite remains which must be coaxed by the most refined art and the subtlest variety.

Starch is no less fattening when conveyed in drinks, such as beer and other beverages of the same kind. The beer-drinking countries are also those where the biggest bellies are found; and certain Parisian families which, in 1817, drank beer for reasons of economy, were rewarded with paunches which they scarcely know what to do with.

101. Continued

A dual cause of obesity results from excess of sleep and want of exercise.

The human body gains a great deal during sleep, and loses very little in the same period, since muscular activity is suspended. It thus becomes essential for the surplus acquired to be reduced by exercise; yet the time for activity is reduced in direct proportion to the time spent in sleep.

By another necessary consequence, heavy sleepers shun everything that promises to be at all tiring; the excess products of assimilation are therefore swept away by the torrent of circulation; they are there charged, by a process of which Nature alone holds the secret, with a little more hydrogen, and fat soon forms, to be deposited by the same agency in the capsules of the cellular tissue.

102. Continued

A last cause of obesity consists of excessive eating and drinking.

We have had occasion to say that it is one of the privileges of mankind to eat without being hungry and drink without being thirsty; and indeed it cannot be a privilege shared by the animals, for it is born of reflection on the pleasures of the table, and the desire to prolong them.

This dual inclination has been found wherever men exist; and it is well known that savages eat to excess and drink themselves into a stupor whenever an opportunity presents itself.

As for ourselves, the citizens of the two worlds, who believe that we stand at the summit of civilization, it is certain that we eat too much.

I am not speaking of the few who, for reasons of avarice or impotence, live alone and apart; the former gloating over the money they are saving, the latter lamenting their inability to do better; I am speaking of all those who, moving about us, are in turn hosts or guests, politely offering or complaisantly accepting; who, when all their needs are satisfied, eat a dish because it is attractive, or drink a wine because it is new to them: I insist that whether they sit every day in fine dining-rooms or only celebrate Sundays and occasionally Mondays, the vast majority eat and drink too much, and huge quantities of food are absorbed every day without need.

This cause, almost always present, acts differently according to the constitution of the individual; and in the case of those who have bad stomachs, its effect is not obesity, but indigestion.

103. Anecdote

We have witnessed with our own eyes an example which half Paris had the opportunity of observing.

Monsieur Lang had one of the most luxurious houses in that city; his table especially was excellent, but his stomach was as bad as his gourmandism was extreme. He did the honours perfectly, and himself ate with a courage worthy of a better fate.

Everything would go well until after the coffee; but soon his stomach would refuse to do its duty, pains would begin, and the wretched gastronome would be forced to throw himself down on a sofa and remain there till next day, expiating the brief pleasures he had tasted in prolonged anguish.

The remarkable thing is that he never changed his ways; as long as he lived, he freely accepted this strange alternation; and never allowed the sufferings of the evening to interfere with next day's dinner.

In the case of those whose stomach is in good shape, overeating acts as described in the previous chapter. Everything is digested and what is not needed for the body's recuperation solidifies and turns into fat.

With the others, chronic indigestion is the rule; their food passes through them without benefiting them, and those who are unaware of the reason are surprised when so many good things fail to produce better results.

It will be seen that I am not dealing exhaustively with the subject; for there are a thousand secondary causes arising out of our habits, occupations, enthusiasms, and pleasures which aid and abet those I have just mentioned.

All of this I bequeath to the successor I planted at the beginning of this chapter, contenting myself with that prelibation which belongs by right to first comers in every sphere.

It is a long time since intemperance first claimed the attention of observers. Philosophers have praised temperance, princes have made sumptuary laws, religion has moralized over gourmandism; but alas, not a mouthful the less has been eaten as a result, and the art of overeating flourishes more and more every day.

Perhaps I shall meet with better luck if I follow a new course; I intend to expose the *physical disadvantages of obesity*; self-preservation will perhaps be a stronger force than morals, more persuasive than sermons, more powerful than laws; for the fair sex, I believe, is quite prepared to open its eyes to the light.

104. Disadvantages of Obesity

Obesity has an unfortunate effect on both sexes since it injures both strength and beauty.

It injures strength because, while increasing the weight of the mass to be moved, it does not increase the motive power; it is also harmful in that it obstructs breathing, and so makes any work impossible which demands the prolonged use of muscular energy.

Obesity injures beauty by destroying the originally established harmony of proportion; because all parts of the body do not fatten equally.

It also injures it by filling up the hollows which are

Nature's shading; thus it is all too common to see faces which were once extremely attractive made almost plain by obesity.

The head of the late government did not escape the effects of this law. He grew extremely fat in the course of his last campaigns; his complexion turned from pale to ashen, and his eyes lost part of their proud fire.

Obesity brings with it a distaste for dancing, walking, and riding, and an inaptitude for every occupation or amusement requiring some degree of agility or skill.

It also opens the way for various diseases, such as apoplexy, dropsy, and ulcers of the legs, and makes all other ailments more difficult to cure.

105. Examples of Obesity

Of heroes who were corpulent, I can remember none but Marius and John Sobieski.

Marius, who was a short man, became as round as he was long, and it may have been his very enormity which terrified the Cimbrian charged with the duty of slaying him.

As for the King of Poland, his obesity came close to being the end of him; for, being forced to flee from a large body of Turkish cavalry, his breath soon failed him, and he would undoubtedly have been done to death if some of his aides-de-camp had not supported him, half unconscious, in his saddle, while others nobly sacrificed their lives to check the enemy.

If I am not mistaken, the Duc de Vendôme, that worthy son of the great Henri, was also a man of remarkable corpulence. He died at an inn forsaken by one and all, and retained enough consciousness to see the last of his servants snatch the cushion from under his head, just as he was giving up the ghost.

History provides many other instances of monstrous obesity; I shall pass over them, to speak a few words of those I have observed with my own eyes.

Monsieur Rameau, my schoolfellow as a boy and later

Mayor of La Chaleur, in Burgundy, was only five feet two inches tall, and weighed five hundred pounds.

Monsieur le Duc de Luynes, beside whom I have often sat at table, became enormous; fat completely ruined his once elegant figure and he spent the last years of his life in a state of almost permanent somnolence.

But the most extraordinary example of this kind I ever saw was a citizen of New York, whom many Frenchmen still alive in Paris may have seen in the street called Broadway, sitting in a huge armchair the legs of which would have supported a church.

Edward was at least five feet ten inches tall, and as fat had blown him out in all directions, he was at least eight feet round. His fingers were like those of that Roman Emperor who used his wife's necklaces as rings; his arms and thighs were tubular, and as thick as an ordinary man's body; and he had feet like an elephant's, half hidden under the flesh of his legs; the weight of fat had drawn his lower eyelids down; but what made him hideous to behold was three spheroidal chins, which hung down for more than a foot over his chest, so that his face looked like the capital of a wreathed column.

In this condition Edward spent his life sitting at the window of a ground-floor room which looked out on to the street, every now and then drinking a glass of ale, a huge pitcher of which was always by his side.

Such an extraordinary figure could not fail to bring passers-by to a halt; but they were not allowed to linger, for Edward soon put them to flight, exclaiming in sepulchral tones: 'What are you staring at me for, like so many wild cats? . . . Get along with you, you lazy body. . . . Be gone, you good for nothing dogs!' and other similar compliments.

I often used to greet him by name, and sometimes stopped for a chat; he assured me that he was neither bored nor unhappy, and that provided death did not disturb him, he would gladly await the end of the world in this fashion.

From what has been said in this chapter it is clear that if obesity is not a disease, it is at least an unfortunate indisposition, into which we nearly always fall through our own fault.

It is also clear that all must wish to avoid it if they are not already afflicted by it, and to be rid of it if they are; and for their benefit we are going to examine the resources made available to us by science with the help of observation.

22. Prevention & Cure of Obesity[1]

106. Introduction

I will begin with a story which proves that courage is essential for both the prevention and the cure of obesity.

Monsieur Louis Greffulhe, whom His Majesty later honoured with the title of Count, came to see me one morning, and told me that, having heard that I had once studied the question of obesity, and being himself seriously threatened by it, he had come to ask my advice.

'Monsieur,' I said, 'not being a qualified physician, I would be within my rights in refusing your request; however, I am at your service, but on one condition, namely that you give me your word of honour that you will follow for one month, and with absolute fidelity, the instructions I am going to lay down for you.'

Monsieur Greffulhe gave the required assurance, shaking hands on it, and the very next day I delivered my *fetwa*, the first article of which ordered him to weigh himself before and after the course of treatment, so as to obtain a mathematical basis on which to judge its efficacy.

A month later Monsieur Greffulhe came back to see me again, and spoke to me in roughly these terms:

'Monsieur, I have followed your prescription as if my life depended on it; and I find that in the last month my weight has decreased by three pounds, and even a little more. But in

---

1. About twenty years ago I began to write an *ex professo* treatise on obesity. My readers will especially regret the preface, which was in dramatic form, and in which I proved to a doctor that fever is much less dangerous than a lawsuit, because the latter, after forcing the plaintiff to make haste, wait, lie, and curse, and robbing him of sleep, happiness, and money for an indefinite period, finally causes him to fall ill and die of vexation; a truth which deserves to be made as widely known as any other.

order to obtain this result, I have been obliged to do such violence to all my tastes and all my habits, in short, I have gone through so much suffering that while thanking you for your good advice, I hereby renounce any good that may come of it, and abandon myself for the future to whatever Providence may ordain.'

After this declaration, which I heard with some sorrow, the end was what it was bound to be; Monsieur Greffulhe grew more and more corpulent, suffered all the disadvantages of extreme obesity, and, at little more than forty years of age, died from the effects of a suffocating malady to which he had become subject.

107. Generalities

Every cure of obesity must begin with these three essential precepts: discretion in eating, moderation in sleeping, and exercise on foot or on horseback.

These are the first resources provided for us by science; but I place very little reliance on them, because I know men and things, and I am aware that no prescription which is not complied with to the letter can be effective.

Now, in the first place, it requires considerable strength of mind to leave the table with an appetite; so long as the need remains one mouthful attracts another with irresistible force; and in general a man will go on eating as long as he is hungry, in spite of the doctors, and even following their example.

Secondly, to suggest to a fat man that he should get up early is to pierce him to the heart; he will tell you that his constitution would never stand it, and that when he has risen early he is good for nothing for the rest of the day; a woman will complain that it gives her rings under the eyes; they will all agree to sit up late, but insist on staying in bed in the morning; and there goes another resource.

Thirdly, riding is an expensive remedy, which suits neither all purses nor all positions.

Suggest riding to a pretty woman who is also fat, and she

will joyfully agree, but on three conditions: first, that she shall be provided with a handsome, lively, and sweet-tempered horse; second, that she shall have a new riding-habit of the very latest cut; and third, that she shall be attended by a squire who is both gallant and good-looking. These conditions can rarely be fulfilled at one and the same time, so farewell to equitation.

Exercise on foot gives rise to many other objections: it is terribly tiring, and causes perspiration and the risk of catching cold; dust ruins the stockings, and stones pierce little shoes, until going on becomes impossible. And if, in the course of these various activities, the shadow of a headache appears, or a pimple the size of a pin's head breaks through the skin, the régime is promptly blamed and abandoned, while the doctor frets and fumes.

So, since it is agreed that whoever wishes to see his paunch diminish, should eat in moderation, sleep little, and take as much exercise as he can, it still remains to seek another way of attaining the same end. Now, there is an infallible method of preventing corpulence from becoming excessive, or of reducing it when it has reached that point. This method, which is based on the surest precepts of chemistry and physics, consists of a diet appropriate to the desired effect.

Of all medical prescriptions, dieting is the best, because it acts incessantly, day and night, in sleep and in waking; its effect is reinforced with every meal, and it ends up by subjugating every part of the individual's constitution. Now, an anti-obesical diet must be governed by the most common and most active cause of obesity; and since it has been proved that fatty congestion is simply due to flour and starch, in man as well as in animals (for, in the case of the latter, this effect is produced every day before our eyes, giving rise to the trade in fattened animals), it may be inferred, as an exact consequence, that a more or less strict abstinence from all floury or starchy food leads to a diminution of flesh.

'Good heavens!' my readers of both sexes are going to exclaim, 'good heavens, what a cruel man the Professor is! Here he is in one word proscribing everything we love –

Limet's white bread, Achard's biscuits, So-and-so's cakes, and all the good things made of flour and butter, flour and sugar, flour, sugar, and eggs! He doesn't even leave us potatoes or macaroni! Who would have expected that of a gastronome who seemed so good-natured?'

'What is this I hear?' I reply, putting on my stern expression, which I only use once a year; 'very well, then, eat and grow fat; grow ugly, heavy, and asthmatic, and die of inflammation of the stomach; I shall be there to take notes, and you will appear in my second edition. . . . What? A single phrase has convinced you? You are terrified and beg me to hold back the thunderbolt? . . . Calm yourselves; I am going to describe your diet and show you that some pleasure still remains for you, in this world in which we live to eat.

'You like bread: very well, you will eat rye bread; the worthy Cadet de Vaux has been praising its virtues for a long time; it is less nutritious and less agreeable too; but that only makes our precept easier to obey. For to be sure of yourselves, you must always avoid temptation. Remember that: it is a sound piece of moral advice.

'You like soup: let it be clear, *à la julienne*, with green vegetables, cabbage, or roots; but croutons, noodles, and thick soups are forbidden.

'For the first course you are free to eat anything, with a few exceptions, such as chicken and rice, and the pastry of hot pâtés. Eat well, but prudently, so that you do not have to satisfy at a later stage a need which will exist no longer.

'The second course is due to appear, and here you will need all your philosophy. Avoid all things floury, in whatever guise they come; for you are still left with the roast and the salad and the green vegetables. And if you must have something sweet afterwards, choose a chocolate custard, or a jelly made with orange or punch.

'Here comes dessert. A new source of danger; but if you have eaten wisely so far, your wisdom will go from strength to strength. Mistrust the savouries (they are always brioches more or less adorned); avert your eyes from the biscuits and macaroons; there still remain all kinds of fruit, jams, and many other things which you will learn to choose for your-self if you adopt my principles.

'After dinner, I prescribe coffee, permit liqueurs, and advise tea and punch on occasion.

'For breakfast, the inevitable rye bread, and chocolate rather than coffee. However, I allow coffee with just a little milk; no eggs, and the rest as you please. But you cannot breakfast too early in the day. When you breakfast late, dinner arrives before digestion is complete; yet you eat no less; and such eating without appetite is a very active cause of obesity, because of its frequent occurrence.'

108. Diet Continued

So far I have simply traced for you, like a kind and rather indulgent father, the limits of a diet which wards off the obesity which is threatening you; let us now add a few precepts against that which has already taken hold of you.

Drink, every summer, thirty bottles of soda-water; a very large glass when you wake up, two before breakfast, and the same number when you go to bed. Prefer for the most part white, light, and sub-acid wines, like those of Anjou. Shun beer like the plague, ask often for radishes, raw artichokes, asparagus, celery, and cardoons. Among meats, prefer veal and fowl; of bread, eat nothing but the crust; in doubtful cases be guided by a doctor who adopts my principles; and at whatever time of life you begin to follow them, you will soon be fresh, pretty, sprightly, healthy, and fit for anything.

Having thus set you on the right road, I must also open your eyes to the pitfalls, for fear that carried away by a desire to lose weight, you overstep the mark.

The pitfall I wish to point out is the habitual use of acids, which ignorant persons sometimes advise, and which have been proved by experience to be invariably harmful.

109. Danger of Acids

There circulates among women a baneful doctrine, which every years brings many young persons to the grave, namely that acids and particularly vinegar, are preventives against obesity.

No doubt continued use of acids is thinning, but only at the expense of freshness, health, and life; and though lemonade is the mildest of them all, few stomachs can stand up to it for long.

The truth I have just enunciated cannot be too widely known; there are few of my readers who could not provide me, out of their own experience, with some observation to bear it out, but of them all I prefer the following, which is in some sort personal to myself.

In 1776 I was at Dijon, taking a law course in the faculty; a chemistry course under Monsieur Guyton de Morveau, then advocate general; and a course of domestic medicine under Monsieur Maret, permanent secretary of the Academy, and the father of Monsieur le Duc de Bassano.

There I struck up a friendship with one of the liveliest girls I have ever known. I say a *friendship*, and this is both strictly true and at the same time somewhat surprising for in those days I was admirably equipped for affinities of a far more exacting nature.

This friendship, then, which must be accepted for what it was, and not for what it might have become, had ripened, from the very first day, into a close familiarity which struck us as perfectly natural, and which was expressed in endless whispered confidences which did not alarm her mother at all, because they were of an innocence worthy of the golden age.

Louise was very pretty, and above all possessed, in a just proportion, that classic fullness of figure which delights the eye and is the glory of the imitative arts. Although I was no more than her friend, I was far from being blind to the charms she displayed or allowed to be guessed at; and perhaps indeed, without my being aware of it, they strength-

ened the chaste sentiment which attached me to her. Be
that as it may, one evening when I had been looking at
Louise more closely than usual, 'My dear,' I said, 'you are
unwell; you seem to have grown thinner.' 'Oh, no,' she
answered, with a smile which seemed tinged with melancholy, 'I am quite well; and if I am a little thinner, why, I
can afford to lose a little in that direction without being any
the poorer.' 'To lose!' I retorted hotly: 'you have no need
to lose or gain; stay as you are, altogether lovely,' and
more phrases of the same sort, which a young man of
twenty always has at his command.

After this conversation, I began to watch this girl with an
interest mingled with anxiety, and soon I saw her colour
fading, her cheeks growing hollow, her charms withering
away. . . . Ah, what a frail and fleeting thing is beauty! At
last, meeting her at a ball (for she still danced as usual), I
persuaded her to sit out two quadrilles; and putting
this time to good use, I made her confess that, tired of the
jests of some of her girl friends who assured her that in less
than two years she would be fatter than Saint Christopher,
and acting on the advice of some other friends, she had set
out to lose weight. To that end she had been drinking a
glass of vinegar every morning for a month: she added
that until that moment she had taken no one into her
confidence.

I shuddered when I heard this confession, for I knew the
full extent of the danger; and the very next morning I told
Louise's mother, who was no less alarmed than I, for she
adored her daughter. No time was lost; doctors arrived,
examined and prescribed. All in vain! The sources of life
were irremediably affected; by the time the danger was first
suspected, there was already no hope left.

And so, through following imprudent advice, dear Louise,
reduced to the dreadful state which accompanies a wasting
sickness, fell asleep for ever, when she was scarcely eighteen
years old.

She died gazing sadly towards a future which, for her,
would never exist; and the thought of having, albeit in-

voluntarily, taken her own life both hastened her end and made it more painful.

She was the first person I ever saw die, for she breathed her last in my arms, while I was raising her, at her request, to see the day. About eight hours after her death, her heart-broken mother begged me to accompany her on a last visit to what remained of her daughter; and we found to our surprise that her face had taken on a radiant ecstatic look it had not had before. I was amazed at the change; her mother took it for a comforting omen. But the case is not uncommon. Lavater mentions it in his *Treatise on the Physiognomy*.

110. Anti-Obesical Belt

Every anti-obesical diet should be accompanied by a precautionary measure which I had forgotten, but ought to have begun with; this consists in wearing day and night a moderately tight belt to hold in the stomach.

In order to appreciate the necessity of this measure, it should be remembered that the spinal column, which forms one of the walls of the intestinal case, is firm and inflexible; whence it follows that all the excess weight acquired by the intestines, as soon as the fat causes them to deviate from the vertical, bears against the various envelopes which form the skin of the belly; and these, though capable of distending almost indefinitely,[1] might not have sufficient resilience to contract again, when relieved of the strain, unless they received mechanical aid which, bearing on the dorsal column itself, becomes its antagonist, and so restores equilibrium. Thus this belt has the dual effect of preventing the belly from yielding to the actual weight of the intestines, and giving it the necessary strength to contract again when that weight decreases. It should never be left off, or the good done during the day will be undone by the freedom of the night;

1. Mirabeau said of an excessively fat man that God had created him only to show how far the human skin could stretch without bursting.

but it causes little discomfort, and the wearer quickly grows accustomed to it.

The patient is not condemned to wear such a belt for life: it may be relinquished without harm when the desired reduction has been achieved and the weight has remained stationary for a few weeks. Naturally a suitable diet must still be observed. It is at least six years since I stopped wearing my own belt.

III. Quinine

There exists a substance which I believe to be actively antiobesical; several observations have brought me to this belief; however, I am ready to accept doubters, and I invite all doctors to experiment.

The substance is quinine.

Ten or twelve persons of my acquaintance used to suffer from prolonged intermittent fevers; they cured themselves, some with homely remedies, powders, etc., the others by continued use of quinine, which never failed to produce results.

All the individuals in the first category who were obese returned to their former corpulence; all those in the second remained permanently rid of their superfluous flesh; and this entitles me to think that it was the quinine which produced that effect, for there was no difference between the people concerned except for the method of treatment.

Rational theory is not opposed to this inference; for on the one hand quinine, by stimulating all the vital forces, may well cause such activity in the circulation as to disturb and dissipate the gases which would otherwise turn into fat; and on the other, it is known that quinine contains a proportion of tannin which may close up the cells which would normally receive fatty congestions. It is even probable that the two effects cooperate and reinforce each other.

It is on the basis of these data, which any reader may verify for himself, that I believe I may recommend quinine to all who desire to rid themselves of excessive fat. And so, *dummodo annuerint in omni medicationis genere doctissimi Facultatis professores,*[1] I think that after one month of a suitable diet, he or she who wishes to grow slender will do well to take, every other day during the next month, at seven in the morning, or two hours before breakfast, a teaspoonful of good red quinine in a glass of dry white wine, and that good results will follow.

Such are the means I recommend to combat an inconvenience as distressing as it is common. I have adjusted them to allow for human weakness as modified by the state of society in which we live.

I have worked on the principle that the stricter the diet, the less effective it proves, because it will be followed either half-heartedly or not at all.

Great efforts of will are rare, and in order to be followed, it is necessary to propose to men only that which comes easily to them, and even, when possible, that which pleases them.

1. 'So long as the learned professors of medicine in all its forms assent . . .' [Ed.]

23. On Thinness

112. Definition

Thinness is the condition of an individual whose muscular flesh, not being filled out with fat, reveals the form and angles of the bony structure.

Different Sorts

There are two sorts of thinness: the first is that which, resulting from the natural disposition of the body, is accompanied by good health and the complete exercise of all the organic functions; the second is that which, being caused by the weakness of certain organs or the defective action of others, gives to the afflicted individual a wretched, puny appearance. I have known a young woman of medium height who weighed only sixty-five pounds.

113. Effects of Thinness

Thinness is no great disadvantage to men; they are no weaker for being thin, and much fitter. The father of the young lady I have just mentioned, though quite as thin as his daughter, was strong enough to lift a heavy chair with his teeth and throw it backwards over his head.

But for women it is a frightful misfortune; for to them beauty is more than life itself, and beauty consists above all in roundness of form and gracefully curving lines. The most elegant outfit and cleverest dressmaker cannot hide certain absences, nor conceal certain angles; and it is a common saying that with every pin she removes, a thin woman, however beautiful she may seem, loses something of her charm.

For the naturally puny there is no remedy; or rather, the Faculty must be called in, and the treatment may be so long drawn out that the cure will probably come too late.

But we see no reason why women who are born thin, yet whose stomach is in order, should be any more difficult to fatten than chickens; and if it takes a little longer, that is because their stomachs are comparatively smaller and because they cannot be subjected, like those devoted birds, to a strict and meticulously executed diet.

This comparison is the gentlest I could find; I had to have one, and the ladies will, I trust, forgive me on the ground of the praiseworthy intentions with which this chapter is written.

114. Natural Predisposition

Nature, various in all her works, has moulds for thinness, just as she has for obesity.

Persons destined to be thin are constructed on an elongated pattern. Their hands and feet are small, their legs lank, the region of the coccyx scantily covered, their ribs apparent, their noses aquiline, their eyes almond-shaped, their mouths large, their chins pointed, and their hair brown.

Such is the general type; some parts of the body may not conform to it, but that is rarely the case.

You may sometimes see thin persons who eat a great deal. All those I have been able to interrogate have admitted to me that they digested badly, that they ... and there you have the reason why they stay as they are.

Puny individuals vary infinitely as to hair and build. They are remarkable for having no salient characteristics, either in their features or their persons; their eyes are dull, their lips colourless, and the combination of their features indicates a lack of energy, weakness, something akin to suffering. It might almost be said of them that they look unfinished, and that in them the torch of life has not been fully lighted.

115. Fattening Régime

Every thin woman wishes to put on flesh; this is an ambition that has been confided to us a thousand times. It is therefore as a final tribute to the all-powerful sex that we shall not look for means of replacing by real shapes those artificial charms, in silk or cotton, which may be seen lavishly displayed in the fashion shops, to the great scandal of the prudish, who pass by horrified and avert their gaze from these chimeras with as much and more care than if the reality was visible to their eyes.

The whole secret of acquiring flesh lies in a suitable diet; all that is needed is to eat with due discrimination.

Given a proper diet, specific instructions as to rest and sleep are scarcely necessary, and you will attain the desired end in any case. For if you take no exercise, the lack of it will help you to put on flesh; and if you take exercise, you will still put on flesh, for you will eat more as a result; and when the appetite is suitably satisfied, the eater is not only refreshed but also acquires flesh where there is a need to acquire it.

If you sleep a great deal, sleep is fattening; if you sleep little, your digestion will be completed the more quickly, and you will eat more.

Thus it is only a question of indicating how those who wish to fill out their figures should always eat; and this task can present no difficulties, after the various principles we have already established.

To solve the problem, we must offer the stomach food which will occupy it without tiring it, and to the assimilative powers material which they can turn into fat.

Let us try to map out the alimentary day of a sylph, whether male or female, who wishes to take material form. *General Rule.* Eat plenty of new bread, baked the same day, taking care to leave the crust.

Before eight o'clock in the morning, and in bed if necessary, drink a bowl of soup thickened with bread or noodles, but not too copious, so that it may be digested rapidly; or, if preferred, a cup of good chocolate.

At eleven o'clock take a breakfast consisting of fresh eggs, scrambled or fried, patties, cutlets, and whatever else you may wish; the essential thing is that there shall be eggs. A cup of coffee will do no harm.

The dinner-hour will be fixed so that breakfast will have been completely digested before you sit down to table; for we are accustomed to say that whenever the ingestion of a meal infringes on the digestion of the previous meal, trouble results.

After breakfast, a little exercise; in the case of men, only if their occupation permits, for duty comes first; the ladies will go to the Bois de Boulogne, the Tuileries, or the drapers' shops, and call on their friends to talk about what they have seen. We consider it a matter of certainty that such talk is eminently medicamental, on account of the great contentment that accompanies it.

For dinner, soup, meat, and fish as desired; but also include rice dishes, macaroni, sugary pastries, sweet creams, charlottes, etc.

For dessert, Savoy biscuits, babas, and other preparations made of flour, eggs, and sugar.

The above diet, though apparently limited in scope, is in fact susceptible of great variety; it admits the whole animal kingdom; and great care must be taken to alter the nature, cooking, and seasoning of the various flour dishes used, and to make them as appetizing as possible, in order to prevent boredom, which would offer an insurmountable obstacle to all subsequent amelioration.

Beer should be drunk for preference; otherwise the wines of Bordeaux or the South of France.

Avoid all acids, except salad, which rejoices the heart. Take sugar with those fruits which can take sugar; make sure that your bath is not too cold; try now and then to go and breathe the pure country air; eat plenty of grapes when they are in season; and do not wear yourself out with too much dancing.

Go to bed about eleven o'clock on ordinary days, and not later than one o'clock in the morning on special occasions.

By following this régime strictly and courageously, you will soon have made up for Nature's shortcomings; health will gain as much as beauty; pleasure will result from one and the other, and grateful accents will echo pleasantly in the Professor's ear.

We fatten sheep, calves, oxen, poultry, carp, crayfish, and oysters; whence I deduce the following general maxim: Everything that eats can be fattened, provided the food is carefully and suitably selected.

24. On Fasting

116. Definition

Fasting is a voluntary abstinence from food, with a moral or religious end in view.

Although fasting is contrary to one of our natural inclinations, or rather one of our most habitual needs, it is nevertheless a custom of the greatest antiquity.

Its establishment is explained as follows by authorities on the subject.

In cases of private bereavement, they say, for example on the death of a father, mother, or beloved child, the whole household went into mourning; the dead person was wept over, washed, embalmed, and then given a funeral suitable to his rank. In such circumstances, there was little thought of eating; the mourners fasted without realizing what they were doing.

In the same way, in cases of public disaster, for example in time of extreme drought or excessive rainfall, cruel wars, or pestilence, in a word, of those scourges which force and industry are powerless to redress, the whole community gave way to tears, and attributed their misfortunes to the wrath of the gods; they humbled themselves before them, and offered up the mortifications of abstinence. The misfortunes came to an end; and convincing themselves that this must be due to their tears and fasting, they continued to resort to the same practices in similar circumstances.

Thus, men afflicted with either public or private calamities gave way to sadness, and neglected food; subsequently they came to look upon this voluntary abstinence as an act of religion.

They believed that by macerating the body when the soul was afflicted, they could stir the gods to pity; as the same idea occurred to every people, it gave rise to mourning, vows, prayers, sacrifices, mortifications, and abstinence.

Finally, Jesus Christ came down on earth, where he sanctified fasting, and every Christian sect has adopted it, with more or less mortification.

117. Fasting as it Used to Be

This practice of fasting, I am bound to remark, has fallen singularly into abeyance; and for the edification of the ungodly, or their conversion, I shall now relate how we went about it in the middle of the eighteenth century.

At ordinary times we breakfasted before nine o'clock on bread, cheese, fruit, and sometimes pâté or cold meat.

Between midday and one o'clock we dined on soup and *pot-au-feu* more or less reinforced according to fortune and circumstances.

About four o'clock the children, and those of their elders who made a point of adhering to the customs of old, took a light meal.

But there were also *suppatory* meals, which began at five o'clock, and lasted indefinitely; these meals were usually very gay, and agreed marvellously with the ladies, who even gave them among themselves to the exclusion of the men-folk. And I find it written in my secret Memoirs that they were the occasion of much scandal and backbiting.

About eight o'clock came supper, consisting of entrée, roast, side-dishes, salad, and dessert; we would then play a game of cards, and so to bed.

In Paris, of course, there were always other suppers of a more exalted order, which began after the play. These were attended, according to the circumstances, by pretty women, fashionable actresses, elegant courtesans, noblemen, financiers, rakes, and wits.

The latest story would be told, and the latest song sung; politics, literature, and the theatre were the subjects of conversation, and love was the order of the day.

Now let us see what happened on fast days.

In the first place, there would be no breakfast, so that everyone had more appetite than usual.

Then, when the time came, you dined as best you might; but fish and vegetables are soon digested, and before five o'clock you were dying of hunger; you pulled out your watch, fretting and fuming, as you worked out your salvation.

At eight o'clock came, not a good supper, but a collation, a word which comes to us from the cloister, because at the end of the day the monks used to gather together to read and discuss the Early Fathers, after which they were allowed a glass of wine.

At this collation neither butter, eggs, nor anything which had had life might be served. We were forced to be content with salad, preserves, and fruit; dishes, alas, of very small value, if you consider the appetites we had in those days; but we were patient for the love of heaven, and went to bed, to begin all over again next day and every day throughout Lent.

As for those who attended the little suppers I have already mentioned, I have been assured they fasted neither then nor at any other time.

The culinary masterpiece of those far-off days was a strictly apostolical collation which none the less had all the appearance of a good supper. Science had successfully solved this problem by means of the toleration granted to fish *au bleu*, vegetable broths, and pastry made with oil.

A strict observance of Lent made possible a pleasure which is unknown to us now, that of 'un-Lenting' at breakfast on Easter Day.

If we look into the matter closely, we find that the basic elements of our pleasures are difficulty, privation, and the desire for enjoyment. All these came together in the act of breaking abstinence, and I have seen two of my great-uncles, both serious, sober men, half swoon with joy when they saw the first slice cut from a ham, or a pâté disembowelled, on Easter day. Now, degenerate race that we are, we could never stand up to such powerful sensations!

118. Origin of the Relaxation of Fasting

I myself have witnessed the relaxation of fasting; it came about by imperceptible degrees.

Children below a certain age were not expected to fast; and expectant mothers or women who thought they were pregnant were exempt by virtue of their condition; they were allowed to eat meat, and were served suppers which sorely tempted the fasters.

Next people began to find that fasting made them irritable, and caused headaches and sleeplessness. Then it was blamed for all the minor ills which plague people in the springtime, such as vernal eruptions, dizziness, bleeding at the nose, and other symptoms of effervescence which accompany the renewal of Nature. And so one person stopped fasting because he thought he was ill, another because he had been ill, a third because he was afraid of falling ill; whence it came about that meatless diets and collations became rarer day by day.

Nor was this all; there came a series of winters severe enough to cause fears of vegetable famine; and the ecclesiastical powers themselves officially relaxed their laws, while employers complained of increased expenses due to meatless meals, some people said it was not God's will that health should be endangered, and men of little faith added that starvation was no way of gaining admittance to paradise.

The duty, however, continued to be recognized, and the priests were nearly always asked for dispensations, which they usually granted, though they insisted on alms-giving as a substitute for fasting.

Finally the Revolution came, filling all minds with cares, fears, and interests of another kind; there was neither time nor opportunity for applying for dispensations to the priests, some of whom were hunted down as enemies of the State, a fact which by no means prevented them from branding the others as schismatics.

To this last cause, which fortunately no longer exists, there was added another no less influential. Our meal-times have completely altered; we eat neither so often nor at the same times as our forebears, and fasting, if it were to be reintroduced, would require a new organization.

This is so true that although I frequent only sage, respectable, and even moderately pious people, I do not believe that in twenty-five years I have seen more than ten meatless meals and a single collation *outside my own house*. Many people might be highly embarrassed in such a position; but I know that St Paul foresaw it, and I take shelter beneath his protection.

Moreover it would be a great mistake to suppose that intemperance has gained by this new order of things.

The number of meals has diminished almost by half. Drunkenness has disappeared, only to be seen on certain days, in the lowest classes of society. Orgies are things of the past, and nowadays a drunken reveller would be treated as an object of contempt. More than a third of Paris is content, in the morning, with the lightest of meals; and if some indulge in the delights of a delicate and studied gourmandism, I scarcely see how they can be blamed for that, for we have seen elsewhere that everybody gains thereby, and nobody loses.

Let us not leave this subject without observing the new direction taken by popular taste.

Every day thousands of men spend at the theatre or in the café the evening which forty years ago they would have spent in the tavern.

No doubt economy gains nothing by this new state of affairs, but it is highly beneficial to the conduct of social life. Manners are polished and civilized at the theatre; in the café newspapers provide instruction; and we avoid the quarrels, diseases, and degradation which are the infallible consequences of frequenting taverns.

25. On Exhaustion

119. Introduction

By exhaustion we mean a state of weakness, languor, and prostration brought about by antecedent circumstances, and impeding the exercise of the vital functions. If we except the exhaustion caused by deprivation of food, we may count three distinct types:

Exhaustion caused by muscular fatigue, exhaustion caused by mental effort, and exhaustion caused by amorous excess.

A remedy common to the three types of exhaustion is the immediate cessation of the acts responsible for this condition, which, if not actually a disease, is at least very close to one.

120. Treatment

After this indispensable introduction, we find gastronomy at hand, ever ready and resourceful.

To the man worn out by the protracted exercise of his muscular strength, it offers good soup, generous wines, cooked meat, and sleep.

To the scholar who has allowed himself to be carried away by the charms of his subject, if offers exercise in the open air to refresh his brain, baths to loosen his aching fibres, poultry, green vegetables, and rest.

Lastly, we shall learn from the following observation what it can do for him who forgets that amorous ardour has its limits, and pleasure its dangers.

121. Cure Effected by the Professor

Hearing one day that one of my best friends (Monsieur Rubat) was unwell, I went to see him, and sure enough found him by the fire, in his dressing-gown, in an attitude of extreme debility.

His appearance alarmed me; his face was pale, his eyes were unnaturally bright, and his lip hung down, exposing the teeth in his lower jaw in a somewhat hideous manner.

I anxiously asked what was the cause of this sudden change; he hesitated; I pressed him, and at last, after a certain show of resistance: 'My dear fellow,' he said, blushing, 'you know about my wife's jealousy, and how much I have suffered from it in the past. Well, these last few days she has been eaten up with it, and it was through trying to prove to her that she has lost none of my affection, and that no portion of the conjugal tribute goes astray to her prejudice, that I reduced myself to this sorry state.' 'Have you forgotten, then,' I said, 'both that you are forty-five years old, and that jealousy is a sickness for which there is no remedy? Don't you know *furens quid femina possit?*'[1] And I made further remarks in the same ungallant strain, for what he had told me had made me very angry.

'And now let us see,' I went on: 'your pulse is faint and slow; what do you propose to do?' 'The doctor has just left,' he said; 'he thought I was suffering from a nervous fever, and prescribed a bleeding, for which purpose he is going to send me a surgeon immediately.'

'A surgeon!' I exclaimed. 'Have nothing to do with him, or you're a dead man! Chase him away like a murderer, and tell him I have taken charge of you, body and soul. By the way, does your doctor know the immediate cause of your trouble?' 'Alas, no; shame prevented me from making a clean breast of it.' 'Very well then, you must send for him at once. I am going to mix you a draught suitable to your condition; in the meantime, drink this.' And I gave him a strong dose of sugar-and-water, which he swallowed with blind trust and simple faith.

Then I left him and ran home to mix, compound, and prepare a magisterial tonic, which the reader will find among my *Miscellanea*[2] together with the various methods

1. '. . . what a furious woman can do?' [Ed.]   2. See Part Two, No . 10.

I adopted to save time; for in such cases a few hours' delay can give rise to irreparable accidents.

I soon returned, armed with my potion, and found him already looking better; the colour was coming back to his cheeks, and his eyes were more normal; but the frightening deformity of the pendulous lip still remained.

The doctor was not long in reappearing; I told him what I had done, and the patient made full confession. At first the physician's brow furrowed in a frown; but soon, looking at us both with a somewhat ironical air, he said to my friend: 'You can hardly be surprised if I failed to recognize a malady so inconsistent with your age and position; and it was really too modest of you to conceal the cause, which could only reflect honour on you. I must also scold you for exposing me to a mistake which might have proved fatal to you. For the rest, my colleague,' and here he made me a bow which I returned with interest, 'has put you on the right road. Take his broth, or whatever he calls it, and if the fever leaves you, as I think it will, breakfast tomorrow on a cup of chocolate, with the yolks of two fresh eggs beaten up in it.'

With these words he took his hat and stick and went off, leaving us strongly tempted to make merry at his expense.

I soon administered a stiff dose of my elixir of life to my patient, who drank it down greedily and asked for more; but I insisted on a two hours' adjournment and gave him the second dose before retiring for the night.

Next day he was free of the fever and almost himself again; he breakfasted according to instructions, drank some more of the potion, and was able to resume his ordinary occupations the following day, but the rebellious lip did not rise again till the third day.

Not long afterwards the affair became common knowledge, and all the ladies discussed it among themselves in a whisper.

Some of them admired my friend, almost all were sorry for him, and the gastronome Professor was praised to the skies.

26. On Death

Omnia mors poscit; lex est, non poena, perire.[1]

122. Introduction

The Creator has imposed on man six great basic necessities which are: birth, action, eating, sleeping, reproduction, and death.

Death is the absolute interruption of the sensual relations, and absolute annihilation of the vital forces, which abandon the body to the laws of decomposition.

These various necessities are all accompanied and softened by certain pleasurable sensations, and death itself is not without its charms when it is natural, that is to say, when the body has passed through the different phases of growth, maturity, old age, and decrepitude.

If I had not resolved to make this a very short chapter, I would call to my aid the doctors who have noted by what imperceptible degrees the living body turns into inert matter. I would quote kings, philosophers, and men of letters, who on the threshold of eternity, far from being a prey to sorrow, had cheerful thoughts, and clothed them in the grace of poetry. I would recall the words of the dying Fontenelle, who on being asked what he could feel, replied: 'Nothing but a certain difficulty in living.' But I prefer simply to declare my own conviction based not only on analogy, but also on several observations which I believe to have been well made, and of which the last is as follows:

I had a great-aunt who lay dying at the age of ninety-three. Although she had been confined to her bed for some time, she was still in possession of all her faculties, and her condition had only been perceived through her gradual loss of appetite and the weakening of her voice.

1. 'Death claims all; dying is not a punishment but a law.' [Ed.]

She had always shown me considerable affection, and I was at her bedside, ready to wait on her solicitously, which did not prevent me from observing her with that philosophic eye which I have always brought to bear on my surroundings.

'Are you there, nephew?' she said to me in a scarcely articulate voice. 'Yes, aunt; I am here at your service, and I think you would do well to drink a little good old wine.' 'Give me some, dear; liquid always goes downwards.' I quickly poured out half a glass of my best wine, and gently lifting her up, held it to her lips. She swallowed it, brightened up immediately, and turning on me her eyes, which had once been very beautiful, she said: 'Many thanks for this last service; if ever you reach my age, you will find that death becomes a need, just like sleep.'

These were her last words; and half an hour later she had fallen asleep for ever.

Doctor Richerand has described the final degradation of the human body and the last moments of the individual so truthfully and philosophically that my readers will be grateful to me for quoting the following passage from his work:

Here is the order in which the intellectual faculties fail and decompose. Reason, that attribute of which man claims to be the sole possessor, is the first to abandon him. First of all he loses the power of associating judgements, and soon afterwards that of comparing, collecting, combining, and linking up several ideas in order to pronounce on their relationship to one another. At this stage we say that the patient is losing his reason, that his mind is wandering, or that he is delirious. His delirium usually resolves around the ideas most familiar to the individual; his ruling passion is easily recognizable from what he says; thus the miser will speak openly of his hidden treasures, while another man will die assailed by religious terrors. Sweet memories of home, you crowd in on the dying exile with all your charm and all your poignancy!

After reason and judgement, the faculty of associating ideas is the next to be struck down by the forces of destruction. The same phenomenon occurs in the state known as *swooning*, as I know from my own experience. For one day, while talking with a friend, I suddenly experienced an insurmountable difficulty in joining together two ideas, on the resemblance between which I wished to base an opinion. The syncope, however, was incomplete; I still retained both memory and sensation; I distinctly heard the people round me say 'He has fainted', and I was aware of their efforts to rouse me from this condition, *which was not disagreeable*.

Memory is extinguished next. The dying man, who in his delirium could still recognize those who approached his bedside, now fails to recognize his closest friends and members of his own family. Finally he ceases to feel; but his senses fail in a definite order: taste and smell give no further sign of their existence; a mist veils his eyes, which assume a sinister expression; but his ear remains sensitive to sound. This is doubtless why the ancients, to make sure that life was extinct, used to shout into the ear of the deceased. When the dying man can no longer smell, taste, see, or hear, there remains the sensation of touch, and he stirs restlessly in his bed, stretching out his arms, and constantly changing his position; he makes movements, as we have already remarked, analogous to those of the foetus in its mother's womb. Death is about to strike, but it cannot frighten him, for he has no more ideas; and he finishes life as he began it, unconsciously.

[Richerand, *New Elements of Physiology,* 9th Ed., vol. ii, p. 600.]

27. Philosophical History of Cooking

123. Introduction

Cooking is the oldest of the arts; for Adam was born fasting, and the new-born child has scarcely made its entry into this world before it utters cries which can only be quieted at its mother's breast.

It is also of all arts the one which has done the most to advance the cause of civilization; it was the need to cook which taught man to use fire, and it was by using fire that man conquered Nature.

Taking an overall view of the subject, we can discern three kinds of *cooking*:

The first, which is concerned with the preparation of food, has retained its original name;

The second is applied to the analysis of food and the verification of its elements, and is usually called *chemistry*;

And the third, which may be called restorative cooking, is better known under the name of *pharmaceutics*.

If their ends are different, they are identical in their common use of fire, furnaces, and the same vessels.

Thus the same piece of beef which the cook turns into soup and *bouilli* is appropriated by the chemist to find out into how many different bodies it can be resolved, while the pharmacist causes it to emerge violently from our bodies, if it happens to give us indigestion.

124. Alimentary Progress

Man is an omnivorous animal; he possesses incisive teeth for dividing fruit, molar teeth for crushing grain, and canine teeth for tearing flesh; and it has been remarked that the closer man approaches to the primitive state, the stronger and more conspicuous are his canine teeth.

It is extremely probable that for a long time the species was frugivorous; it was confined to such a diet by necessity, for man is the clumsiest of the animals, and his means of attack are very limited as long as he is unarmed. But that instinct for improvement which is inseparable from his nature was not slow to develop; the very consciousness of his weakness led him to seek means of arming himself; he was impelled to the same end by the carnivorous instinct revealed in his canine teeth; and as soon as he was armed, he preyed on all the animals surrounding him, and made them his food.

This instinct of destruction still survives; children will almost invariably kill any small animals which are left in their care, and would eat them if they were hungry.

It is not to be wondered at that man decided to feed on flesh; his stomach is too small, and fruit contains too few animalizable elements to restore his strength in full; he could nourish himself better with vegetables, but such a diet calls for arts which have only come in the course of centuries.

The first weapons must have been the branches of trees, and these were followed by bows and arrows.

It is particularly noteworthy that wherever man has been found, in whatever climate or latitude, he has always been found armed with bows and arrows. Such uniformity is difficult to explain. It is not easy to see how the same sequence of ideas occurred to the minds of individuals faced by entirely different circumstances; we can only attribute it to some cause hidden in the mists of time.

Raw flesh has only one disadvantage, namely, its viscous nature, which causes it to stick to the teeth; apart from that, it is not unpleasant to the taste. Seasoned with a little salt, it is easily digested, and is obviously more nutritious than any sort of cooked meat.

'*Mein Gott*,' said a Croat captain, who dined with me in 1815, 'a man can eat well without all these trimmings. When we are in the field and feel hungry, we shoot down the first animal that comes our way, cut off a good hunk of flesh, salt it a little (for we always carry a supply of salt in our *sabre-tasche*[1]), and put it under the saddle, next to the horse's back; then we gallop for a while after which [moving his jaws like a man tearing meat apart with his teeth] *gnian, gnian, gnian*, we feed like princes.'

When the sportsmen of Dauphiné go shooting in the month of September, they likewise provide themselves with a supply of salt and pepper. If they kill a plump blackcap, they pluck it, season it, carry it for a while in their hats, and then eat it. They declare that this bird, treated like this, tastes even better than when it is roasted.

Moreover, if our remote ancestors ate all their meat raw, we have not entirely lost the habit ourselves. The most delicate palate will respond very well to Arles and Bologna sausages, smoked Hamburg beef, anchovies, freshly salted herrings, and other such things, which have never been subjected to fire, but which stimulate the appetite for all that.

125. Discovery of Fire

After man had been content for a long time to eat as the Croats eat, he discovered fire; this again was a chance discovery, for fire does not exist on earth spontaneously; the inhabitants of the Marianas Islands had no knowledge of it.

126. Grilling

Once fire had been discovered, the instinct for improvement led man to place his meat close to the flames, in order to dry it, and later to put it on the embers, in order to cook it.

Meat so treated was found to be much better; it acquires

1. The *sabre-tasche*, or sabre-pouch, is a sort of bag decorated with a coat of arms and suspended from the baldric in which light-cavalrymen wear their sabres; it plays an important part in the tales which soldiers tell among themselves.

greater consistency, becomes easier to chew, and develops, through the browning of the osmazome, an aroma which has not yet ceased to please.

However, it was eventually perceived that meat cooked on the embers of a fire cannot be kept clean; for it always brings away particles of ash or cinder which are difficult to remove. This disadvantage was overcome by piercing it with skewers, which were then placed over the glowing embers, with their ends resting on stones of a suitable height.

Such was the origin of grilling, that simple but savoury method of cooking; for all grilled meat is extremely tasty, through being partially smoked.

Matters were not much further advanced in the days of Homer; and I hope the reader will enjoy the following account of how Achilles entertained in his tent three of the most eminent of the Greeks, one of them a king.

I dedicate this account to the ladies, because Achilles was the most handsome of the Greeks, and because his pride did not prevent him from weeping when Briseis was taken from him; for them too I have chosen the elegant translation of Monsieur Dugas-Montbel, a gentle and complaisant author, and no mean gourmand for a Hellenist:

Majorem jam crateram, Moenetii fili, appone,
Meraciusque misce, poculum autem para unicuique;
Charissimi enim isti viri meo sub tecto.
Sic dixit: Patroclus dilecto obedivit socio;
Sed cacabum ingentem posuit ad ignis jubar;
Tergum in ipso posuit ovis et pinguis caprae
Apposuit et suis saginati scapulam abundantem pinguedine.
Huic tenebat carnes Automedon, secabatque nobilis Achilles,
Eas quidem minute secabat, et verubus affigebat.
Ignem Moenetiades accendebat magnum, deo similis vir;
Sed postquam ignis deflagravit, et flamma exstincta est,
Prunas sternens, verua desuper extendit.
Imspersit autem sale sacro, a lapidibus elevans.
At postquam assavit et in mensas culinarias fudit,
Patroclus quidem, panem accipiens, distribuit in mensas
Pulchris in canistri, sed carnnerm distribuit Achilles.
Ispe autem adversus sedit Ulyssi divino,

Ad parietem alterum. Diis autem sacrificare jussit
Patroclum suum socium. Is in ignem jecit libamenta.
Hi in cibos paratos appositos manus immiserunt;
Sed postquam potus et cibi desiderium exemerunt,
Innuit Ajax Phoenici: intellexit autem divinus Ulysses,
Implensque vino poculum, propinavit Achilli ...[1]

'At once Patroclus obeys the commands of his trusty companion. Meanwhile Achilles sets a vessel near the sparkling flames which contains the shoulders of a ewe and a fat goat, and the broad back of a succulent pig. Automedon holds the meat, while god-like Achilles carves; he cuts it into pieces, and pierces them with iron spikes.

'Patroclus, a man like the immortals, lights a great fire. As soon as the burnt wood gives out no more than a dying flame, he lays across the embers two long spears supported by two massive stones, and sprinkles the sacred salt.

'When the meat is ready, and the banquet ready, Patroclus distributes bread around the table in rich baskets; but Achilles himself chooses to serve the meat. Then he sits down facing Ulysses, at the other end of the table, and bids his companion sacrifice to the gods.

'Patroclus casts the first-fruits of the meal into the flames, and all of them set their hands to the dishes which have been prepared and served to them. When in the abundance of the feast they have chased away hunger and thirst, Achilles motions to Phoenix; Ulysses sees the sign, fills his great cup with wine, and addressing the hero says: 'Hail, Achilles ...'

Thus we see that a king, a king's son, and three Greek generals dined very well on bread, wine, and grilled meat.

We must assume that when Achilles and Patroclus themselves saw to the preparing of the feast, they were doing exceptional honour to their distinguished guests; for it was

1. I have not transcribed the original text, which few people would have understood; but I have thought fit to give the Latin version, because that language, which is more widely known, moulds itself perfectly on the Greek, and lends itself better than our own to the details and simplicity of this heroic meal.

customary to leave the cares of cookery to slaves and women, as Homer informs us in the *Odyssey* when he describes the meals of the suitors.

The entrails of animals, stuffed with blood and fat, were then regarded as a great delicacy; this dish was in fact a sort of black pudding.

At that time and doubtless long before, poetry and music were linked with the pleasures of the feast. Venerable bards sang of the marvels of nature, the loves of the gods, and the feats of warriors; they fulfilled a sort of priestly function, and it is probable that godlike Homer himself was born into this favoured order of men; he could never have reached such heights if his poetic studies had not begun in childhood.

Madame Dacier observed that nowhere in Homer is any mention made of boiled meat. The Hebrews were more advanced on account of their stay in Egypt. They had pots which could be placed on the fire, and it was in such a vessel that the soup was made which Jacob sold so dearly to his brother Esau.

It is extremely difficult to guess how man first succeeded in working metals; Tubal-Cain, it is said, was the first to acquire the art.

In the present state of our knowledge, we work on metals with other metals; we take hold of them with iron tongs, forge them with iron hammers, and cut them with steel files; but I have never yet met with anyone who could explain to me how the first tongs were made and the first hammer forged.

127. *Banquets of the Orientals and the Greeks*

Cookery made rapid progress once man was equipped with vessels, whether of bronze or pottery, capable of resisting fire. It became possible to season meat and to cook vegetables; broths, gravies, and jellies were evolved, all following naturally on one another.

The oldest books which have come down to us make

honourable mention of the feasts of Eastern kings. It is not hard to believe that monarchs who reigned over lands so fertile in all things, but especially in spices and perfumes, kept sumptuous tables. Details, however, are lacking; we only know that Cadmus, who brought writing to Greece, had been cook to the King of Sidon.

It was among those soft and pleasure-loving peoples of the East that the custom arose of eating reclining on couches arranged around the banqueting table.

This effeminate refinement was not received with equal readiness everywhere. Nations which set particular store by strength and courage, or which regarded frugality as a virtue, held out against it for many years; but Athens adopted it, and for a long time the practice remained general throughout the civilized world.

Cooking and its amenities were held in high regard by the Athenians, as was natural in a nation so elegant and eager for novelty; kings, rich citizens, poets, and scholars led the way, and philosophers themselves did not feel called upon to refuse pleasures derived from the breast of Nature.

From what we read in the ancient authors, we cannot doubt that their banquets were magnificent occasions.

Hunting, fishing, and trade provided them with most of the foods which we still hold in high esteem, and the demand was great enough to make the price of those foods excessively high.

All the arts contributed to the adornment of their tables, round which the guests reclined on couches covered with rich crimson rugs.

They made a point of enhancing the pleasures of good cheer by agreeable conversation; and table-talk became a science.

The songs, which usually began with the third course, now lost their old severity, and were no longer confined to the praise of gods, heroes, and historic feats. The joys of friendship, pleasure, and love were sung with a sweetness and harmony which our harsh, dry tongues can never hope to equal.

The wines of Greece, which we still find excellent, were examined and classified by connoisseurs, from the mildest to the headiest; and there were meals at which the whole gamut of wines was run, and at which, contrary to the custom of our times, the glasses grew larger in proportion to the increasing goodness of the wine.

The prettiest women embellished these voluptuous gatherings even further; dances, games, and every sort of diversion prolonged the delights of the evening. Pleasure was breathed in through every pore, and more than one Aristippus, arriving under Plato's banner, departed under that of Epicurus.

Scholars vied with one another to write about an art which procured such exquisite delights. Plato, Athenaeus, and others have preserved their names for us. But alas, their works have perished; and if there is one to be regretted above all the rest, it is the 'Gastronomia' of Achestrades, the friend of one of the sons of Pericles.

Such was the condition of cookery among the Greeks;[1] and such it remained until the day when a handful of men who had settled on the banks of the Tiber extended their dominion over the neighbouring states, and ended by overrunning the world.

128. Banquets of the Romans

So long as the Romans fought only to secure their independence, or to subjugate neighbours as poor as themselves, good cheer was unknown to them. Their very generals were ordinary ploughmen, and lived on vegetables, etc. Frugivorous historians never fail to praise those early times, when frugality was held in high regard. But when their conquests had extended into Africa, Sicily, and Greece,

---

1. 'Despite these happy efforts, Athens never reached the heights of the culinary art; the reason for this is that she indulged too much in sweet things, fruits and flowers; she never had the refined flour bread of Imperial Rome, nor the latter's Italian spices, cunning sauces and Rhenish white wines.' – De Cussy.

when they had feasted at the expense of their defeated foes in countries where civilization was more advanced than in their own, they began to bring back to Rome preparations which had appealed to them in foreign lands, and there is every reason to believe that these imports were well received.

The Romans had sent a deputation to Athens, to bring back the laws of Solon; later they went there for instruction in philosophy and letters. While polishing up their manners, they came to know the pleasures of the table; and there returned to Rome not only orators, philosophers, rhetoricians, and poets, but also cooks.

With time and the succession of triumphs which enriched Rome with the wealth of the entire world, the luxury of their tables reached an almost incredible point.

Nothing was left untasted, from the ostrich to the cicada, from the dormouse to the wild boar;[1] in their search for new methods of seasoning they tried anything which could stimulate the palate, and employed many substances the use of which is beyond our understanding, such as assafoetida, rue, etc.

1. *Glires Farsi : Glires isicio porcino, item pulpis ex omni glirium membro tritis, cum pipere, nucleis, lasere, liquamine, farcies glires, et sutos in tegula positos, mittes in furnum, an farsos in clibano coques.*
['Stuffed Dormice: Stuff the dormice with pork forcemeat and the minced flesh taken from all parts of the dormice, along with pepper, nut kernels, assafoetida, and fish sauce, stitch them up and put them in a clay dish in the oven, or bake them when stuffed in a pot oven.' – Ed.]
Dormice were considered a great delicacy; scales were sometimes placed on the table for weighing them. Martial has a well-known epigram on the subject of dormice (XIII, 59):
> *Tota mihi dormitur hiems, et pinguior illo*
> *Tempore sum quo me nil nisi somnus alit.*
['All my winter is spent in sleep, and I'm fatter at that season when I've only sleep to feed me.' – Ed.]
Lister, the gourmand physician of a gourmand queen (Queen Anne), dwelling on the advantage of using scales in cookery, observes that if twelve larks weigh less than twelve ounces, they are scarcely eatable; that if they weigh exactly twelve ounces, they are worth eating; but that if they weigh thirteen they are fat and delicious.

The known world was laid under contribution, and their armies and travellers brought truffles and guinea-fowl from Africa, rabbits from Spain, pheasants from Greece (where they had migrated from the banks of the Phasis), and peacocks from the farthest ends of Asia.

The wealthier Romans took great pride in their gardens, and grew not only such familiar fruits as pears, apples, figs, and grapes, but also new fruits introduced from various foreign parts: the apricot from Armenia, the peach from Persia, the quince of Sidon, the raspberry from the valleys of Mount Ida, and the cherry which Lucullus had brought back from the kingdom of Pontus. The fact that all these fruits were imported into Italy, in widely different circumstances, is proof that the impulse was general, and that everyone considered it his proud duty to contribute to the enjoyment of the sovereign people.

Among comestibles, fish was regarded as an object of luxury. Preferences were established in favour of certain kinds, and had particular reference to the latitude in which they had been caught. Fish from distant waters were shipped to Rome in jars full of honey; and when individual specimens exceeded the normal size, they were sold at very high prices, owing to the keen demand among consumers, some of whom were richer than kings.

Drinks were the object of no less eager and attentive study. Greek, Sicilian, and Italian wines were all highly prized by the Romans; and as their price depended on the district or the year of their growth, a kind of birth certificate was inscribed on every amphora:

O nata mecum consule Manlio.[1] (Horace).

Nor was this all. In obedience to that instinct for improvement which we have already mentioned, ways were sought of increasing the bouquet and the flavour of wines; floral essences, spices, and drugs of various kinds were infused into them, and the preparations which contemporary writers

---

1. 'O [wine-jar] born with me when Manlius was consul.' [Ed.]

have handed down to us under the name of *condita* must have burnt the mouth and had a profoundly irritating effect on the stomach.

Thus already, at that period, the Romans dreamed of alcohol, which was not discovered until more than fifteen centuries later.

But their amazing taste for luxury found its most fervent expression in the accessories of the table.

The finest material and most talented workmanship were used for all the equipment required for the banquet. The number of courses gradually increased up to and beyond twenty, and with each new course everything that had been used in the previous course was removed.

There were special slaves allotted to each convivial function, and those functions were carefully distinguished. The rarest perfumes scented the banqueting hall. Heralds proclaimed the merits of dishes worthy of special attention, announcing their claims to an ovation. In short, nothing was forgotten which might sharpen the appetite, sustain attention, or prolong enjoyment.

This luxury was not without its aberrations and oddities. Such were those feasts at which the birds and fishes served could be counted by the thousands, and those dishes which had no merit but their great cost, like the one composed of the brains of five hundred ostriches, and another which contained the tongues of five thousand talking birds.

In the light of these examples it seems to me easy to believe in the fabulous sums spent on his table by Lucullus, and the costliness of those banquets he held in the hall of Apollo, at which it was his rule to exhaust every known means of gratifying his guests' sensuality.

129. Resurrection of Lucullus

Those glorious days might dawn again before our own eyes; to renew the marvels of that time we lack nothing but a Lucullus. Let us suppose that a man of enormous wealth wishes to celebrate some great financial or political triumph, and to honour the occasion with a memorable feast for which no expense is to be spared.

Let us suppose that he summons all the arts to adorn the banqueting-hall, orders his cooks to devote all their resources to the fare, and instructs his *sommeliers* to treat the guests to the choicest contents of his cellars;

That he has two plays performed for them, at this solemn dinner, by the most accomplished actors;

That during the meal, music, vocal as well as instrumental is rendered by the most renowned artists;

That he has engaged the prettiest and most graceful dancers of the Opera to perform a ballet in the interval between dinner and coffee;

That the evening culminates in a ball which brings together two hundred women chosen for their beauty and four hundred men chosen for their elegance;

That the buffet provides an inexhaustible supply of hot drinks, cold drinks and iced drinks;

That about the middle of the night a cunningly composed collation is served to fill everyone with renewed vigour;

That the servants are both handsome and well dressed, and, as a last refinement, the Amphitryon takes it on himself to convey his guests both from and back to their homes in comfort.

If such a banquet were well prepared, well planned, well organized, and well conducted, everyone who knows Paris will agree with me that there would be enough in the next day's memoirs to make Lucullus's own steward turn in his grave.

In pointing out what would have to be done today to rival the feast of that splendid Roman, I have sufficiently enlightened the reader as to what accessories were considered indispensable at a banquet in those days; they included actors, singers, mimes, clowns, and everything which could serve to increase the enjoyment of guests who had been invited with the sole object of giving them pleasure.

What was done among the Athenians, next among the Romans, then among our ancestors in the Middle Ages, and finally among ourselves nowadays, has its source in the nature of man, who impatiently seeks the end of any journey he begins, and in a certain anxiety which torments him whenever the sum-total of life at his disposal is not fully occupied.

130. Lectisternium et Incubitatium

Like the Athenians, the Romans ate in a reclining position; but they came to adopt the habit in a rather round-about way.

They used couches at first for only the sacred feasts held in honour of the gods; then the chief magistrates and leading citizens adopted them, and before long the custom became general. It was retained until the beginning of the fourth century of the Christian era.

These couches, which had originally been just ordinary simple benches, with a covering of skins stuffed with straw, soon received their share of the luxury which invaded everything connected with banquets. They were made of the rarest woods, encrusted with ivory, gold, and sometimes precious stones; the cushions were exquisitely soft, and the rugs which covered them were decorated with magnificent embroidery.

The same couch usually held three persons, who lay on their left side, supporting themselves on their elbow.

Was this attitude, which the Romans called *lectisternium*, more comfortable or more convenient than that which we have adopted, or rather, to which we have returned? I think not.

From the physical point of view incubation requires a certain expenditure of energy in order to maintain equilibrium; and the arm muscles cannot support the weight of part of the body for long without a certain discomfort.

From the physiological point of view there is also something to say: ingestion proceeds in a less natural manner; the food goes down less smoothly and settles less evenly in the stomach.

Above all, the ingestion of liquids or the action of drinking was a far more difficult matter; extreme care must have been required to avoid spilling wine from the huge cups which glittered on the tables of the great; and it was doubtless during the reign of *lectisternium* that someone coined the proverb 'There's many a slip 'twixt cup and lip'.

Nor can it have been any easier to eat cleanly in a reclining position, especially if we consider that many of the guests wore long beards, and used their fingers, or at the very most a knife to convey food to their mouth; for the use of forks is a modern innovation; none were discovered in the ruins of Herculaneum, although a great many spoons were found there.

It is to be feared too that decency was occasionally outraged during meals at which the bounds of temperance were frequently exceeded on couches shared by both sexes, and when it was no rare thing to see some of the guests asleep together.

> *Nam pransus jaceo, et satur supinus*
> *Pertundo tunicamque palliumque.*[1]

In fact the first attack on the *lectisternium* was made on moral grounds.

As soon as the Christian religion, having survived the persecution which stained its cradle with blood, had obtained some influence, its ministers lifted up their voices against the excesses of intemperance. They cried out against the length of meals, at which every pleasure was indulged and every one of their precepts flouted. Having themselves chosen an austere way of life, they set gourmandism among the capital sins, bitterly denounced the promiscuity of the sexes, and above all else attacked the custom of eating on couches, a practice which they held to be the outcome of culpable softness and the chief cause of the abuses they deplored.

Their threatening voices were heard; couches ceased to adorn the banqueting hall; man returned to the old way of

1. 'I'm lying here after lunch, flat on my back and full of food, boring a hole through tunic and cloak.' [Ed.]

sitting at table; and, by a rare piece of good fortune, this change, prescribed on moral grounds, did not detract in the slightest from the pleasures of the table.

131. Poetry

During the period we are now concerned with convivial poetry underwent a new change, and acquired in the mouths of Horace, Tibullus, and other writers roughly contemporary with them, a soft and languorous character quite foreign to the muses of Greece:

> *Dulce ridentem Lalagem amabo,*
> *Dulce loquentem.*[1] (Horace).

> *Quaeris quot mihi basiationes*
> *Tuae, Lesbia, sint satis superque.*[2] (Catullus.)

> *Pande, puella, pande capillulos*
> *Flavos, lucentes ut aurum nitidum:*
> *Pande, pcella, collum candidum,*
> *Productum bene candidas humeris.*[3] (Gallus.)

132. Invasion of the Barbarians

The five or six centuries which we have just reviewed in the course of a few pages were great times for cookery, and for all who loved and cultivated the culinary art; but the arrival of the Northern races, or rather their irruption, changed everything completely, and those glorious days were followed by a long and terrible period of darkness.

On the appearance of the barbarians, the culinary art vanished, together with all the sciences of which it is the companion and consolation. Most of the cooks were mass-

1. 'I'll still love Lalage with her sweet chatter and her sweet smile.' [Ed.]

2. 'You ask me, Lesbia, how many of your kisses would be enough for me and more.' [Ed.]

3. 'Sweetheart, spread out your yellow hair, shining like gleaming gold; stretch out your white neck, sweetheart, which rises gracefully from your white shoulders.' [Ed.]

acred in their masters' palaces; others fled rather than cater for their country's oppressors; and the few who stayed to offer their services had the shame of seeing them refused. Those fierce mouths and scorched gullets were insensible to the gentle charms of delicate fare. Huge haunches of beef and venison, immeasurable quantities of the strongest liquors, were enough to please them; and as the usurpers never laid aside their arms, most of their meals degenerated into orgies, and the banqueting-hall was frequently the scene of bloodshed.

However, it is not in the nature of things for excess to be of long duration. The victors finally wearied of cruelty; they allied themselves with the vanquished, took on a tincture of civilization, and began to taste the delights of social life.

This change was reflected in their meals. A host now invited his friends, not so much to fill their bellies as to offer them a feast; they, in turn, perceived that an effort had been made to please them; a more decent joy animated them, and the duties of hospitality began to take on a quality of affection.

These improvements, which took place about the fifth century of our era, received a further impetus under Charlemagne; and we learn from his Capitularies that that great king took personal pains to ensure that his realm should minister to the luxury of his table.

Under Charlemagne and his successors, hospitality assumed a chivalrous and gallant aspect; the ladies embellished the court with their charms, and distributed rewards for valour; pages dressed in gold, and high-born maidens whose innocence did not always exclude the desire to please, bore pheasants with gilded claws and peacocks with outspread tails to the tables of princes.

It is interesting to observe that this was the third time that women, who had been segregated by the Greeks, the Romans, and the Franks, were summoned to grace the banqueting-hall. Only the Ottomans have remained deaf to their appeal; but terrible storms now threaten that unsociable race, and before thirty years have elapsed the thunderous voice of the cannon shall proclaim the emancipation of the odalisques.

The movement, once begun, has gone on, gathering strength with every generation, down to our own day.

Women, even of the highest rank, busied themselves in their own homes with the preparation of food, holding it to be part of the duties of hospitality, which continued to be observed in France until the end of the seventeenth century.

Under their pretty hands food sometimes underwent astonishing transformations; they served up eels with serpents' tongues, hares with cat's ears, and other such frivolities. They made great use of the spices which the Venetians were beginning to bring from the East, and of the perfumed essences of Arabia; thus fish was sometimes cooked in rose-water. The luxury of the table consisted above all else in an abundance of dishes; and matters went so far that our kings felt obliged to curb excess by means of sumptuary laws, which, however, met the same fate as those drawn up in similar circumstances by Greek and Roman legislators. They were laughed at, evaded, and forgotten, and only remained in the statute-books as historic monuments.

Good cheer, then, continued to be enjoyed as far as possible, especially in abbeys, convents, and monasteries; because the wealth accumulated by those establishments was less exposed to the hazards and dangers of the internal warfare which afflicted France for so long.

Since it is certain that the ladies of France have at all times taken a hand in what was done in their kitchens, to a greater or lesser degree, we may safely conclude that the indisputable pre-eminence which French cooking has always enjoyed in Europe is due to their intervention, and that it was chiefly acquired through a vast number of cunning, light, and delicious preparations which only women could ever have conceived.

I have said that good cheer was enjoyed as far as possible; but there were times when it was an impossibility. Sometimes even the suppers of kings were at the mercy of chance.

We know that in the civil wars they could not always be sure of a meal; and one evening Henri IV would have had a very poor supper, if he had not had the good sense to admit a burgher to his table, who was the fortunate possessor of the only turkey in the town where the king was due to pass the night.

Meanwhile, the art of cooking progressed by imperceptible degrees; the crusaders endowed it with the shallot, torn from the plains of Ascalon; parsley was imported from Italy; and long before the days of Louis IX, sausage-makers were turning pork to good account, thus laying the foundations of those fortunes of which we have memorable examples before our eyes.

Pastrycooks were equally successful, and the products of their industry had a place of honour at every banquet. When Charles IX ascended the throne, they already formed an important corporation; and that monarch granted them certain statutory privileges, including that of making sacramental wafers.

About the middle of the seventeenth century, the Dutch introduced coffee into Europe[1]. Soliman Aga, that powerful Turk so admired by our forefathers, gave them their first taste of it in 1660; in 1670 it was put on sale to the public by an American at Saint-Germain Fair; and the first café was opened in the Rue Saint-André-des-Arts, adorned with mirrors and marble tables, rather like the café of today.

Sugar began to make its appearance about the same time;[2] and Scarron, complaining of his sister's avarice, which led her to reduce the size of the holes in her sugar-

1. The Dutch were the first Europeans to export coffee-plants from Arabia; they took them to Batavia, and later brought them to Europe. Monsieur de Reissout, a lieutenant-general in the Artillery, sent for a specimen from Amsterdam, and presented it to the Jardin du Roi; this was the first ever seen in Paris. Monsieur de Jussieu has left a description of it; in 1673, it seems, it was an inch in diameter and stood five feet high. The fruit is very pretty and looks rather like a cherry.

2. Whatever Lucretius may have said, sugar was unknown to the ancients. It is a product of art; and without crystallization, the cane only yields an insipid and worthless liquid.

castor, shows us at least that in his day that utensil was already in general use.

It was in the seventeenth century too that brandy came to be more widely drunk. Distilling, the idea of which had been brought back by the returning crusaders, had until then remained a mystery practised by only a small number of adepts. About the beginning of the reign of Louis XIV stills became commoner, but it was only under Louis XV that brandy became really popular; and it is only a few years since alcohol was first extracted in a single operation, after countless unsuccessful experiments.

Finally, the same period witnessed the introduction of tobacco; so that sugar, coffee, brandy, and tobacco, those four substances of such importance to both trade and treasury, are scarcely two centuries old.

133. Age of Louis XIV and Louis XV

It was under these auspices that the age of Louis XIV began: and in his brilliant reign the art of banqueting made the same immense progress as all the other arts.

The memory still lingers of the fêtes of those days, which brought all Europe to France, and of those tournaments at which the lances and armour of chivalry shone their last in the sun, before giving place to the savage bayonet and the brutal cannon.

All those fêtes culminated in sumptuous banquets; for such is the nature of man, that he can never be completely happy so long as his taste remains ungratified; and this imperious need has even won control over grammar, to such a degree that to express perfection in anything, we say that it has been done with taste.

By a necessary consequence, those who arranged the preparation of these feasts became men of note; and not without reason, for they had to combine many different qualities, namely inventive genius, the power of organization, a sense of proportion, a talent for discovery, firmness to exact obedience, and unfailing punctuality.

It was on these great occasions that the *surtout* or centre-piece was first seen, a magnificent device which, combining sculpture with painting, offered a pleasing spectacle to the eye, and sometimes a setting suited to the circumstances or the hero of the fête.

The fête called for grandiose and even gigantic efforts on the part of the cook; but soon smaller assemblies and daintier meals became the fashion, calling for more intelligent planning and a more scrupulous attention to detail.

In the private dining-rooms of royal favourites, and at suppers given by courtiers and financiers to a chosen few, culinary artists won admiration for their talents, and strove, in a praiseworthy spirit of rivalry, to surpass one another's feats.

Towards the end of the reign of Louis XIV the names of the most famous cooks were almost always coupled with those of their patrons, who took pride in the association. These twin merits were united; and the most illustrious names appeared in the cookery-books, beside the preparations they had patronized, invented, or given to the world.

This sort of association no longer exists today; not that we are less fond of good food than our ancestors, far from it; but we are less interested in the name of the man who rules over the kitchens. Applause by inclination of the left ear is the only tribute we pay to the artist who has delighted our senses; and the restaurateur, who is the public's cook, is the only one to obtain that monetary praise which makes him the equal of millionaires. *Utile dulci.*

It was for Louis XIV that the prickly pear, which he called *the good pear,* was imported from the Middle East; and it is to his old age that we owe the invention of liqueurs.

The monarch sometimes suffered from extreme debility, and that lack of vitality which often afflicts a man after the age of sixty; brandy was accordingly mixed with sugar and essences, to make potions for him, which after the fashion of the day were called *cordials.* Such was the origin of the liquorist's art.

It is interesting to note that at about the same time the art of cooking flourished at the English court. Queen Anne was a real gourmand; she did not scorn to converse with her cook, and English cookery-books contain many recipes bearing the designation 'after Queen Anne's fashion'.

While Madame de Maintenon was in a position of power the culinary art remained at a standstill in France; but it resumed its upward progress under the Regency.

The Duc d'Orléans, a witty prince and one worthy to have friends, invited them to meals as choice as they were well devised. I am able to state on unimpeachable authority that those meals were particularly remarkable for delicate sauces, fish *à la matelote* as appetizing as if it had just come out of the water, and turkeys gloriously truffled.

Truffled turkeys, whose fame and price go soaring ever higher! Kind stars, whose appearance makes gourmands of every category scintillate, radiate, and tripudiate!

The reign of Louis XV proved no less favourable to the culinary art. Eighteen years of peace more than sufficed to heal all the wounds of sixty years of war; the wealth created by industry and disseminated by trade, or acquired by tax farmers, put an end to inequality of fortune, and the spirit of conviviality spread through all classes of society.

Beginning from this period[1] there began to be generally

1. According to information I have collected from the inhabitants of several regions, a dinner for ten persons was composed, about 1740, as follows:

First course	Bouilli
	An entrée of veal cooked in its own juice
	An *hors-d'œuvre*
Second course	A turkey
	A dish of vegetables
	Salad
	A *crème* (sometimes)
Dessert	Cheese
	Fruit
	A pot of preserves

The plates were changed only three times, namely after the soup, for the second course, and for dessert.

Coffee was very rarely served but it was quite common to serve a cherry brandy or a carnation liqueur, which at that time was a novelty.

observed in all meals more order, cleanliness, and elegance; and various refinements were introduced which have been of greater importance year by year, until they now threaten to exceed all bounds and to become utterly ridiculous.

In this reign too, kept women and the *petites maisons* called for efforts on the part of cooks which were of considerable benefit to their art.

Great facilities are available to anyone catering for a large party and healthy appetites; with meat, game, venison, and a few large fishes, he can easily contrive a meal for sixty persons.

But to gratify mouths which never open except in a simper, to tempt vapourish women, to stir *papier mâché* stomachs, and to rouse spindly creatures whose appetites are only ephemeral whims, requires more genius, penetration, and sheer hard work than the solution of one of the most difficult problems in the geometry of the infinite.

134. Louis XVI

Having now arrived at the reign of Louis XVI and the period of the Revolution, we do not intend to provide a detailed account of the changes we ourselves have witnessed; we shall content ourselves with a broad survey of the various improvements which have taken place since 1774 in the art of banqueting.

Those improvements have been directed either at the art itself or at the customs and social institutions connected with it; and although these two orders of things continually interact, we have thought fit, for the sake of clarity, to consider them separately.

135. Improvements in the Art

The ranks of every profession concerned with the sale or preparation of food, such as cooks, caterers, pastrycooks, confectioners, provision-merchants, and the like, have multiplied in ever-increasing proportions; and proof that this increase has only come about in response to a real need may be seen in the fact that their number has not had a harmful effect on their prosperity.

Physics and chemistry have been called in to help the culinary art; the most distinguished scientists have not thought it beneath them to give their attention to our basic needs, whether the labourer's ordinary *pot-au-feu* or those transparent extracts which are never served except in vessels of crystal or gold.

New professions have arisen; that, for example, of the *petit-four* pastrycook, who occupies a place between the pastrycook proper and the confectioner. His domain comprises preparations made from butter, sugar, eggs, and flour, such as biscuits, macaroons, fancy cakes, meringues, and similar delicacies.

The art of preserving food has also become a profession in itself, whose aim is to offer us at all times of the year things peculiar to one particular season.

Immense progress has been made in horticulture; tropical fruits grow in hot-houses beneath our very eyes; various types of vegetables have been cultivated or imported, among them the cantaloup melon which bears none but sound fruit, thus daily giving the lie to the proverb.[1]

Wines have been imported from all over the world, and arranged with our own in a regular order; Madeira to open up the way, French wines to accompany the main courses, and African and Spanish wines to crown the meal.

French cookery has annexed dishes of foreign extraction, such as curry and the beefsteak; relishes, such as caviare and soy; drinks, such as punch, negus, and others.

Coffee has come into general use as a food in the morning, and after dinner as an exhilarating and tonic drink. A wide variety of vessels, utensils, and other accessories has been invented, so that foreigners coming to Paris find many ob-

---

1. 'To find a good melon you must try fifty.' It seems that melons such as we grow now were unknown to the Romans: what they called *melo* and *fispo* were just cucumbers which they ate with very sharp sauces. (Apicius, *De Re Coquinaria*.)

jects on the table, the names of which they do not know and the purpose of which they often dare not ask.

From all these facts we may draw the general conclusion that at the time of writing everything that precedes, accompanies, or follows a meal is done with an orderly method which indicates a desire to please such as should warm the heart of every guest.

136. Latest Improvements

The word *gastronomy* has been revived from the Greek; it sounds sweetly in French ears, and although imperfectly understood, simply to pronounce it is enough to bring a joyful smile to every face.

We have begun to distinguish gourmandism from greed and gluttony; it has come to be regarded as an admissible inclination, a social quality welcome to the host, profitable to the guest, and beneficial to the art: and gourmands are now classed with all other enthusiasts who share a common predilection.

The spirit of conviviality has spread through all classes of society; invitations are issued more frequently; and every host aims at offering his guests such delicacies as he himself has encountered as a guest in more exalted spheres.

As a result of the pleasure we have come to take in one another's company, we have adopted a more convenient distribution of our time, devoting the hours between dawn and dusk to business and reserving the remainder for the pleasures which accompany and follow the feast.

The breakfast party has become an institution, a meal with a character all its own on account of the dishes composing it, the gaiety of the conversation, and the casual dress which is permitted.

Another novelty is the tea-party, an extraordinary meal in that, being offered to persons who have already dined well, it supposes neither appetite nor thirst, and has no object but distraction, no basis but delicate enjoyment.

Political banquets have likewise come into fashion during

the last thirty years, being given whenever it has been necessary to bring influence to bear on a large number of wills; as meals, they call for lavish fare to which nobody pays the slightest attention, and they are only enjoyable in retrospect.

Finally, the restaurant has made its appearance; a completely new and inadequately recognized institution, the effect of which is that any man with three or four pistoles in his purse can immediately, infallibly, and simply for the asking, procure all the pleasures of which taste is susceptible.

28. On Restaurateurs

137. Introduction

A restaurateur is a person whose trade consists in offering to the public an ever-ready feast, the dishes of which are served in separate portions, at fixed prices, at the request of each consumer.

The establishment is called a *restaurant*, and the person in charge of it the *restaurateur*. The list of dishes, bearing the name and price of each, is called the *carte*, or bill of fare, while the record of the dishes served to the customer, together with the relevant prices, is called the *carte à payer*, or bill.

Few among the crowds which patronize our restaurants every day pause to think that the man who founded the first restaurant must have been a genius endowed with profound insight into human nature.

We shall therefore aid the process of reflection and follow the thread of ideas which gave rise to this most popular and convenient institution.

138. Origin

About 1770, after the glorious days of Louis XIV, the intrigues of the Regency, and the long and peaceful ministry of Cardinal Fleury, the visitor to Paris still found few resources in the way of good cheer.

He was forced to have recourse to the fare provided by his innkeeper, which was generally bad. There were one or two hotels boasting a *table d'hôte*, but with few exceptions they offered only the barest necessities, and moreover served their meals at a fixed hour.

The visitor, it is true, could fall back on caterers; but they only supplied complete meals, and anyone who wished to entertain a few friends was obliged to order his requirements in advance; so that the stranger who had not the good fortune to be invited to dine at some rich house would leave our capital in total ignorance of the resources and delights of French cookery.

An order of things harmful to such everyday interests could not last; and already there were a few thinking men who dreamed of a change for the better.

At last a man of judgement appeared who decided that an active cause could not remain without effect; that with the same need recurring every day about the same times, consumers would flock to a place where they could be certain of that need being pleasantly satisfied; that if a wing of chicken were detached in favour of the first comer, a second would be sure to arrive who would be content with the leg; that the removal of a first slice in the obscurity of the kitchen would not put the remainder of the joint to shame; that nobody would mind a slight increase in price when they had received good, prompt, clean service; that if each guest were able to quibble over the price and quality of the dishes he ordered, there would be no end to the inevitable difficulties of the undertaking, but that a variety of dishes, combined with fixed prices, would have the advantage of suiting all purses.

This man thought of many other things, as may easily be imagined. He was the first restaurateur, and created a profession which is bound to make the fortune of anyone who exercises it with good faith, order, and ability.

139. Advantages of the Restaurant

The advent of the restaurant, which was adopted first by France, has proved a boon to all citizens, and of great importance to the culinary art.

1. By this means, a man may dine at whatever hour suits him, according to the circumstances in which he is placed by his business or pleasure;

2. He can be sure of not going beyond the sum which he

thinks fit to spend on his meal, for he knows the price of every dish beforehand;

3. Having once come to a reckoning with his purse, the consumer may indulge at will in a light, heavy, or exotic meal, wash it down with the best French or foreign wines, flavour it with coffee, and perfume it with the liqueurs of both worlds, and all with no limit but the vigour of his appetite or the capacity of his stomach. The restaurant is the gourmand's paradise;

4. It is also a boon for the traveller, the foreigner, the man whose family is temporarily staying in the country, and for all, in a word, who have no cooking facilities at home, or are temporarily deprived of them.

Up to the date we mentioned above (1770), the rich and powerful had almost a monopoly of two great advantages: they alone travelled rapidly, and they alone constantly enjoyed good cheer.

With the advent of the new coaches which cover fifty leagues in twenty-four hours, the first of these privileges has disappeared; the advent of the restaurateur has destroyed the second; thanks to him, good cheer has become generally available.

Anyone with fifteen or twenty pistoles at his disposal, who sits down at the table of a first-class restaurateur, eats as well and even better than if he were at the table of a prince; for the feast which is offered him is just as splendid, and moreover, having every conceivable dish at his command, he is undisturbed by any personal consideration.

140. A Restaurant Examined

The interior of a restaurant, examined in some detail, offers to the keen eye of the philosopher a spectacle well worth his interest, on account of the variety of situations contained within it.

The far end of the room is occupied by a host of solitary diners, who order loudly, wait impatiently, eat rapidly, pay, and depart.

At another table is a family from the country, content with a frugal meal, yet relishing one or two unfamiliar dishes, and obviously enjoying the novelty of their surroundings.

Nearby sit a husband and wife, Parisians, from the evidence of the hat and shawl hanging above their heads; it is clearly a long time since they had anything to say to each other; they are going to the theatre, and it is a safe bet that one of them will fall asleep during the performance.

Farther on are two lovers, judging by the attentions of one, the coquetry of the other, and the gourmandism of both. Pleasure shines in their eyes; and, from the choice that governs the composition of their meal, the present serves both to illuminate the past and foreshadow the future.

In the centre of the room is a table surrounded by regular patrons, who as a rule obtain special terms, and dine at a fixed price. They know the names of all the waiters, who let them into the secret of what is freshest and newest; they are like the stock-in-trade of a shop, like a centre of attraction, or to be more precise, like the decoys used in Brittany to attract wild duck.

There are also a number of those individuals whom everyone knows by sight, and no one by name. These people are as much at ease as if they were at home, and quite often try to strike up a conversation with their neighbours. They belong to a type only met with in Paris, which has neither property, capital, nor employment, but spends freely for all that.

Finally, there are one or two foreigners, usually Englishmen; these last stuff themselves with double portions, order all the most expensive dishes, drink the headiest wines, and do not always leave without assistance.

The accuracy of our description may be verified any day of the week; and if it succeeds in rousing curiosity, perhaps it may also serve as a moral warning.

141. Disadvantages

There can be no doubt that the availability and attraction of the restaurateur's wares may lead many people to indulge themselves beyond the limit of their faculties, and that this may cause indigestion, in the case of delicate stomachs, and some untimely sacrifices to the basest of Venuses.

But what is far more dangerous in our opinion to the social order is the fact that solitary reflection breeds egoism, by accustoming the individual to consider no one but himself, to hold aloof from his surroundings, and to show no consideration for others; and from their behaviour before, during, and after meals, it is an easy matter, in ordinary society, to single out from a party of guests those who normally eat in restaurants.[1]

142. Rivalry

We have said that the advent of the restaurateur proved of great importance to the culinary art.

In fact, as soon as experience showed that a well-made *ragoût* was enough to make its inventor's fortune, self-interest, that most powerful of incentives, kindled every imagination and set every cook to work.

Analysis has revealed edible parts in substances formerly considered worthless; new foodstuffs have been discovered, the old ones improved, and both combined in a thousand variations. Foreign inventions have been imported, and the whole world laid under contribution, until a single meal may constitute a complete course of alimentary geography.

143. Fixed-price Restaurants

While the culinary art thus rose to higher flights, in point of price as of discovery (for novelty must always be paid for), the same motive, namely the hope of gain, impelled it in the opposite direction, at least in the matter of expense.

---

1. Among other things, when a dish of ready-cut food is being handed round, they help themselves and put it down in front of them, without passing it to the neighbour whose needs they are unaccustomed to considering.

Certain restaurateurs made it their aim to combine good cheer with economy, and by catering for modest incomes, which necessarily predominate, to make sure of attracting large numbers.

They sought out, among inexpensive substances, those which by skilful preparation could be made reasonably appetizing.

They found inexhaustible resources in the form of meat, which in Paris is always good, and salt-water fish, of which there is never a shortage; and by way of complement, there were fruit and vegetables, made cheaper by the latest methods of cultivation. They calculated what was strictly necessary to fill a stomach of ordinary capacity, and to quench any but an abnormal thirst.

They observed that there are many foods which owe their excessive price only to novelty or the time of year, but which can be supplied a little later, when this obstacle has ceased to exist; and in the end they reached a point when, at a profit of twenty-five to thirty per cent, they were able to offer their customers, for two francs or even less, an ample dinner, and one which any gentleman can be content with, since it would cost at least a thousand francs a month to maintain a table so well and variously furnished in a private house.

From this point of view, the restaurateur may be said to have rendered a signal service to that important part of the population of any great city which consists of foreigners, military men, and clerks; he was led by his own self-interest to the solution of a problem apparently contrary to it, namely, how to make good cheer available at a moderate price, and even cheaply.

The restaurateurs who have followed this course have been just as richly rewarded as their colleagues at the opposite end of the scale; they have met with fewer reverses, and their fortune, though slower to materialize, is far surer, for if they make a smaller profit, they make it every day, and it is a mathematical truism that when an equal number of units are brought together at a given point, they produce an equal total, whether they are brought together by tens, or one by one.

Connoisseurs still recall the names of several artists who have shone in Paris since the invention of the restaurant: names such as Beauvilliers, Méot, Robert, Rose, Legacque, the brothers Véry, Henneveu, and Baleine.

Some of these establishments owed their prosperity to special causes: for example, the Veau Qui Tette to sheep's trotters; the — to grilled tripe; the Frères Provençaux to cod cooked with garlic; Véry to truffled entrées, Robert to dinners ordered in advance; Baleine to the care he took to procure excellent fish; and Henneveu to the mysterious private rooms on his fourth floor. But of all these heroes of gastronomy, none has more right to a biographical notice than Beauvilliers, whose death was announced in the newspapers of 1820.

144. Beauvilliers

Beauvilliers, who set up in business in 1782, was for more than fifteen years the most famous restaurateur in Paris.

He was the first to combine an elegant dining-room, smart waiters, and a choice cellar with superior cooking; and when several of the restaurateurs we have mentioned above tried to equal him, he never lost ground to them, because he had only a few steps to take to keep level with the progress of the art.

During the two successive occupations of Paris, in 1814 and 1815, vehicles of all nations were constantly at his door; he knew all the heads of foreign contingents, and learned to speak all their languages as well as was necessary for his business.

Towards the end of his life, Beauvilliers published a work in two octavo volumes, entitled *The Art of Cookery*. This work, the fruit of long experience, bears the seal of enlightened practice, and still commands the same respect it was accorded on its first appearance. Never before had the culinary art been expounded with such method and accuracy. This book, which has run into several editions, considerably simplified the task of writing the various works which have succeeded, but never surpassed it.

Beauvilliers was the possessor of a prodigious memory; he could recognize and greet, after an interval of twenty years, persons who had only eaten once or twice in his establishment. In certain cases he also had a method of procedure peculiar to himself. When he was told that a party of wealthy people had sat down at one of his tables, he would approach them with an obliging air, kiss the ladies' hands, and appear to honour his guests with special attention.

He would point out here a dish to be avoided and there one to be ordered at once, before it was too late; a third which nobody dreamed of ordering, he would order himself, at the same time sending for wine from a cellar to which he alone had the key; in a word, he assumed so gracious and engaging a tone, that all these additional items seemed so many favours on his part. But this amphitryonic role lasted only a moment; having played it, he withdrew from the scene; and before long the swollen bill, and the bitterness of Rabelais's quarter of an hour, amply demonstrated the difference between a host and a restaurateur.

Beauvilliers made his fortune, unmade it, and made it again several times over; we do not know in what circumstances death overtook him; but his tastes were so extravagant that we do not think his heirs can have inherited a great fortune.

145. *The Gastronome in the Restaurant*

It will be found, on examining the bill of fare at various leading restaurants, notably those of the Véry brothers and the Frères Provençaux, that anyone who patronizes such an establishment has a choice, for the elements of his dinner, of at least

12 soups,
24 *hors-d'œuvre,*

15 or 20 beef entrées,
20 mutton entrées,
30 chicken or game entrées,
16 or 20 veal dishes,
12 pastry dishes,
24 fish dishes,
15 roasts,
50 side dishes,
50 dessert dishes.

In addition, the fortunate gastronome can wash his meal down with at least thirty kinds of wine, from Burgundy to Cape wine and Tokay, and with twenty to thirty kinds of liqueur, not to mention coffee and mixed drinks, such as punch, negus, syllabub, and the like.

Of these various component parts of a connoisseur's dinner, the principal parts are of French origin, such as the meat, fowl, and fruit; some are imitated from the English, such as beef-steak, Welsh rarebit, punch, etc., some come from Germany, such as the sauerkraut, Hamburg smoked beef, Black Forest fillets; some from Spain, such as the *olla podrida, garbanços,* Malaga raisins, Xerica pepper-cured ham, and dessert wines; some from Italy, such as the macaroni, Parmesan cheese, Bologna sausages, polenta, ices, and liqueurs; some from Russia, such as the dried meat, smoked eels, and caviare; some from Holland, such as the salt cod, cheeses, pickled herring, curaçao, and anisette; some from Asia, such as the Indian rice, sago, curry, soy, Schiraz wine, and coffee; some from Africa, such as the Cape wines; and lastly, some from America, such as the potatoes, pineapples, chocolate, vanilla, sugar, etc.; all of which provides sufficient proof of the statement we have made elsewhere: that a meal such as may be had in Paris is a cosmopolitan whole, in which every part of the world is represented by its products.

29. A Model Gourmand

146. The Story of Monsieur de Borose

Monsieur de Borose was born about 1780. His father was secretary to the king. He lost his parents early in life, and found himself the possessor of a private income of forty thousand livres. Such a sum was a fortune in those days; now, it is only just enough to keep the wolf from the door.

A paternal uncle saw to his education. He learned Latin, not without feeling some surprise that when everything could be expressed in French, so much trouble should be taken over learning to say the same things in other words. Nevertheless, he made progress, and when he came to Horace, was completely converted, finding so much pleasure in the consideration of ideas so elegantly clad, that he went to great pains to familiarize himself with the language spoken by that witty poet.

He also learned music, and after several experiments, decided in favour of the piano. He shunned the more complicated difficulties of that musical implement,[1] and, reducing it to its proper function, contented himself with becoming sufficiently proficient to be able to accompany song.

But in this respect he was considered superior even to the professors of the art, because he never sought to draw attention to himself; he made neither eyes nor arms,[2] but con-

1. The piano was made to assist musical composition and accompany song. Played alone it has neither warmth nor expression. The Spaniards have a word, *bordonear*, to express the action of playing stringed instruments.

2. Musical slang: *to make eyes* is to gaze heavenwards, as if about to swoon; *to make arms* is to raise the elbows and shoulders as though overcome by emotion; *to make 'brioches'* is to miss an intonation or play a wrong note.

scientiously performed the duty of every accompanist, of supporting and making the most of the singer.

Protected by his youth, he lived unscathed through the worst days of the Revolution; called to the colours when his turn came, he hired a substitute who bravely went to war and died on the battlefield in his place; whereupon, armed with his deputy's death certificate, he found himself well placed to rejoice at our triumphs or weep over our reverses.

Monsieur de Borose was of medium height, but admirably proportioned. As for his face, it was cast in a sensual mould, and we shall give some idea of it if we say that if Gavaudon of the Variétés, Michot of the Théâtre-Français, and the vaudevillist Désaugiers had been brought together in the same room with him, all four would have seemed members of the same family. On the whole, it was generally agreed that he was a handsome fellow, and he sometimes had reason to believe it.

Choosing a profession he found no easy matter; he tried several, but discovered some objection to them all, and finally settled down to a life of busy leisure; that is to say, he joined several literary circles, sat on the charity board of his district, subscribed to various philanthropical institutions, and what with these and his estate, which he managed wonderfully well, he had, like any other man, his affairs and correspondence.

On reaching the age of twenty-eight, he thought it time he married, refused to meet his future wife except at table, and, at the third interview, felt sufficiently convinced that she was at once pretty, good-natured, and intelligent.

Borose's conjugal bliss, however, was not of long duration; he had been married scarcely eighteen months when his wife died in childbed, bequeathing him everlasting grief at her untimely departure, and, by way of consolation, a daughter whom he called Herminie, and of whom we shall say more later.

Monsieur de Borose found no lack of pleasure in his various occupations. However, he discovered in time that even in the choicest company one meets pretentiousness, patronage, and even a little jealousy. All these defects he put down to humanity, which is nowhere perfect, and performed his duties no less assiduously; but obeying, albeit unconsciously, the decree impressed on his features by fate, he gradually came to depend more and more on the pleasures of taste.

Monsieur de Borose used to say that gastronomy was nothing but reflective appreciation applied to the art of amelioration.

He said with Epicurus[1]:

Was man made to spurn the gifts of nature? Does he come on earth only to pick bitter fruit? For whom are the flowers which the gods cause to grow beneath the feet of mortals? . . . We only do the will of Providence, if we abandon ourselves to the various penchants it suggests to us; our duties are laid down by its laws, our desires by its inspiration.

He said with the Sebusian sage that good things are for good people; otherwise we should be reduced to the absurd belief that God created them for sinners.

Borose's first task was to see his cook, to whom he sought to reveal the true significance of his functions.

He told him that the skilful cook, who could well be a man of science in theory, was always one in practice; that the nature of his functions set him between the chemist and the physician; he even went so far as to say that the cook, being charged with the maintenance of the animal machine, was superior to the pharmacist, whose usefulness is only occasional.

And he added, in the words of a learned and witty doctor, that a cook must have mastered the art of modifying food by the action of fire, an art unknown to the ancients. This is an art which nowadays calls for profound study, for a man must have pondered for a long time over the products of our globe to make skilful use of seasonings, to disguise the bitterness of certain dishes, to make others more savoury, and to select the best ingredients. The European cook outshines all others in the art of contriving these marvellous mixtures.[2]

His words did not fall on deaf ears; and henceforth the

1. Albert, *Physiologie des passions*, vol. i, p. 241.
2. *Ibid*, vol. i, p. 196.

chef,[1] duly filled with a sense of his importance, always lived up to the dignity of his calling.

Time, reflection and experience soon taught Monsieur de Borose that, the number of dishes in a meal being more or less determined by custom, a good dinner is not much dearer than a bad one; that it does not cost five hundred francs more a year to drink only very good wines; and that everything depends on the will of the master, the order he establishes in his household, and the energy he instils into all those whose services he hires.

Built on these fundamental concepts, Borose's dinners rose to a classic and solemn eminence; the fame of their excellence was spread abroad; it became a matter of pride to have been invited to partake of them; and there were some who boasted of their charms without ever having tasted them.

Monsieur de Borose never invited any of those self-styled gastronomes who are really mere gluttons, whose bellies are abysses, and who eat up all of everything everywhere. He found among his best friends no lack of delightful guests who, while they savoured each dish with truly philosophical attention and gave this study all the time it demands, never forgot that a moment comes when reason says to appetite: *Non procedes amplius* (Thou shalt go no further).

It often happened that shopkeepers came to him with delicacies of supreme distinction, and gladly sold them to him at a reduced price because they knew very well that these delicacies would be consumed calmly and with due reflection, that they would be talked about in society, and that the reputation of their shops would grow as a result.

The number of guests at Monsieur de Borose's dinners rarely exceeded nine, and the dishes were never very numerous; but the master's insistence, and his exquisite taste, had succeeded in making those dishes perfect. His table was

---

1. In a well-ordered household, the cook is called the chef. He has under him the entrée assistant, the pastrycook, the roaster, and the scullions (the pantry is a separate institution). The scullions are the cabin-boys of the kitchen; like them, they are frequently beaten, and like them, they sometimes work their way upwards.

always furnished with the season's choicest products, whether in point of rarity or precocity; and the meal was served with a care which left nothing to be desired.

The conversation during the meal was always general, always gay, and not infrequently instructive; this last quality was due to a very special precaution taken by Borose.

Every week a distinguished but impecunious man of learning, whom he lodged at his own expense, descended from his seventh floor and laid before him a list of subjects suitable for discussion at table. These the host was careful to put forward as soon as the topics of the day showed signs of exhaustion; and this device not only revived the conversation but also cut short those political discussions which obstruct both ingestion and digestion.

Twice a week he invited ladies, being careful so to arrange matters in such a way that each found among the guests a cavalier to wait exclusively on her: a precaution which gave enormous pleasure, for the strictest prude feels humiliated when she is unnoticed.

On those days, and those alone, a modest game of écarté was permitted; on others, none were allowed but piquet and whist, both grave and thoughtful games, and hallmarks of a careful upbringing. But more often the evening was spent in pleasant conversation, interspersed with a few songs which Borose accompanied with the skill we have already mentioned, earning applause to which he was by no means insensible.

On the first Monday of each month, Borose's curé dined with his parishioner, sure of being received with the greatest consideration. The conversation that day was of a more serious character, but not such as to exclude a few innocent pleasantries. The good priest found it impossible to resist the charm of these dinners, and sometimes caught himself wishing that every month contained four first Mondays.

On the same day young Herminie would emerge from Madame Migneron's establishment,[1] where she was a

1. Madame Migneron Remy directs, at No. 4 rue de Valois, Faubourg de Roule, an educational establishment under the patronage of

boarder; and more often than not that lady would accompany her pupil. With each visit Herminie revealed a new grace; she adored her father, and when he gave her his blessing, and kissed her bowed head, no two beings in the world were happier than they.

Borose was always careful to see that the money he spent on his table should serve the best moral purpose.

He gave his custom only to such tradesmen as were conspicuous for the uniform quality of their wares and the moderation of their prices; he recommended these tradesmen to his friends, and helped them if the need arose, for he was accustomed to say that people in too much of a hurry to make their fortune are often indifferent to the means they employ.

His wine-merchant soon grew rich, for he declared him to be innocent of adulteration, a quality rare even among the Athenians in the days of Pericles, and none too common in the nineteenth century.

We believe it was he who gave advice and guidance to Hurbain, the restaurateur in the Palais-Royal who provides for two francs a dinner which would cost over twice that sum elsewhere, and whose road to fortune is all the surer in that the number of his clients increases daily in direct proportion to the moderation of his prices.

The food which was removed from our gastronome's table was never left to the discretion of the servants, who were compensated amply; anything which retained a good appearance was sent to a destination indicated by the master of the house.

Well informed, through his position on the charity board, of the needs and morals of many of the people under his jurisdiction, he was certain of bestowing his gifts in the proper quarters; and left-over portions which were still very desirable – for example, the tail-end of a fat pike, the crest of

---

Madame la Duchesse d'Orléans; the premises are superb, the tone excellent, the masters the best in Paris, and, what most impresses the Professor, with all these advantages the fees are such as to suit quite modest incomes.

a turkey, a piece of fillet steak, or some pastry – would occasionally banish hunger or be the cause of joy.

But in order to make these offerings still more beneficial, he took care to announce them for Monday morning, or the morning after a feast-day, thus obviating the cessation of work on holidays, combating the disadvantages of 'holy Monday',[1] and making sensuality the antidote of debauchery.

When Monsieur de Borose discovered, in the third or fourth class of tradespeople, an exemplary young couple whose prudent conduct indicated the qualities on which the prosperity of nations is founded, he paid them the compliment of a visit and made a point of asking them to dinner.

On the appointed day, the young woman would invariably meet ladies who talked to her about the management of a household, and the husband, men who would discuss commerce and industry with him.

These invitations, the motive of which was well known, came to be regarded as a distinction, and all strove to deserve them.

In the meantime young Herminie grew and developed in the shelter of the rue de Valois; and we owe our readers a portrait of the daughter, as an integral part of her father's biography.

Mademoiselle Herminie de Borose is quite tall (5 feet 1 inch), and her figure combines the lightness of a nymph with the grace of a goddess.

Sole fruit of a happy marriage, her health is perfect, and

1. Most of the workers in Paris work on Sunday morning to finish the job they have in hand, deliver it to their employer, and are then paid for it; after which they go off to enjoy themselves for the rest of the day.

On Monday morning they gather together in groups, pool whatever money is left to them, and do not separate until every sou is spent.

This state of affairs, which was almost universal ten years ago, has been partly remedied by the owners of workshops, and by such associations as thrift clubs; but the evil is still a serious one, and much time and labour is lost to the profit of places of pleasure gardens, restaurants, public-houses, and taverns inside and outside the city.

her physical strength remarkable; she is not afraid of the sun's heat, the longest walk leaves her undismayed.

From a distance you would think her dark, but a closer inspection shows her hair to be chestnut, her eyebrows black, her eyes pale blue.

Most of her features are Grecian, but her nose is Gallic, and so charming that a committee of artists, after discussing it at three successive dinners, decided that the most French of types is at least as worthy as any other to be immortalized by brush, chisel, and graving tool.

The feet of this young person are remarkably small and shapely; the Professor has praised and even flattered her so often on the subject, that on New Year's Day 1825, with her father's approval, she made him a present of a pretty little black satin shoe, which he sometimes shows to the elect, and which he uses to prove that extreme sociability influences forms as well as characters; for he maintains that a small foot, such as we prize so highly nowadays, is the product of art and culture, is hardly ever found among peasants, and almost always denotes a person whose ancestors have lived in comfort for a long time past.

When Herminie has drawn back the forest of her hair with a comb, and confined a simple tunic within a belt of ribbons, she looks utterly charming, and neither flowers, pearls, nor diamonds could add anything to her beauty.

Her conversation is easy and unaffected, and few would suspect that she knows all our best authors; but there are times when she grows excited and then the aptness of her comments betrays her secret; as soon as she realizes this, she blushes and lowers her eyes, and her blushing cheeks offer proof of her modesty.

Mademoiselle de Borose plays equally well on harp and piano; but she prefers the former instrument, moved by some instinctive partiality for the celestial harps played by the angels, and the golden harps celebrated by Ossian.

Her voice, too, has a heavenly sweetness and purity, though this does not prevent her from being a little shy; however, she sings without needing to be pressed, but never fails, before beginning her song, to bestow a bewitching glance on her audience, so that she might sing out of tune, like so many others, and nobody would notice it.

She has not neglected needlework, a source of innocent pleasure and an ever-present antidote to boredom; she works like a fairy, and whenever any innovation is made in that sphere, the first sempstress of the *Père de Famille* always comes to teach it to her.

Herminie's heart has not yet spoken, and so far filial piety has filled her cup of happiness; but she is passionately fond of dancing.

When she takes her place in a quadrille, she seems to grow two inches taller, and you would think she is about to take flight; yet her dancing is restrained, and her steps unpretentious; she is content to glide lightly round the room, a charming, graceful figure; but now and then there appears a hint of latent powers, and we suspect that if she chose to exert herself, Madame Montessu would have a rival:

Even when a bird walks, we see that it has wings.

With this sweet girl, whom he had taken away from her boarding-school, and in the enjoyment of his carefully administered fortune and the well-deserved esteem of the world, Monsieur de Borose was living a happy life, and looking forward to its long continuation; but hope is always deceitful, and no man can tell the future.

About the middle of last March, Monsieur de Borose was invited to spend a day in the country with some friends.

It was one of those prematurely hot days which are the forerunners of spring: from beyond the horizon came some of those low rumblings which have given rise to the proverbial saying that 'Winter is breaking his neck'; but this did not deter the party from setting out on a walk. Soon, however, the sky took on a threatening appearance, dark clouds gathered, and a terrible storm broke, with thunder, rain, and hail.

The friends ran for shelter wherever they could find it, and Monsieur de Borose sought refuge under a poplar-tree whose lower branches, spread out like an umbrella, seemed to promise him protection.

Fatal refuge! The top of the tree rose into the very clouds as if in search of the electric fluid, and the rain, streaming down its branches, served as a conductor. Soon a frightful crash was heard, and the unlucky walker fell dead, without even having time to breathe a last sigh.

Thus cut off by the death which Caesar wished for, and which offered no cause for complaint, Monsieur de Borose was buried with due form and ceremony. A long procession, on foot and in carriages, followed his hearse to the cemetery of Père Lachaise; his praise was on all lips, and when a friendly voice pronounced a moving speech over his grave, it found an echo in the hearts of all who were present.

Herminie was overwhelmed by this unexpected disaster; she gave way to neither convulsions nor hysteria, and did not hide her grief in bed; but she wept so copiously, so bitterly, and so long for her father, that her friends hoped that the very excess of her grief would be its remedy; for we are not strong enough to endure such anguish for long.

Sure enough, time has had its unfailing effect on that young heart; Herminie can now speak her father's name without bursting into tears; but she talks of him with such sweet piety, ingenuous sorrow, and undying love, and in such profound accents that it is impossible to hear her and not share her emotion.

Happy the man to whom Herminie one day grants the right to accompany her and lay a funeral wreath upon her father's tomb.

In a side chapel of the church of —, there may be seen every Sunday at the midday Mass a tall, lovely girl, accompanied by an old lady. Her figure is charming, but a thick veil masks her features. Yet those features must be well known, for all around the chapel stand a host of youths suddenly turned devout, all of them most elegantly clad, and some of them extremely handsome.

147. An Heiress's Suite

One day as I was entering the place Vendôme from the rue de la Paix, I was stopped by the suite of the richest heiress in Paris, who was then unmarried, returning from the Bois de Boulogne.

The cavalcade was composed as follows:

1. The desirable lady herself, mounted on a handsome bay, which she was managing skilfully, and wearing a full-skirted blue riding-habit and a black hat with white feathers;

2. Her tutor, riding by her side, with the grave features and self-important bearing proper to his functions;

3. A group of twelve to fifteen aspirants, each seeking to attract attention, one by his ardour, another by his horsemanship, a third by his melancholy;

4. A magnificent carriage, ready in case of rain or fatigue, with a fat coachman and a footman no larger than your fist;

5. Mounted servants in every sort of livery, following pell-mell.

They rode by . . . and I resumed my meditations.

30. Bouquet

148. Gastronomical Mythology

Gasterea is the Tenth Muse; the delights of taste are her domain.

The whole world would be hers if she wished to claim it; for the world is nothing without life, and all that lives takes nourishment.

Her chief delight is to linger on hillsides where the vine grows, or the fragrant orange-tree in groves where the truffle comes to perfection, and in regions abounding in game and fruit.

When she deigns to show herself, she appears in the guise of a young girl; round her waist is a flame-coloured girdle; her hair is black, her eyes sky-blue, and her figure full of grace; as beautiful as Venus, she is also extremely pretty.

She rarely shows herself to mortals; but her statue consoles them for her invisibility. Only one sculptor has ever been allowed to contemplate her countless charms, and such was the skill of that fortunate artist that anyone who sees his work thinks he recognizes in it the features of his greatest love.

Of all the places where she has an altar, Gasterea loves best that city, the queen of all the world, which imprisons the Seine between the steps of its palaces.

Her temple is built on that famous hill to which Mars gave his name; it stands there on a mighty plinth of white marble, and a hundred steps lead up to it from all sides.

Deep inside that hallowed rock are those mysterious chambers where Art puts Nature to the question, and subjects her to his laws.

There air and water, iron and flame, controlled by skilful hands, divide and make whole again, pulverize and amalgamate to produce effects beyond the understanding of the common herd.

And thence issue, at predetermined times, marvellous recipes whose authors prefer to remain nameless, for their happiness is in their conscience, their reward in the knowledge that they have extended the frontiers of their art and won new pleasures for mankind.

The temple, a unique monument of simple and majestic architecture, is supported by a hundred columns of Eastern jasper, and lit by a dome built to resemble the very vault of heaven.

We shall not attempt a minute description of the marvels that edifice contains; enough to say that the sculptures adorning its pediment, like the bas-reliefs which decorate its walls, are devoted to the memory of men who have deserved well of their fellows by useful discoveries, such as the application of fire to the needs of life, or the invention of the plough.

Far from the dome, and within the sanctuary, the statue of the goddess stands; her left hand rests on a stove, and in her right she holds the product dearest to her worshippers.

The canopy above her head is of crystal, supported by eight pillars of the same material, and those pillars, continuously bathed in electric light, cast a glow about the holy place which has something of the divine about it.

The cult of the goddess is simple: every day at sunrise her priests enter and remove the floral wreath adorning her statue, placing a new wreath in its stead, and singing in unison one of the many hymns composed in praise of the immortal goddess who showers such blessings on mankind.

These priests are twelve in number, and the eldest is their leader; they are chosen from among the most learned of men, and the most handsome, other things being equal, are given preference. Their age is the age of maturity; they are bound to grow old, but never senile: from that fate the air they breathe in the temple preserves them.

The festivals of the goddess are equal in number to the days of the year, for she never ceases to bestow her benefits on mankind; but there is one day specially devoted to her honour: that is the twenty-first of September, called the 'grand gastronomical gaudy-day'.

On that solemn day the queen of cities is wreathed from early morning in a cloud of incense; the people, crowned with flowers, throng the streets singing the praises of the goddess; the citizens greet one another by the most endearing and familiar names; all hearts are full of the kindliest feelings; the air is laden with sympathy, and breathes love and friendship far and wide.

Part of the day is given over to these rejoicings; then, at the appointed hour, the crowd makes its way to the temple, where the sacred banquet is to be held,

In the holy of holies, at the feet of the goddess's statue, stands the table reserved for the priesthood; and a second table laid for twelve hundred persons is ready beneath the dome for guests of both sexes. All the arts have combined to adorn these solemn boards, and nothing so elegant was ever seen in the palaces of kings.

Slow of step, and solemn of face, the priests arrive; they are clad in tunics of white Kashmir wool, edged with pink embroidery, the folds contained by girdles of the same colour; health and goodwill are written on their features; they greet one another, and take their seats.

Already servants, clothed in fine linen, have set the first dishes before them; these are no common preparations, made to appease vulgar cravings; nothing is served at this august table but what has been found worthy of it and belongs by choice of matter and skilful craft to transcendental spheres.

The venerable diners too are worthy of their functions: their talk is calm and full of substance, touching the marvels of nature and the power of art: they eat slowly and savour every morsel; the movement of their jaws is smooth and gentle; each bite seems to have its special accent; and if they happen to pass their tongues along their gleaming lips, the author of the favoured dish wins for himself immortal glory.

The drinks, following one another at intervals, are worthy of the feast; twelve maidens pour them, chosen, for this day alone, by a jury of painters and sculptors; they are clothed in the ancient Athenian style which favours beauty but without offending modesty.

The priests of the goddess make no hypocritical pretence of averting their gaze, while pretty hands pour for their pleasure the choicest liquors of both worlds; although they may admire the Creator's fairest handiwork, virtuous restraint rules their conduct, and their manner of giving thanks and of drinking expresses this dual sentiment.

Around this mysterious table kings, princes, and illustrious foreigners perambulate; they walk in silence, watching closely, for they have come from all parts of the world to seek instruction in the great and difficult art of eating well, an art of which whole nations are still ignorant.

While these things are taking place in the sanctuary, universal joy reigns among the guests at the table beneath the dome.

The chief cause of their gaiety is as follows: no man is seated beside the woman to whom he has already said all he has to say. Such is the will of the goddess.

Chosen and summoned to this vast table are the savants of both sexes who have enriched the art with new discoveries, hosts who graciously fulfil the duties of French hospitality, cosmopolitan sages to whom society owes useful or agreeable imports, and those charitable men who nourish the poor with the rich spoils of their superabundance.

The table is in the form of a circle, enclosing a wide space in which a crowd of carvers and distributors offer and parade all that the guests could possibly desire from the farthest corners of the earth.

There, admirably displayed, is all that generous Nature created for the nourishment of man. These treasures are multiplied a hundredfold not only by association with one another, but also by the metamorphoses to which they are subjected by art. That magician has drawn the two worlds together, confused countries, and shortened distances; the air is heavy with the fragrance of these cunning preparations, and balmy with intoxicating fumes.

Meanwhile young boys as handsome as they are well dressed move around the circle's outer rim, constantly offering the guests delicious wine in cups which have now the rich glow of the ruby, now the more modest hue of the topaz.

Now and then skilled musicians, seated in the galleries of the dome, fill the temple with the melodious strains of a simple but subtle harmony.

Then heads are raised, the attention caught, and for a while all conversations cease, to be resumed before long with greater charm; for this new gift from the gods seems to refresh the imagination and make every heart beat faster.

When the pleasures of the table have run their allotted course, the twelve priests draw near; they come to join the banquet, to mingle with the guests and sip with them that Mocha which the lawgiver of the East allows his disciples. The perfumed fluid steams in gold-edged vessels and the fair acolytes of the sanctuary go round the company distributing sugar to sweeten its bitterness. They are charming creatures, yet such is the influence of the air breathed in Gasterea's temple, that no woman's heart there feels a twinge of jealousy.

At last the high priest intones a hymn of thanksgiving, all voices join in, together with the instruments; heartfelt homage rises to the heavens, and the service is at an end.

Only then does the popular banquet begin; for there is no true festival in which the people have no share.

Tables stretching farther than the eye can see are set up in every street, in every square, in front of every palace. People sit down wherever they happen to be, all ranks and ages and districts mingling together; and happiness shines in every face.

Although the great city is now just one immense refectory, the generosity of private individuals ensures abundance, while a paternal government watches to see that order is maintained, and that the limits of sobriety are not exceeded.

Soon brisk and lively music is heard, announcing the dance, that exercise youth loves so well.

Vast halls have been prepared, with well-sprung floors, and there is no lack of all kinds of refreshment.

Crowds gather in them, some to dance, some to encourage the dancers, some to be spectators only. Laughter greets a few old men who, warmed by a short-lived flame, offer beauty an ephemeral homage; but the cult of the goddess and the solemnity of the day excuse everything.

Far into the night the merry-making continues; joy is general, movement universal, and it is with regret that the clock is heard announcing the hour for rest. But none resists the summons: each reveller goes home content with his day, to fall asleep full of hope for the events of a year begun under such happy auspices.

Part Two

Transition

If my readers have followed me so far with that attention which I have sought both to rouse and to maintain, they will have seen that I have never lost sight of a twofold aim: first, to determine the basic principles of *gastronomy*, so that it may take that place among the sciences which is its undeniable right; secondly, to propose an exact definition of what is meant by *gourmandism* and to distinguish, once and for all, between that social quality and the vices of gluttony and intemperance with which it has been so regrettably confused.

This ambiguity was introduced by intolerant moralists who, carried away by excessive zeal, chose to see excess in what was nothing more than intelligent enjoyment; for the treasures of creation were not made to be trampled underfoot. Later it was further propagated by unsociable grammarians, who defined in the dark and laid down the law *in verba magistri*.

It is time to have done with such an error, for nowadays everyone understands the difference between gourmandism and gluttony. No one today would not confess with pride to a tinge of gourmandism, just as no one would fail to feel insulted if accused of gluttony, voracity, or intemperance.

On these two cardinal points, it seems to me that what I have already written amounts to proof positive, and must suffice to persuade all but those who refuse to be convinced. I could therefore lay down my pen and regard my self-appointed task as finished; but in the course of exploring a subject connected with every aspect of life, I have remembered many things which seemed worth setting down on paper: anecdotes hitherto unknown to the public, witticisms born under my very eyes, recipes of the highest distinction, and other similar *hors-d'oeuvres*.

Scattered about in the theoretical part of my work, they

would have destroyed its continuity; but collected here, I hope they will give pleasure to the reader, not only as a source of entertainment, but also because they contain a number of experimental truths and practical developments.

As I warned my readers earlier, I must also be allowed to indulge in a little autobiography, such as occasions neither comment nor argument. I have sought a reward for my work in this part of it where I find myself with my friends again. For it is when the light of life is burning low that the word *I* grows dearest, and friends are necessarily part of it.

However, I will not deny that in reading over the more personal passages I felt a few qualms of apprehension.

This uneasiness was the result of my own most recent reading, and the comments made on certain memoirs to be found in everybody's library.

I was afraid that some malicious person, suffering from insomnia and indigestion, might exclaim: 'Here's a Professor who thinks very highly of himself! Here's a Professor who never tires of paying himself compliments! Here's a Professor who. . . . Here's a Professor whom . . . !'

To which I shall reply in advance, putting myself on guard, that someone who speaks ill of no man has every right to treat himself with some indulgence; and that I can see no reason why I, who have always been innocent of all thoughts of hatred, should be cut off from my own benevolence.

With this reply, which is firmly based on reality, I believe I may rest in peace in the shelter of my philosopher's robe: and as for those who persist in finding fault with me, I hereby declare them to be bad sleepers. *Bad sleepers!* This is a new insult, and I intend to take out a patent for it, being the first to have discovered that it is an excommunication in itself.

Miscellanea

1. The Curé's Omelette

Everybody knows that for the past twenty years the throne of beauty in Paris has been occupied by universal agreement by Madame R—. It is common knowledge too that she has a very charitable nature, and at one time took an active interest in most of the enterprises whose object is the alleviation of distress, which is sometimes more acutely felt in the capital than anywhere else.[1]

Wishing to consult the curé of — one day in connexion with one of these matters, she called on him about five o'clock in the afternoon, and was astonished to find him already at table.

The fair inhabitant of the rue du Mont-Blanc believed that everybody in Paris dined at six; she did not know that ecclesiastics usually begin early because many of them are in the habit of partaking of a light collation in the evening.

Madame R— made as if to withdraw, but the curé begged her to stay; perhaps because the affair to be discussed was not such as to interfere with his dinner, perhaps because a pretty woman can never be an unwelcome visitor, or perhaps because he saw that nothing was wanting but an interlocutor to turn his dining-room into a positive gastronomical Elysium.

For his table was covered with an immaculate cloth; old wine sparkled in a crystal decanter; the white porcelain was of the choicest quality; the dishes were kept warm with boil-

1. Those people are most to be pitied whose needs are unknown; for in justice to the citizens of Paris, it must be said that they are charitable by nature and generous almsgivers.

In the year X, I was paying a small weekly pension to an aged nun, who lived in a sixth-floor attic, and whose body was half paralysed. The worthy woman received enough help from her neighbours to enable her to live in reasonable comfort and to feed a lay sister who had taken pity on her.

ing water; and a maidservant, both neat and canonical, stood ready to receive his orders.

The meal was a compromise between frugality and refinement. A bowl of crayfish soup had just been removed, and on the table were a salmon-trout, an omelette and a salad.

'My dinner,' said the curé with a smile, 'may tell you something which perhaps you are unaware of; today is a day of abstinence according to the rules of the Church.' Our dear friend bent her head in assent, and it is said that she blushed slightly but this in no way prevented the curé from proceeding with his meal.

Work had already begun on the trout, the upper end of which was in the process of consumption; the sauce proclaimed the skill of a master, and inward satisfaction was written on the priestly brow.

When he had finished the trout, he set to work on the omelette, which was round, swollen, and done to a turn.

At the first impact of the spoon, some thick gravy, agreeable to the senses of both sight and smell, escaped from the paunch, till the whole dish seemed full of it; and dear Juliette confessed that it made her mouth water.

This sympathetic reaction was not lost upon the curé, accustomed as he was to studying the passions of mankind; and as if in answer to a question which Madame R— had studiously refrained from asking he said: 'This is a tunny omelette; my cook makes them beautifully, and few people have tasted them without congratulating me.' 'I can well believe it,' replied the denizen of the Chaussée-d'Antin; 'I have never seen such an appetizing omelette on our worldly tables.'

Next came the salad. (I commend salad to all those who have faith in me; it refreshes without weakening, and soothes without irritating: I often call it the rejuvenator.)

The dinner did not interrupt their conversation. The business which had occasioned the visit was discussed, as well as the war raging at that time, topics of the day, the hopes of the Church, and other such table-talk as makes a bad dinner passable and embellishes a good one.

Dessert came in due course, consisting of a Septmoncel cheese, three queening apples, and a pot of preserves.

Finally, the maid brought up a little round table, of the sort which used to be called a pedestal table, and placed on it a cup of hot and limpid Mocha, the aroma of which filled the room.

After sipping his coffee, the curé said grace, adding, as he rose from his chair: 'I never drink spirits; they are a luxury which I offer my friends, but make no use of myself. I am saving them up to fall back on in my old age, if God in His goodness spares me till then.'

Meanwhile, time had not stood still: the clock struck six, and Madame R— hurried back to her carriage, for that day she had invited a few friends to dinner, including myself. She arrived late, as is her custom; but arrive at last she did, still deeply moved by what she had seen and smelt.

Throughout the meal nothing was talked of but the curé's dinner, and especially his tunny omelette. Madame R— praised it for its size, roundness, and general appearance, and all this being granted, the entire company agreed that it must have been exquisite, each working out a perfect sensual equation in his own manner.

This subject being finally exhausted, others took its place, and it was forgotten. But I, in my capacity as a propagator of useful truths, thought it my duty to rescue from obscurity a dish which I believe to be as wholesome as it is delicious. I therefore instructed my master cook to obtain the recipe in its minutest details; and I now offer it to all gourmands with the more pleasure in that I have never found it in any cookery-book.

Recipe for Tunny Omelette

Take, for six persons, two soft carps' roes, wash well, and blanch for five minutes in slightly salted boiling water.

Have ready a piece of fresh tunny, about the size of a hen's egg, and a small shallot, cut in pieces.

Chop up and mix well the roes and tunny, place the whole

in a pan with a sizeable piece of the best butter, and fry until the butter is thoroughly melted. This is what gives the omelette its special flavour.

Then take a second piece of butter, at discretion, mix parsley and chives into it, and place in the fish-shaped dish intended for the omelette; squeeze the juice of one lemon over it, and place on the fire.

Next beat up twelve eggs (the fresher the better); add the fried roe and tunny, and mix thoroughly.

Then cook the omelette in the usual way, taking care to make it long, thick, and soft. Turn it out neatly into the dish prepared as above, and serve at once.

This dish is to be reserved for special breakfasts, gatherings of connoisseurs who know what they are about and eat deliberately; if it is washed down with good old wine, wonders will be seen.

Theoretical Notes

1. The roe and tunny should be fried lightly and not allowed to brown, or they will harden, which would prevent them from mixing well with the eggs.

2. The dish should be hollow, to allow the sauce to collect so that it can be served with a spoon.

3. The dish should be slightly warmed, for if it were cold, the porcelain would draw the heat out of the omelette, leaving too little to melt the *maître d'hôtel* sauce on which it rests.

2. Eggs in Gravy

One day I was travelling with two ladies whom I was escorting to Melun.

We had started none too early, and we arrived at Montgeron with an appetite which threatened destruction to any foodstuffs we encountered.

Vain threats: the inn at which we alighted, though pleasant enough outwardly, was empty of all provisions; three coaches and two post-chaises had preceded us, devouring everything in their path, like the locusts of Egypt.

So said the cook.

However, I saw a spit turning in front of the fire, laden with a very handsome leg of mutton at which the ladies from sheer force of habit darted extremely coquettish glances.

Alas, those shafts were wasted! The leg of mutton belonged to three Englishmen, who had brought it with them, and who sat patiently awaiting it over a bottle of champagne.

'But at least,' I said, half in anger and half in supplication, 'couldn't you scramble these eggs for us in the gravy from that leg of mutton? We would be quite content with them and a cup of white coffee.' 'Why, certainly,' the host replied; 'the gravy is our property by law, and I'll do what you ask at once.' Whereupon he began carefully breaking the eggs.

When I saw that he was fully occupied, I went up to the fire, and, taking a travelling-knife from my pocket, inflicted a dozen deep wounds on the forbidden joint, so that its juices should escape down to the last drop.

I was then careful to join in the business of cooking the eggs, for fear that some misappropriation might take place to our disadvantage. When they were done, I took possession of them and carried them off to the room which had been prepared for my companions and myself.

There we made a feast of them, laughing uproariously to think that we were in fact swallowing all the substance of the mutton, leaving our English friends to chew the residue.

3. National Victory

During my stay in New York, I sometimes spent the evening in a kind of café-tavern kept by a certain Little, where turtle soup could be obtained in the morning, and in the evening all the forms of refreshment usual in the United States.

Generally I took with me the Vicomte de la Massue and Jean-Rodolphe Fehr, a former broker in Marseilles, both of whom were exiles like myself; I would treat them to a *Welsh rabbit*[1] washed down with ale or cider, and the evening would pass off gently with talk of our misfortunes, pleasures, and hopes.

At this tavern I made the acquaintance of a Jamaican planter called Mr Wilkinson, and also of a man who was presumably a great friend of his, for he never left his side. This last individual, whose name I never discovered, was one of the most extraordinary men I have ever met; his face was square, his eyes very bright, and he seemed to scrutinize everything with the greatest attention; but he never spoke, and his features were as blank as those of a blind man. However, when he heard a joke or a witty remark, his face lighted up, and opening a mouth as wide as the bell of a horn, he emitted a prolonged noise resembling both laughter as we understand it, and the neighing sound the English call a horse-laugh; after which everything returned to normal, and he relapsed into his habitual silence; the effect was that of a flash of lightning piercing a cloud. Mr Wilkinson himself seemed about fifty years of age, and had the manners and appearance of a gentleman.

These two Englishmen appeared to enjoy our company,

1. *Welsh rabbit* is the epigrammatical English name for a piece of cheese toasted on a slice of bread. The concoction is certainly not as substantial as a rabbit; but it brings on a thirst, makes wine taste good, and is a perfectly acceptable savoury for a small party.

and had already several times, and with very good grace, shared the frugal collation which I used to offer my two friends, when one evening Mr Wilkinson took me aside, and announced his intention of inviting all three of us to dinner.

I thanked him; and considering myself entitled to act in an affair in which I was obviously the principal, accepted on behalf of us all; whereupon the party was fixed for the next day but one, at three o'clock.

The evening then proceeded as usual; but as I was leaving, the waiter took me on one side and informed me that the Jamaicans had ordered an excellent meal; that they had given orders for particular attention to be paid to the liquid refreshment, because they regarded their invitation as a challenge to the best drinker; and that the man with the large mouth had declared that he had every hope of drinking the Frenchmen under the table all by himself.

This news would have been enough to make me decline the invitation if I could have done so honourably, for I have always avoided orgies of that kind; but this was impossible. The Englishmen would have told all and sundry that we had been afraid to give battle, and that their very presence had been enough to make us turn tail; and so, though fully aware of the danger, we obeyed the maxim of Marshal de Saxe: the cork was drawn, and we were prepared to drink the wine.

I was not without certain misgivings; but at least it was not for myself that I felt afraid.

Since I was younger, taller, and more vigorous than our hosts, I felt certain that my constitution, virgin of any Bacchic excess, would triumph over the two Englishmen's, which were doubtless worn out by unbridled spirituous indulgence.

No doubt, alone against the other four combatants, I would have been proclaimed the winner; but such a triumph being purely personal, would have been singularly weakened by the defeat of my compatriots, who would have been carried from the field in the hideous state inseparable from such disasters. I wished to spare them that indignity; in a word, I wanted a national and not an individual triumph. I accordingly summoned Fehr and La Massue to my apartment, and gave them a formal and severe harangue on the subject of my fears: I urged them whenever possible to drink a little at a time, to empty a few glasses surreptitiously while I distracted our adversaries' attention, and above all to eat slowly and nurse their appetites throughout the meal, because food mixed with wine tempers its ardour, and prevents it from rushing violently to the head; finally, we shared between us a dish of bitter almonds, which I had heard possessed the property of moderating the fumes of wine.

Thus morally and physically armed, we set out for Little's, where we found the Jamaicans waiting for us; and very soon afterwards dinner was served. It consisted of a huge piece of roast beef, a roast turkey, boiled vegetables, raw cabbage salad, and a jam tart.

We drank in the French fashion, that is to say, the wine was served from the beginning: it was a very good claret, which was then much cheaper than in France, owing to the recent arrival of several shiploads, of which the last few had sold badly.

Mr Wilkinson did the honours admirably, calling on us to set to, and setting the example; his friend seemed buried in his plate, said not a word, studied us with side-long glances, and laughed out of the corners of his mouth.

For my part, I was delighted with my two acolytes. La Massue, though endowed with a mighty appetite, toyed with his food like a finicky woman, while Fehr disposed of a few glassfuls of wine now and then, skilfully emptying them into a beer-mug at the end of the table. As for myself, I stood up fair and square to the two Englishmen, and as the meal proceeded, so my confidence increased.

After the claret came port, and after the port Madeira, to which we confined ourselves for a long time.

Dessert had now been served, composed of butter, cheese, coconuts, and hickory nuts, and the time had come for toasts.

We drank copiously to the power of kings, the liberty of

peoples, and the beauty of the ladies; we also toasted, with Mr Wilkinson, the health of his daughter Mariah, who, he assured us, was the prettiest girl in all Jamaica.

After the wine came spirits, that is to say, rum, brandy, whisky, and raspberry-brandy; I saw that we were in for a warm time. I feared those spirits, and avoided them by asking for some punch; and Little himself brought in a huge bowl, doubtless ordered beforehand, which held enough for forty. We have no vessels of such capacity in France.

The sight of it revived my courage; I ate five or six pieces of toast with fresh butter on them, and felt my strength returning to me. Then I took careful stock of my surroundings; for I was beginning to feel some anxiety as to how all this was going to end. My two friends seemed fairly fresh, and were cracking hickory nuts between drinks. Mr Wilkinson's face was a dark crimson, his eyes bleary and his air subdued; his friend remained silent, though his head was steaming like a pan of boiling water, and his great mouth had gathered into a pout. I could see that catastrophe was near at hand.

Sure enough, Mr Wilkinson, waking up with a start, leapt to his feet and in a loud voice intoned the national air of 'Rule, Britannia': but he could go no further; his strength gave way, and he sank back into his chair, and from there slipped under the table. His friend, seeing his condition, gave vent to one of his noisiest guffaws, bent down to help him up, and collapsed beside him.

It is impossible to express the satisfaction I felt at this sudden turn of events, nor the weight it lifted from my mind. I rang the bell at once. Little came upstairs, and after I had uttered, in the official phrase: 'See that these gentlemen are properly attended to,' we drank their health with him in a final glass of punch. Soon the waiter arrived, and, with the help of his underlings, took possession of our vanquished foes and carried them out feet first,[1] Mr Wilkinson still trying to sing 'Rule, Britannia', and his friend as still as death.

1. This phrase is used in English of persons who are carried out either dead or drunk.

Next morning the New York newspapers gave a substantially accurate account of what had happened, which was repeated in every paper in the Union; and as they added that the Englishmen had taken to their beds as a result of this affair, I went to see them. I found the friend completely stupefied by the effects of violent indigestion, and Mr Wilkinson confined to his chair by an attack of gout, probably brought on by our Bacchic contest. He seemed touched by my visit, and said to me, among other things: 'My dear sir, you are very good company indeed, but too hard a drinker for us.'

4. Ablutions

I wrote earlier that the Roman vomitory offended the delicacy of our own conventions; but I am afraid this was a piece of rashness on my part, and that I must now retract. Let me explain:

About forty years ago, or thereabouts, there were a few people in high society, nearly all of them ladies, who used to rinse their mouths out at the end of a meal.

To this end, as soon as they left the table, they turned their backs on the company; a servant handed them a cup of water, they took a mouthful, and promptly spat it out into the saucer; the servant carried off both cup and saucer, and the operation, or the way in which it was carried out, went almost unnoticed.

We have changed all that.

In houses where a point is made of following the latest fashions, servants, at the end of dessert, distribute bowls of cold water among the guests, in each of which stands a goblet of hot water. Whereupon, in full view of one another, the guests plunge their fingers in the cold water, as if to wash them, fill their mouths with the hot, gargle noisily, and spit it out into the goblet or the bowl.

I am not the only person to have spoken out against this useless, indecent, and disgusting innovation.

Useless, because in the case of people who know how to eat, the mouth is clean at the end of a meal, having been cleansed either by the fruit or by the last glasses of wine drunk at dessert. As for the hands, they should not be used in such a way as to soil them; and besides, has not everyone a napkin to wipe them on?

Indecent, because it is a generally recognized principle that any sort of ablution should take place in private.

And above all *disgusting,* for the prettiest and freshest

mouth loses all its charms when it usurps the functions of the evacuatory organs: what then if the mouth is neither fresh nor pretty? And what shall be said of those monstrous chasms which open up to reveal pits that would seem bottomless, if it were not for the sight of shapeless, time-corroded stumps? *Proh pudor!*

Such is the pass to which we have been brought by a pretentious affectation of cleanliness, foreign alike to our tastes and our manners.

Once certain limits have been passed, there is no saying where we shall stop, and heaven knows what purification may next be imposed on us.

Ever since the official appearance of these new-fangled bowls I have been grieving night and day. A second Jeremiah, I deplore the vagaries of fashion; and all too well informed by my travels, I never now enter a dining-room without trembling at the thought that my eyes might fall upon the odious *chamber-pot*.[1]

---

1. It is common knowledge that there are, or were a few years ago, dining-rooms in England where it was possible for a man to answer the call of Nature without leaving the room: a curious facility, but one which perhaps had fewer disadvantages in a land where the ladies withdraw as soon as the men begin to drink wine.

5. The Professor is Taken in and a General Defeated

A few years ago the papers announced the discovery of a new perfume, extracted from the *hemerocallis,* a bulbous plant with a very pleasant smell not unlike that of jasmine.

Now, I am inquisitive by nature and much addicted to strolling; and one day these two causes combined to propel me as far as the Faubourg Saint-Germain in search of that perfume, or the charmer of nostrils, as the Turks call it.

There I was welcomed as befits a connoisseur, and from the tabernacle of a well-stocked chemist's shop a little box, carefully wrapped up, which appeared to contain two ounces of the precious crystals, was brought out for me; a piece of politeness which I reciprocated by leaving three francs behind me, in accordance with that law of compensation whose sphere and principles Monsieur Azaïs enlarges every day.

A member of the common herd would there and then have unwrapped, opened, sniffed, and tasted; but that is not the professorial way. Here, it seemed to me, was a case calling for withdrawal: I accordingly returned home, and before long, comfortably ensconced in my sofa, I prepared to experience a new sensation.

I took the fragrant box from my pocket, and released it from the wrappings in which it was still swathed: there were three separate pamphlets, all dealing with *hemerocallis*, its natural history, growth, and flower, and the bliss to be derived from its perfume, whether that perfume was concentrated in pastilles or merged in pharmaceutical preparations, or whether it came to the table dissolved in alcoholic liquors or mixed with ice-cream. I carefully perused the three pamphlets, first, to indemnify myself as fully as possible for the compensation mentioned above, and secondly, to prepare myself for a proper appreciation of this new treasure extracted from the vegetable realm.

Then, with due reverence, I opened the box, imagining it to be full of pastilles. But to my surprise and disappointment, I found, at the top, a second edition of the three pamphlets I had just read, and underneath, almost as an afterthought, some two dozen of the lozenges in pursuit of which I had ventured into the noble Faubourg.

The first thing I did was to taste one or two; and in deference to truth I must admit that I found those pastilles extremely agreeable; but this only made me regret all the more that, contrary to appearances, they were so few in number; and indeed, the more I thought about it, the more I thought I had been taken in.

I accordingly got up with the intention of returning the box to its author, even if he refused to refund my money; but the movement showed me my grey hairs in a glass: I could not help laughing at my indignation, and I sat down again, bottling up my rancour. It can be seen that it has lasted well.

I was held back, too, by a special consideration; for this was a matter concerning chemists, and only four days before I had been a witness of the extreme imperturbability of that respectable brotherhood.

My readers must resign themselves to reading yet another anecdote. I am in the mood for telling stories today (17 June, 1825). May God grant it be not a public calamity!

Well, then, I went one morning to call on my friend and fellow townsman, General Bouvier des Éclats.

I found him striding up and down his room in a state of considerable agitation, with a crumpled manuscript in his hands which I took to be a piece of poetry.

'Look at this,' he said, giving it to me, 'and tell me what you think of it; you are a good judge of such things.'

I took it, and running my eye over it, found to my surprise that it was a bill for medicine supplied; so that it was not in my capacity of a poet that I was being consulted, but in that of a pharmacologist.

'Come, now, my friend,' I said, returning his property to him, 'you know the ways of the body you have set to work; true, the limits may have been a little overstepped, but what have you a smart coat, three orders, and a bullion-fringe hat for? Those are three aggravating circumstances, and you can't expect to be let off lightly.' 'Be quiet,' he said crossly; 'this bill is quite unacceptable. But you will be able to see my extortioner for yourself; I have sent for him, and he is on his way. I rely on you to back me up.'

He was still talking when the door opened, and there entered a meticulously dressed man of about fifty-five; he was tall and very dignified, and his features would have been of a uniformly solemn cast if there had not been something faintly sardonic about the relationship between his eyes and his mouth.

He walked over to the fireplace, but refused to be seated; and I was then privileged to listen to the following dialogue, which I faithfully committed to memory:

THE GENERAL: Sir, the bill you have sent in is a real apothecary's bill, and . . .

THE SINISTER MAN: Sir, I am not an apothecary.

THE GENERAL: What are you then, sir?

THE SINISTER MAN: Sir, I am a chemist.

THE GENERAL: Very well, Mister chemist, your boy has doubtless told you that . . .

THE SINISTER MAN: Sir, I have no boy.

THE GENERAL: Who was that young man, then?

THE SINISTER MAN: Sir, he is my pupil.

THE GENERAL: What I wished to tell you, sir, was that your drugs . . .

THE SINISTER MAN: Sir, I do not sell drugs.

THE GENERAL: What do you sell then, sir?

THE SINISTER MAN: Sir, I sell medicine.

There the discussion ended. The general, ashamed of having uttered so many solecisms, and of being so ignorant of the pharmaceutical tongue, lost his head, forgot what he had intended to say, and paid every penny that was asked of him.

6. The Dish of Eel

There lived in Paris, in the rue de la Chaussée-d'Antin, an individual called Briguet, who had risen from a coachman to be a horse-dealer, and had made a small fortune in the process.

He had been born at Talissieu, and having decided to end his days there, he married a woman of modest means who had formerly been employed as a cook by Mademoiselle Chevenin, once known to all Paris as the Ace of Spades.

As soon as an opportunity came his way of acquiring a small property in his native village, he took advantage of it, and settled there with his wife towards the end of 1791.

In those days it was usual for all the parish priests in a diocese to meet together once a month, each playing host in turn, to discuss ecclesiastical affairs. The discussion took place after a celebration of High Mass, and was followed by a dinner.

The whole affair was known as *the conference*; and the priest at whose house it was due to be held always made preparations in advance to entertain his brethren well and fittingly.

Now, when it was the turn of the curé of Talissieu, it so happened that one of his flock presented him with a magnificent eel, over three feet long, taken from the limpid waters of Serans.

Delighted at finding himself the possessor of so noble a fish, the priest was afraid that his cook might be unable to do justice to it; he therefore sought out Madame Briguet, and paying due homage to her superior skill, begged her to set her seal upon a dish worthy of an archbishop, and which would do the greatest honour to his dinner.

She, as a docile member of his flock, raised no objection, saying that she was all the readier to comply with his request in that there was still in her possession a little box containing certain rare condiments which she had used in the service of her former mistress.

The eel, then, was cooked with care and served with distinction. It not only looked magnificent and smelt delicious, but when it was tasted, words could not be found to express its praise; and so it disappeared, body and sauce, down to the last particle.

Now it so happened·that at dessert the reverend men were stirred in an unaccustomed manner, and as a result of the inevitable influence of matter on mind, their conversation took a ribald turn.

One told tales of his college escapades, another teased his neighbour about some scandalous rumour; in a word, the conversation was entirely given up to the sweetest of the deadly sins; and, what was most remarkable, they were quite unconscious of their wickedness, so cunningly did the devil do his work.

They separated late, and my private information goes no further on the subject of that day. But at the next conference, when the same guests came together again, they were ashamed of the things they had said, apologized to one another for the accusations they had made, and ended up by attributing everything to the dish of eel; so that, while admitting that it had been delicious, they none the less agreed that it would be unwise to put Madame Briguet's skill to a second test.

I have inquired in vain after the exact nature of the condiment which had worked such wonders, with all the more interest in that nobody had complained of its being dangerous or corrosive.

The artist herself pleaded guilty to serving a highly spiced crayfish sauce, but I am convinced that she was not telling me everything.

7. The Asparagus

A servant came one day to inform Monseigneur Court-
ois de Quincey, Bishop of Belley, that an asparagus of marvellous size was emerging from a certain bed in his kitchen
garden.

The entire household promptly sallied out to verify the
fact; for in bishops' palaces, as everywhere else, men are
delighted to have something to do.

The news was found to be neither false nor exaggerated.
The plant had broken through the earth's crust, and already
showed above ground; the head of it was round, shiny, and
mottled, and gave promise of a column too thick to be en-
circled by the hand.

There were cries of admiration at the sight of this horti-
cultural phenomenon; all agreed that the right of severing
it from its root belonged to the Bishop alone, and the local
cutler was immediately instructed to make a knife suited for
that exalted function.

In the days that followed the asparagus did nothing but
grow in grace and beauty; its progress was slow but steady,
and soon the white part could be seen, where the esculent
properties of the vegetable come to an end.

The harvest-time being thus proclaimed, a good dinner
was eaten by way of preparation, and the operation ad-
journed until the return from the post-prandial walk.

Then the Bishop advanced, armed with the official instrument, and, bending down with dignity, set about separating
the proud plant from its stem, while the whole episcopal
court waited impatiently to examine its fibres and texture.

But to their surprise, disappointment and dismay, the pre-
late rose up empty-handed. . . . The asparagus was made of
wood.

The joke, which perhaps went a little far, was the work of

Canon Rosset, a native of Saint-Claude, who was wonderfully skilful as a turner, and painted admirably too.

He had fashioned the fake plant to perfection, buried it secretly, and raised it little by little every day, to imitate the process of natural growth.

The Bishop scarcely knew how to take this hoax (for it was no less); but seeing signs of hilarity already appearing on the features of all present, he smiled; and that smile was followed by a general explosion of Homeric laughter: the evidence was accordingly taken away, and the offender left unpunished; and for that one evening at least, the asparagus-statue was granted the honours of the drawing-room.

8. The Trap

The Chevalier de Langeac once had a sizeable fortune, which had filtered away by way of the usual outlets which beset any rich and handsome young man.

He had collected what was left, and in Lyons, with the help of a small government pension, he led an agreeable life in the best society; for experience had taught him the value of moderation.

Though still gallant, he had retired from the service of the ladies; he still enjoyed playing cards with them, being equally proficient in all the usual games; but defended his money against them with all the sang-froid of a man who has renounced their favours.

Gourmandism had gained by the loss of his other inclinations; he may be said to have made it his profession; and as he was also very good company, he received more invitations than he could possibly accept.

Lyons is a city of good cheer; on account of its situation, it abounds in Bordeaux, Hermitage, and Burgundy wines; the game from the surrounding hills is excellent; the lakes of Geneva and Le Bourget contain the best fish in the world; and connoisseurs swoon at the sight of Bresse fowls, of which Lyons is the principal market.

The Chevalier de Langeac, then, was always sure of a place at the best tables in the town, but the one he liked best of all was that of Monsieur A—, a wealthy banker and distinguished gastronome. This preference the Chevalier put down to the bond of friendship they had contracted in their schooldays. Cynics (for there are some of those everywhere) attributed it to the fact that Monsieur A—'s kitchen was presided over by the ablest pupil of Ramier, a remarkable cook who flourished in those far-off days.

Be that as it may, towards the end of the winter of 1780

the Chevalier de Langeac received a letter from Monsieur A— inviting him to supper ten days later (for suppers were still fashionable in those days); and it is written in my secret memoirs that he trembled with joy at the thought that such long notice promised a solemn occasion and a banquet of the highest order.

On the day in question, at the appointed hour, he arrived at Monsieur A—'s house, and found ten guests already gathered there, all friends of joy and good cheer; the word *gastronome* had not yet been borrowed from the Greek, or at least was not in general use as it is today.

Soon a substantial meal was served, comprising, among other things, a huge roast sirloin, a richly garnished chicken fricassée, a piece of veal which held out every promise, and a very fine stuffed carp.

All this was well and good, but scarcely corresponded, in the Chevalier's eyes, to the hopes roused in him by his ultra-decadary invitation.

He was struck, too, by another odd circumstance: the guests, all men of good appetite, either ate nothing or scarcely touched their food; one was suffering from a headache, another from a chill, a third had dined late, and so on with all the rest. The Chevalier was astonished at the chance which had brought so many anti-convivial dispositions together that evening, and, holding himself in honour bound to act on behalf of all these invalids, set about his food with a will, plied his knife with precision, and brought great powers of intussusception into play.

The second course was built on no less solid foundations: a huge Crémieu turkey faced a very fine pike *au bleu*, flanked by six traditional side-dishes (not including salad) among which a dish of macaroni cheese was generously conspicuous.

At this sight the Chevalier felt his waning powers revive, while the others looked as if they were about to breathe their last. Exalted by a change of wines, he gloated over their importance, and drank their health in a long succession of toasts, which also served to wash down a large helping of pike which had followed the *entrecuisse* of the turkey.

The side-dishes in turn received a suitable welcome, and so he continued, gloriously and valiantly, leaving room for no more dessert than a piece of cheese and a small glass of Madeira; for sweets had never had a place among the Chevalier's preferences.

We have seen how the evening had already provided him with two surprises; first the too solid nature of the fare, and secondly the indisposition of all the other guests; a third, of a very different order, awaited him.

For instead of bringing in dessert, the servants cleared everything from the table, linen as well as plate, laid fresh covers for the guests, and placed in front of them four new entrées, the smell of which rose to the heavens.

These entreés were sweetbreads with crayfish sauce, soft roes truffled, a stuffed and larded pike, and partridge wings in chestnut cream.

Like Ariosto's old magician, who, having the beautiful Armida in his power, made impotent efforts to dishonour her, the Chevalier was appalled at the sight of so many good things which he could no longer enjoy; and he began to suspect his host's intentions.

The other guests, on the contrary, all felt their strength revive: appetite returned, headaches fled away, mouths seemed to grow wider in ironic smiles; and now it was their turn to drink to the Chevalier, whose powers were exhausted.

However, he refused to be put out of countenance, and seemed ready to bear up against the storm; but at the third mouthful Nature rebelled, and his stomach threatened to let him down. He was forced against his will into inactivity, and proceeded, to use the musical term, to mark time.

His feelings can be imagined when a third change was rung, and he saw snipe brought in by the dozen, white with fat and sleeping on official toast, together with a pheasant – then a rare bird – from the banks of the Seine, a fresh tunny, and pastry and side-dishes of unsurpassed elegance.

He thought hard, and was on the point of staying where

he was, continuing the struggle, and dying bravely on the field of battle. Such, right or wrong, was the call honour made on him; but soon egoism came to his aid, and brought him round to a more moderate way of thinking.

He reflected that in such a case prudence is not cowardice; that death by indigestion always invites ridicule, and that the future probably held many compensations for the present disappointment: he therefore made up his mind, and throwing down his napkin: 'Sir,' he said to the banker, 'no gentleman exposes his friends like this; you have acted perfidiously, and I shall never speak to you again.' So saying, he walked out.

His departure caused no great stir; it announced the success of a plot designed to confront him with a good meal which he would be unable to enjoy; and everyone was in the secret.

The Chevalier sulked longer than might have been expected; and a great deal of tact was needed to appease his wrath; in the end, however, he returned with the garden warblers, and had forgotten the affair by the time truffles were in again.

9. The Turbot

Discord tried one day to part one of the utmost united couples in the entire capital. To be precise, the day was a Saturday; the trouble concerned the cooking of a turbot; it occurred in the country, and the place was Villecrêne.

The fish, which looked as if it had been intended for some more glorious fate, was to be served up the next day at a gathering of good people of whom I was one; it was fresh and plump and as lustrous as could be wished; but its proportions so far exceeded all available vessels, that no one knew how it should be cooked.

'Well,' said the husband, 'we will cut it in two.'

'Would you dare dishonour the poor creature like that,' said the wife. 'We must, my dear, for there's no other way. Come, send for the chopper, and the thing will be done in no time.' 'Wait a little, dear, we still have plenty of time; besides, you know our cousin is coming; he is a Professor, and I feel sure that he will be able to solve our problem.'

'A Professor solve our problem? Nonsense!' And a trustworthy report suggests that he who spoke thus seemed to put little trust in the Professor; and yet I was that Professor! *Schwernoth!*

The problem was probably on the point of being solved in the Alexandrine way, when I arrived at the charge, nose to windward, and with the appetite which always comes at the end of a journey, at seven in the evening, when the smell of a good dinner greets the nostrils and tempts the taste-buds.

On entering the house, I tried in vain to pay the usual compliments; there was no reply, for the simple reason that no one had listened to my greeting. Soon the all-absorbing question was put to me almost in a duet; after which the two performers fell silent together, my cousin looking at me with eyes which seemed to say: 'I hope we can find a solution,' and her husband showing by his scornful, supercilious air that he was sure I would never succeed, while his left hand rested on the formidable chopper, which had been brought at his request.

Both these expressions gave place to one of lively curiosity when in grave and oracular tones I pronounced these solemn words: 'The turbot will remain whole up to the moment of its official presentation.'

Already I was certain of success, because in the last resort I would have proposed baking it in the oven; but as that method might have presented certain difficulties, I said nothing as yet and silently made my way to the kitchen, myself at the head of the procession, the husband and wife serving as acolytes, the servants playing the part of the faithful, and the cook *in fiocchi* bringing up the rear.

The first two rooms contained nothing that suited my purpose; but when I came to the scullery, a copper met my gaze, small, but firmly embedded in its furnace; at once I saw how it might be used, and, turning to my suite: 'Have no fear,' I cried, with that faith which moves mountains: 'The turbot will be cooked whole, it will be cooked by steam, it will be cooked here and now.'

And straight away, although it was already dinner-time, I set everyone to work. While some lit the furnace, I made a sort of hurdle, of the exact size of the giant fish, from a fifty-bottle pannier. On this hurdle I spread a layer of roots and savoury herbs, on which the fish was laid, after being well scoured, well dried, and suitably salted. A second layer of the same seasoning was spread on the turbot's back. Then the hurdle with its load was placed over the copper, which had been half-filled with water; and the whole was covered with a small wash-tub, round which some dry sand was heaped, to prevent the steam from escaping too easily. Soon the water was boiling; and before long steam filled the interior of the wash-tub, which was removed at the end of half an hour, when the hurdle was lifted off the copper with the turbot done to a turn, very white and splendid to behold.

The operation being complete, we hurried to sit down at

table, with appetites whetted by delay, labour, and success, so that some time passed before we arrived at the happy moment, mentioned by Homer, when abundance and variety of fare had banished hunger.

The following day, at dinner, the turbot was served up before the honourable guests, and all were loud in admiration of its splendid appearance. Then the master of the house himself described the providential means by which it had been cooked; and I was praised not only for the timeliness of my invention, but also for its effect; for after careful degustation, it was unanimously agreed that the fish, cooked in this way, was incomparably better than if it had been cooked in a turbot-kettle.

This verdict astonished no one, since, not having passed through boiling water, it had lost none of its basic elements, but, on the contrary, had absorbed all the flavour of the seasoning.

While my ears tingled with the compliments being heaped upon me, my eyes sought more sincere compliments in the visible post-mortem verdict of the guests; and I perceived, with secret satisfaction, that General Labassée was so pleased that he smiled after every mouthful; that the curé sat entranced, with neck outstretched and eyes fixed on the ceiling; and that of two academicians who were present, both gourmands and men of wit, one, Monsieur Auger, had the sparkling eyes and radiant features of a successful author, while Monsieur Villemain, the other, sat with head bent forward and chin to the west, like a man listening attentively.

All this is worth remembering, for there are few country houses that do not contain all that is needed to construct the apparatus which I used on this occasion, and to which recourse can be had whenever it is necessary to cook some object which comes unexpectedly to hand and exceeds ordinary dimensions.

Yet my readers would never have had an account of this great adventure if it had not seemed to me to be bound to lead to results of more general utility.

For, as everyone knows who understands the nature and effects of steam, its temperature equals that of the liquid from which it rises; it can even be raised a few degrees above that point by a slight concentration, and it continues to accumulate as long as it finds no issue.

From this it follows that, in similar circumstances, simply by increasing the capacity of the wash-tub used as a cover in my experiment – for example, by substituting an empty cask for it – it would be possible to cook by steam, both promptly and economically, several bushels of potatoes, roots of every kind, and in fact anything heaped on the hurdle and covered by the cask, whether intended as food for man or beast: and all this would cook in a sixth of the time, and with a sixth of the fuel required just to bring a cauldron of twenty gallons of water to the boil.

I believe that this simple device can be usefully employed in any house containing a sizeable copper, whether in town or country; and for that reason I have described it in detail, so that anyone may learn and profit by it.

I also believe that not nearly enough use is made of steam-power for household purposes, and I earnestly hope that one day the bulletin of the Society for Encouragement will inform the agricultural world that the subject has already occupied my attention.

p.s. One day, at a Professorial committee meeting at No. 14 rue de la Paix, I related the true story of the steamed turbot. When I had finished, my neighbour on the left turned to me and said reproachfully: 'Was I not there myself? And did I not join in the chorus of approval?'

'Certainly,' I replied, 'you were there, next to the curé, and you played your part in an irreproachable manner; do not imagine that . . .'

The plaintiff was Monsieur Lorrain, a remarkably sensitive degustator and a financier both amiable and wise, who has tied up in port the better to gauge the effects of the storm, and is thus worthy in more respects than one of a first-class nomination.

10. Three Fortifying Prescriptions Devised by the Professor to Meet the Case of Meditation

I

Chop up six large onions, three carrots, and a handful of parsley, place in a casserole with a piece of best fresh butter, and heat until brown.

When this mixture is ready, add six ounces of sugar-candy, twenty grains of powdered amber, a piece of toast, and three bottles of water; boil for three quarters of an hour, adding fresh water to replace what is lost in boiling, so that the volume of liquid remains the same.

Meanwhile, kill, pluck, and clean an old cock, and pound it in a mortar, flesh and bone, with an iron pestle; also mince two pounds of the best beef.

This done, mix these two kinds of meat together, adding a sufficient quantity of salt and pepper.

Place in a casserole, on a hot fire, and heat well, adding a little fresh butter now and then, so as to fry the mixture well without allowing it to stick.

When it is browned, in other words, when the osmazome is roasted, strain the broth in the first casserole, and pour gradually into the second. When it is all poured in, let it boil well for three quarters of an hour, taking care again to add enough hot water to keep up the level of the liquid.

At the end of that time the operation is complete, and you have a draught which is invariably effective, provided that the patient's stomach, despite a general weakness due to one of the causes I have mentioned, is still in good working order.

The instructions for use are as follows: on the first day, a cupful every three hours, until the patient goes to sleep at night; on each succeeding day, one large cupful in the morning, and the same night, until the three bottles are exhausted. If the patient is kept on a light but nutritious diet, such as leg of chicken, fish, sweet fruit, and preserves, it will only very rarely be found necessary to repeat the treatment. On the fourth day he will be able to resume his ordinary occupations, and must try to live more prudently in the future, *if possible*.

If the amber and sugar-candy are left out, a very savoury soup can be obtained by this process, a soup worthy to grace a dinner of connoisseurs.

Four old partridges can be substituted for the old cock, and a piece of leg of mutton for the beef; the preparation will be neither less effective nor less agreeable as a result.

The method of mincing the meat and browning it before adding the liquid can be used on all occasions when time is short. It is based on the fact that meat treated in that way reaches a much higher degree of heat than when it is placed in water; it may therefore be employed whenever a good rich soup is required, without the necessity of waiting five or six hours for it, as often happens, especially in the country. It goes without saying that nobody who resorts to this method will fail to glorify the Professor.

II

It is well for everyone to know that though amber, considered as a perfume, may be bad for those of the profane who have delicate nerves, taken internally it is a supremely exhilarating tonic; our forefathers used it freely in their cooking, and were never any the worse for it.

I have been told that Marshal de Richelieu, of glorious memory, was in the habit of sucking amber lozenges; and for my part, on days when the burden of age seems more than usually heavy, when thought is a labour and some unknown force weighs upon me, I mix into a cup of strong chocolate as much amber, pounded with sugar, as would make a lump the size of a bean, and always find that I feel better for it. By means of this tonic, the action of life is made easy, thought flows freely, and I do not experience the insomnia which would infallibly follow a cup of coffee taken with the intention of producing the same effect.

III

Prescription 1 is intended for robust constitutions, strong characters, and for those in general whose exhaustion is due to excessive activity.

I once had occasion to devise another prescription, far pleasanter to the taste and milder in its effects, which I reserve for weak constitutions and indecisive characters – in a word, for those who are easily exhausted; it is as follows:

Take a knuckle of veal weighing at least two pounds, split in four lengthwise, flesh and bone, and brown with four sliced onions and a handful of watercress; when it is nearly done, pour on three bottles of water and boil for two hours, taking care to replenish what is lost by evaporation, and you will have an excellent veal broth; add a modest quantity of pepper and salt.

Pound separately three old pigeons and twenty-five live crayfish; mix and brown as described in 1, and when you see that the heat has penetrated the mixture, and that it is beginning to stick, pour on the veal broth and stoke the fire well for one hour. Then strain the enriched broth, which may be taken by the patient morning and evening, or preferably in the morning only, two hours before breakfast. It also makes a delicious soup.

I was induced to devise this last prescription by a pair of writers who, seeing me in a fairly positive mood, put their trust in me, and, as they said, had recourse to my lights.

They followed the treatment, and had no reason to regret it. The poet, who before had been simply elegiac, turned romantic; the lady, who had only a rather insipid novel with a catastrophic ending to her credit, wrote another and much better one, which ended with a happy marriage. It can be seen that in each case there was an increase of power, and I believe, in all conscience, I may claim a little of the credit for that.

11. The Bresse Chicken

On one of the first days of January this present year, 1825, a young married couple, Monsieur and Madame de Versy by name, were guests at an oyster breakfast.

Such meals are charming, not only because they are composed of tempting dishes, but also because of the gaiety which usually distinguishes them; however, they have the disadvantage of upsetting the rest of the day's arrangements. This was the case on the present occasion. When dinner-time arrived, the pair sat down at table; but it was a mere formality. Madame took a little soup, Monsieur drank a glass of wine and water; some friends dropped in, a game of whist was played, the evening drew to a close, and the couple retired to their bed.

About two o'clock in the morning, Monsieur de Versy awoke, feeling restless; he yawned, and tossed and turned so much that his wife grew alarmed, and asked if he was unwell. 'No, my dear, but I appear to be hungry; I was thinking of that beautiful white Bresse chicken which we were offered for dinner and to which we gave such a cold reception.' 'My dear, to tell the truth, I am as hungry as you are, and now that you have thought of that chicken it must be sent for and eaten.' 'What an idea! The whole house is asleep, and tomorrow everybody will laugh at us.' 'If the whole house is asleep, the whole house must wake up, and we shall not be laughed at for the simple reason that no one will know about it. Besides, who knows if between now and tomorrow one of us may not starve to death? I don't intend running that risk. I'm going to ring for Justine.'

No sooner said than done; and the poor girl, who had supped well and was sleeping as only those can sleep who are nineteen years old and untroubled by love,[1] was duly awakened.

She arrived all untidy and bleary-eyed, and sat down yawning and stretching her arms.

But this had been an easy task; it still remained to rouse the cook, and that was no small matter; she grumbled, neighed, growled, roared, and snorted. In the end, however, she got out of bed and set her vast circumference in motion.

In the meantime Madame de Versy had put on a dressing-jacket, her husband had made himself presentable, while Justine had spread a cloth on the bed, and brought in the indispensable accessories to an improvised feast.

When everything was ready, the chicken appeared, to be torn apart on the spot and remorselessly devoured.

After this first exploit, husband and wife shared a large Saint-Germain pear, and ate some orange marmalade.

In the intervals they drained a bottle of Graves wine to the dregs, and declared several times, with variations, that they had never had a more delightful meal.

However, this meal came to an end, as all things must in this world. Justine cleared away the incriminating evidence, and went back to bed; and the conjugal curtain fell upon the participants in the feast.

Next morning, Madame de Versy hurried round to see her friend Madame de Franval, and recounted all that had happened in the night; and it is to that lady's indiscretion that the public owes the present revelation.

She never fails to add that when Madame de Versy came to the end of her story, she coughed twice and blushed furiously.

1. *A pierna tendida* (Spanish).

12. Pheasant

The pheasant is an enigma, the answer to which is revealed only to the initiate; they alone can savour it in all its excellence.

Every substance has its esculent apogee; some attain it before they reach their full development, such as capers, asparagus, grey partridges, spoon-fed pigeons, etc.; some when they reach their natural prime, such as melons, most kinds of fruit, mutton, beef, venison, and red partridges; and some when they begin to decompose, such as medlars, woodcock, and, above all, pheasant.

This last bird, eaten within three days of its death, has an undistinguished taste. It is neither as delicate as a fowl, nor as fragrant as a quail.

Cooked at the right time, its flesh is tender, sublime, and tasty, for it partakes of both poultry and venison.

This desirable stage is reached just as the pheasant begins to decompose; only then does its fragrance develop, combining with an oil which, to be formed, requires a period of fermentation, like the oil of coffee, which is only obtained by roasting.

This moment is made manifest to the senses of the profane by a faint odour, and by a change in the bird's belly; but the inspired few divine it by a sort of instinct which moves them on certain occasions, as, for example, when a skilled cook decides at a glance to take a fowl from the spit or to leave it for a few more turns.

As soon as the pheasant has reached this stage, but no sooner, it is plucked and carefully larded with the freshest and crispest bacon.

It is not for nothing that we say that the pheasant must not be plucked too soon; careful experiments have shown that those kept in feather are much more fragrant than those which have been kept plucked for a long time, either because contact with the air neutralizes part of the flavour, or because a part of the juice which nourishes the feathers is reabsorbed, and helps to enrich the flesh.

After the bird has been plucked and larded, it is now ready to be stuffed; and this is done in the following way:

Have ready a brace of woodcock; bone and draw them, laying the liver and entrails on one side and the flesh on the other.

Take the flesh, and mince it with steamed ox-marrow, a little grated bacon, pepper, salt, herbs, and a sufficient quantity of good truffles to produce enough stuffing to fill the interior of the pheasant.

You will be careful to insert the stuffing in such a way that it cannot escape; quite a difficult business sometimes, when the bird is fairly high. There are various methods, however, one of which is to tie a crust of bread over the opening with a piece of thread, so that it serves as a stopper.

Then cut a slice of bread two inches longer at each end than the pheasant laid lengthwise; take the woodcocks' livers and entrails, and pound with two large truffles, an anchovy, a little grated bacon, and a piece of good fresh butter.

Spread this paste evenly over the bread, and place it beneath the pheasant prepared as above, so that it is thoroughly soaked with all the juice which exudes from the bird while it is roasting.

When the pheasant is cooked, serve it up gracefully reclining on its bed of toast; surround it with bitter oranges, and have no fear of the result.

This savoury dish is best washed down with good wine from Upper Burgundy; I derived this truth from a series of observations which cost me more trouble than a table of logarithms.

A pheasant cooked in this way would be worthy to set before angels, if they still walked the earth as in the days of Lot.

But what am I saying? The thing has been done. A stuffed

pheasant was prepared before my very eyes by the good chef Picard, at the Château de la Grange, the home of my charming friend Madame de Ville-Plaine, and carried to the table by her steward Louis, stepping with processional dignity. It was as carefully scrutinized as one of Madame Herbault's hats; it was studiously savoured; and throughout this learned work the ladies' eyes shone like stars, their lips gleamed like coral, and their faces were pictures of ecstasy. (See my *Gastronomical Tests*.)

I have done more: I have offered such a dish to a group of judges of the Supreme Court, who know that it is sometimes necessary to lay aside the senatorial toga, and to whom I proved without much trouble that good cheer is Nature's compensation for the cares of the bench.

After careful consideration the President announced in a grave voice the word *Excellent*! All heads bowed in agreement, and the verdict was unanimous.

I had observed, during the period of deliberation, that the noses of those venerable men were agitated by marked olfactory twitchings, that their august brows shone with calm serenity, and that about the corners of each judicial mouth there played something which might almost have been a smile.

But these remarkable effects are in the nature of things. For a pheasant cooked in accordance with the foregoing recipe, already distinguished enough in itself, is impregnated from outside by the savoury juices of the roasting bacon, while from inside it absorbs the fragrant gases given off by the woodcock and truffles. Meanwhile, the toast, richly garnished already, is also soaked with the three varieties of gravy which exude from the roasting bird.

Thus of all the good things brought together, not a single particle escapes appreciation; and such is the virtue of this dish that I consider it worthy of the most august of tables.

Parve, nec invideo, sine me liber ibis in aulam.[1]

1. 'Little book, you'll go without me to the palace, nor do I grudge you this.' [Ed.]

13. Gastronomical Industry of the Émigrés

> In all of France, by hook or crook,
> You'll find no lass who cannot cook.
>
> *Belle Arsène, Act* III.

In an earlier chapter I revealed the enormous advantages France derived from gourmandism in the circumstances of 1815. The same national talent proved no less useful to the *émigrés*; and those among them who had a gift for the alimentary art found it of immense value to them.

While I was in Boston, I taught the restaurateur Jullien[1] how to scramble eggs with cheese. This dish was new to the Americans, and became so much the rage that Jullien, in payment of his debt of gratitude to me, sent me, in New York, the rump of one of those delicious little roe-deer which are shot in Canada in the winter, which was pronounced excellent by the chosen company I convened for the occasion.

Captain Collet was another who made a great deal of money in New York in 1794 and 1795, from the ices which he made for the citizens of that mercantile community. The women in particular found so novel a delicacy irresistible, and nothing could be more amusing than the little grimaces they made when eating them. They were at a loss to understand how anything could be kept so cold in a temperature of ninety degrees.

I remember meeting a Breton gentleman in Cologne who had done very well for himself as a restaurateur; and I could go on citing examples of this kind indefinitely; but I prefer to relate, as being rather more peculiar, the story of a Frenchman who made his fortune in London through his skill in mixing salad.

He was a Limousin, and his name, if I remember aright, was d'Aubignac or d'Albignac.

---

1. Jullien was prospering in 1794. He was an able fellow, who claimed to have been cook to the Archbishop of Bordeaux. If God spared him, he must have made a considerable fortune.

One day, although his expenditure on food was considerably restricted by his straitened circumstances, he went to dine in one of the most celebrated London taverns; for he was among those who maintain that a man can dine well off a single dish, provided that dish is an excellent one.

He was finishing a plate of succulent roast beef when one of a party of young men of good family, who were dining at a neighbouring table, got up, came over to him, and said politely: 'Mr Frenchman, your countrymen are said to excel in the art of salad-making; would you do my friends and myself the favour of mixing one for us?'

D'Albignac consented after a little hesitation, called for what he considered necessary for the production of the required masterpiece, devoted every care to the task, and was fortunate enough to see his efforts crowned with success.

While measuring out his doses, he answered frankly the questions which were put to him about his situation; he explained that he was in exile, and confessed, not without blushing slightly, that he was in receipt of help from the English government: a circumstance which doubtless authorized one of the young men to slip a five-pound note into his hand, which, after a feeble show of resistance, he accepted.

He left his address with them, and was only mildly surprised when a few days later he received a letter begging him, in the warmest terms, to come and mix a salad at one of the finest mansions in Grosvenor Square.

Seeing a chance of lasting profit, d'Albignac did not hesitate for a moment, and arrived punctually at his destination, armed with a few new seasonings which he considered likely to bring his work to a higher degree of perfection.

He had had time to ponder on the task he had to perform; accordingly, his efforts were again successful, and on this occasion he received a gratification so generous that in his own interest he could not have refused it.

The young men for whom he had first officiated had, it may be presumed, extolled almost to the point of exaggeration the virtues of the salad he had seasoned for them. The second company were still louder in their approval, so that d'Albignac's fame spread rapidly; he became known as the 'fashionable salad-maker', and in that land which is always avid for novelty, all the most elegant personages in the capital of the three kingdoms were soon dying for a salad of the French gentleman's making. 'I am dying for it' is the time-honoured expression:

> Hot is the ardour of a nun's desire,
> But nothing to an Englishwoman's fire.

D'Albignac, as a wise man, profited by the infatuation of which he became the object; he soon had a carriage to convey him more quickly to the various places where he was summoned, and a servant carrying in a mahogany case all the ingredients he had added to his repertory, such as different sorts of vinegar, oils with or without fruity flavour, soy, caviare, truffles, anchovies, ketchup, meat extracts, and even yolks of egg, which are the distinguishing feature of mayonnaise.

Later, he had similar cases manufactured, which he fitted out completely and sold by the hundred.

In the end, by following his chosen path carefully and consistently, he realized a fortune of over eighty thousand francs, which he brought to France with him when times had improved.

Back in his native land, he did not amuse himself adorning the streets of Paris, but preferred to make suitable provision for his future. He invested sixty thousand francs in government stock, which then stood at fifty, and with the remaining twenty thousand bought a modest estate in Limousin, where he is probably still living happy and contented, since he knows how to limit his desires.

These details were given to me some time ago by a friend of mine who had known d'Albignac in London, and had met him again during his stay in Paris.

14. More Memories of Exile

The Weaver

In 1794 Monsieur Rostaing[1] and I were in Switzerland, showing a calm face to adversity, and preserving our love for the homeland which was persecuting us.

We came to Mondon, where I had some relatives, and were taken in by the Trolliet family with a kindness I have always remembered with gratitude.

This family, one of the oldest in the country, is now extinct, the last male representative having left only a daughter, who herself has borne no sons.

At Mondon a young French officer was pointed out to me who plied the trade of weaver; and this is how he came to do so.

He was a young man of very good family, and passing through Mondon on his way to join Condé's army, found himself sitting at table next to an old man whose features displayed that combination of gravity and animation which painters give to the comrades of William Tell.

Over dessert they talked; the officer made no secret of his position, and received several marks of interest from his neighbour, who sympathized with him for being forced, so early in life, to give up all that was dearest to him, and drew his attention to the justice of Rousseau's maxim, to the effect that every man should learn a trade to fall back on in adversity and earn his living anywhere. As for himself, he declared that he was a weaver, a childless widower, and contented with his lot.

There the conversation ended; the officer left the next

1. Baron Rostaing, my relative and friend, now Military Governor of Lyons. A first-class administrator, he has perfected a system of military accountancy so clear that it is bound to be adopted in time.

day, and shortly afterwards took his place in the ranks of Condé's army. But from what he saw both inside and outside the army, he realized that he could never hope to return to France by that door. It was not long before he underwent some of those unpleasant experiences which sometimes befell men who had no qualification apart from their zeal for the royal cause; and later on he was made the victim of a piece of favouritism, or something of the sort, which seemed to him a crying injustice.

Then the old weaver's advice came back to him; he pondered over it for a while, and then, having made up his mind, left the army, returned to Mondon, called on the weaver, and asked to be taken on as his apprentice.

'I will not miss this chance of doing a good deed,' the old man answered. 'You shall eat at my table; I know only one thing, and that I will teach you; I have only one bed, and that you shall share with me; you shall work like that for a year, and after that you shall set up on your own account, and live happily in a land where work is honoured and encouraged.'

The very next day, the officer set to work, and succeeded so well that at the end of six months his master declared that he had nothing more to teach him, that he considered himself sufficiently repaid for the care he had taken of him, and that henceforth whatever he did should be to his own profit.

When I came to Mondon, the new artisan had already earned enough money to buy himself a loom and a bed; he worked with remarkable assiduity, and so much interest was taken in him that the best houses in the town had come to an arrangement to ask him to dinner by turns every Sunday.

On that day he donned his uniform and resumed his rightful position in society; and as he was both charming and intelligent, everybody made much of him. But on Mondays he turned weaver again, and having grown accustomed to this dual way of life, seemed not dissatisfied with his lot.

The Faster

To this picture of the advantages of industry I am going to add another of a directly opposite kind.

I met in Lausanne an *émigré* from Lyons, a tall and hand-some youth, who in order to avoid work had hit upon the idea of only eating twice a week. He would have starved to death with the best grace in the world if a worthy merchant of the town had not opened a credit for him at a tavern, where he was allowed to dine free on Sunday and Wednesday every week.

On each of these days the exile would enter the tavern, stuff himself to the oesophagus, and take his leave, not with-out carrying off a fairly large piece of bread, which he was allowed to do under the terms of the agreement.

This supplementary fare he husbanded as best he could, drinking water when his stomach hurt him, and spending part of his time in bed in a not unpleasant state of som-nolence, until the time came for his next meal.

When I met him, he had been living like this for three months; he was not ill, but there was such an air of languor about all his person, his features were so drawn, and there was something so Hippocratical about the space between his nose and ears, that he was painful to behold.

I marvelled that he should submit to such anguish rather than use the resources of his person, and invited him to din-ner at my inn, when he acquitted himself in an awe-inspiring manner. But I never repeated the offence, because I prefer a man to fight against adversity, and to comply, when necess-ary, with the sentence passed on the whole human race: *Thou shalt work.*

The Lion d'Argent

What good dinners we had in those days at Lausanne, at the Lion d'Argent!

For the sum of fifteen batz (2 fr. 25 c.) we could enjoy three full courses, including excellent game from the surrounding mountains and delicious fish from Lake Geneva, all of which we humectated with as much as we pleased of an ordinary white wine, as limpid as rock-water, which would have made even a madman drink.

The top end of the table was always occupied by a canon of Notre-Dame de Paris (I hope he is still alive), who had made himself at home there, and in front of whom the *Kellner* never failed to place whatever was best on the menu.

He did me the honour of picking me out and summoning me to his side, in the capacity of aide-de-camp; but I had not enjoyed this distinction for long before the tide of events swept me off to America, where I found refuge, work, and peace.

Stay in America

. . . .

Battle

I will close this chapter with the story of an experience of mine which proves that nothing is sure in this world of ours and that misfortune sometimes overtakes us at the very moment when we least expect it.

I was leaving for France after a stay of three years in the United States; and my time there had gone so pleasantly that all I asked of heaven (and my prayer was answered), in the emotion of departure, was that I might be no unhappier in the Old World than I had been in the New.

The happiness I enjoyed there was chiefly due to the fact that from the day of my arrival among the Americans, I spoke their language,[1] dressed like them, took care not to be

---

1. I sat next to a Creole one day at dinner, who had been living in New York for two years and still did not know enough English to be able to ask for bread. I expressed my astonishment at this. 'Bah,' he replied, shrugging his shoulders, 'do you think I am fool enough to take the trouble to learn the language of such a gloomy people?'

wittier than they, and praised all their ways; thus repaying the hospitality they showed me by a form of condescension which I consider essential and which I commend to all who may find themselves in a similar position.

I was therefore leaving in peaceful fashion a land where I had lived at peace with all men, and there could have been no featherless biped in all creation whose love for his fellows was more real than mine, when there occurred an incident, quite independent of my will, which came very close to involving me in tragedy.

I was on board the steamer which was to take me from New York to Philadelphia; and you must know that in order to make this journey safely, it is necessary to profit by the turn of the tide.

It was slack water then, that is to say, the tide was about to ebb, so that the time had come to start; yet there was no sign of any movement being made to cast off.

There were a great many of us Frenchmen aboard, including a certain Gautier, who should still be living in Paris: a good fellow who ruined himself in his attempts to build *ultra vires* the house which forms the south-western corner of the Ministry of Finance.

The cause of the delay was soon made known to us: it was due to the non-arrival of two Americans, for whose benefit the ship was being held back, although this exposed us to the risk of being caught by low tide, and thus taking twice as long to reach our destination; for the sea waits for no man.

Hence loud complaints, chiefly from the French; for a Frenchman's passions are much fiercer than those of the inhabitants of the farther shores of the Atlantic.

I myself not only took no part in the outcry, but scarcely noticed it, for my heart was full of sorrow and I was wondering what Fate held in store for me in France. But soon I heard a crash, and saw that it came from Gautier's giving an American cheek a slap which would have felled a rhinoceros.

This act of violence produced absolute bedlam. The

words *Frenchmen* and *Americans* having been uttered several times in anger, the quarrel assumed a national character; and somebody proposed nothing less than to throw us all into the sea: a difficult undertaking, I might add, for there were eight of us against eleven of them.

Now I, to all appearances, was the one who seemed likely to offer the most resistance to *transboardation*; for I am tall and broad, and was then only thirty-nine. That was doubtless why the enemy decided to launch against me their most imposing warrior, who now came and squared up to me.

He was as tall as a steeple, and proportionately heavy; but sizing him up with a marrow-piercing glance, I saw that he was of a lymphatic temperament, that his face was puffy, his eyes dull, his head small, and his legs like a woman's.

'*Mens non agitat molem*,' I said to myself; 'let us see what he's made of, and then die if need be.' And aloud I addressed him as follows, like one of Homer's heroes:

'Do you[1] think you can bully me, you damned rogue? By God, you'll do no such thing ... I'll throw you overboard like a dead cat ... If I find you too heavy, I'll cling to you with hands, legs, teeth, nails, everything, and if I can't do any better, we'll sink together to the bottom. I would give my life gladly to send a dog like you to hell. Now let's go! ...'[2]

Hearing these words, which were doubtless matched by my bearing (for I felt the strength of Hercules in me), my man shrank a full inch, his arms fell to his sides, and his cheeks sagged; in a word, he displayed such obvious signs of fear that one of his comrades – probably the one who had pushed him forward – made as if to intervene; and he did well, for I was thoroughly roused, and that native of the

---

1. There is no thee-ing and thou-ing in English; even a carter whipping his horse will shout: 'Go, sir; go, sir, I say.'

2. In lands governed under English law, assault is always preceded by an exchange of insults; for the English have a saying, 'High words break no bones.' Frequently this is as far as it goes, and the law makes a man think twice before striking; for he who strikes the first blow breaks the peace, and will always be condemned to pay a penalty, whatever the result of the fight.

New World was on the point of discovering that those who bathe in the waters of the Furens[1] have sinews of steel.

Meanwhile a few words of peace had begun to be heard in the other part of the ship; the arrival of the latecomers caused a diversion, and the seamen had to see to the business of setting sail; so that while I was still in warlike posture the tumult suddenly ceased.

Matters even improved; for when all was quiet again I went to look for Gautier, intending to rebuke him for his quick temper, and found him at table with his victim, in the presence of a splendid ham and a pitcher of beer which stood a cubit high.

1. A limpid river which, rising above Rossilon, passes close to Belley and joins the Rhône above Peyrieux. The flesh of the trout caught in it is pink, that of the pike as white as ivory. *Gut! Gut! Gut!* (German).

15. The Bundle of Asparagus

One fine day in the month of February, walking through the Palais-Royal, I stopped before the shop of Madame Chevet, the most famous provision-merchant in Paris, who has always been extremely kind to me; and noticing a bundle of asparagus, the thinnest of which was fatter than my index finger, I asked her the price of it. 'Forty francs, Monsieur,' she replied. 'They are certainly very fine, but at such a price no one but the King or some prince will be able to eat them.' 'You are mistaken; such luxuries never find their way into palaces; what kings and princes want is goodness, not magnificence but for all that, my bundle of asparagus will sell, and this is how it will happen.

'At the present moment there are at least three hundred rich men in Paris, bankers, capitalists, merchants, and others, who are kept at home by gout, fear of catching cold, doctor's orders, or other causes which do not prevent them from eating; they sit by the fire, racking their brains to think of something to tempt their appetite, and when they have tired themselves out to no purpose, they send their valet out on the same quest. The valet will come to me, see the asparagus, and return with his report; and they will be sent for at once no matter what the price. Or perhaps a pretty woman will pass this way with her lover, and say to him: "Look, my dear, what lovely asparagus! Do let us buy them! You know what delicious sauce my maid makes for them!" Well in such a case no lover worth his salt will refuse or bargain. Or it may be a wager, or a baptism, or a sudden rise in Government stock. How am I to tell? In a word, the dearest things go more quickly than anything else, because in Paris the course of life brings about so many extraordinary circumstances that there is always some justification for them.'

As she was talking, two fat Englishmen, who were strolling by arm in arm, stopped in front of us, and immediately their faces lit up with admiration. One of them had the miraculous bundle wrapped up without so much as asking the price, paid for it, tucked it under his arm, and carried it off, whistling 'God Save the King'.

'There, Monsieur,' said Madame Chevet with a laugh, 'there you have a possibility which I hadn't mentioned, but which is as common as any of the others.'

16. The Fondue

The *fondue* originated in Switzerland, and is nothing more nor less than eggs scrambled with cheese, in certain proportions revealed by time and experience. I shall give my readers the official recipe a little later.

It is a wholesome, savoury, appetizing dish, and being quickly cooked, is always useful when guests arrive unexpectedly. But I am only writing about it here for my own satisfaction, and because the word recalls an incident still talked of by the old people of Belley.

About the end of the seventeenth century, a certain Monsieur de Madot was nominated to the see of Belley, and arrived to take up his appointment.

Those whose function it was to receive him and do him the honours of his palace had prepared a feast worthy of the occasion, and had drawn upon all the culinary resources of the day to celebrate His Grace's advent.

Among the side-dishes shone a copious *fondue*, to which His Grace freely helped himself. But to everyone's surprise, deceived by its exterior, he mistook it for a *crème* and ate it with a spoon, instead of using the fork employed for that purpose since time immemorial.

All the guests, astounded by this curious behaviour, glanced at one another out of the corners of their eyes, smiling imperceptibly. Respect, however, tied all tongues, for a bishop from Paris can do nothing at table that is not well done, particularly on the day of his arrival.

But the incident was noised abroad, and the very next day, whenever two people met, the first would ask: 'Have you heard how the new bishop ate his *fondue* last night?' 'I have indeed,' the other would reply; 'he ate it with a spoon. I had it from an eye-witness.' The town told the story to the country; and by the end of three months it was common knowledge throughout the diocese.

The remarkable thing is that the incident did not shake the faith of our fathers. There were a few innovators who spoke up in favour of the spoon; but they were soon forgotten; the fork triumphed, and more than a hundred years later one of my great-uncles could still enjoy the joke, and would laugh uproariously as he told me how Monsieur de Madot had once eaten *fondue* with a spoon.

Recipe for Making Fondue

As found among the papers of Monsieur Trollet, steward of Mondon, in the Canton of Berne.

Take as many eggs as are required for the number of your guests, and weigh them.

Next take a piece of good Gruyère cheese weighing a third, and a piece of butter weighing a sixth, of that weight.

Break and beat up the eggs in a casserole; after which, add the cheese, grated or sliced, and the butter.

Set the casserole over a brisk fire, and stir with a wooden spoon until the mixture is suitably thick and soft; put in a little salt, or none, according to whether the cheese is more or less old, and a strong dose of pepper, which is one of the essential features of this ancient preparation; serve in a lightly warmed dish, send for your best wine, drink it down, and you will see wonders.

17. Disappointment

All was quiet one day in the Écu de France inn at Bourg-en-Bresse, when suddenly a loud rumble of wheels was heard, and a superb berlin in the English style drove up, drawn by four horses, and particularly remarkable for the presence on the coachman's seat of two very pretty chambermaids, snugly enveloped in a rug of scarlet cloth, lined and edged in blue.

At this sight, which indicated a milord travelling by short stages, Chicot (for that was the innkeeper's name) ran out cap in hand; his wife stood waiting on the doorstep; the maids nearly broke their necks hurrying downstairs, and the stable-lads ran up, already counting on a generous tip.

The two chambermaids were helped down from their perch, not without blushing a little, on account of the difficulties of the descent; and the berlin brought forth, first, a short, fat, red-faced, paunchy milord; second, two long, pale, red-haired misses, and third, a milady who seemed to be between the first and second stages of consumption.

It was milady who spoke up for the party.

'Innkeeper,' she said, 'let my horses be well cared for; show us to a room where we can rest, and have some refreshments served to my chambermaids; but I wish the whole to cost not more than six francs; take your measures accordingly.'

This economical phrase had no sooner been uttered than Chicot put on his cap again, his wife withdrew indoors, and the maids returned to their posts.

The horses were led to the stable, where they were allowed to watch the other animals feed; the ladies were shown into a room upstairs; and the two chambermaids were provided with glasses and a jug of the purest water.

The six francs stipulated by milady were received sourly as a paltry recompense for all the trouble caused and the hopes dashed to the ground.

18. Wonderful Effect of a Classic Dinner

'Alas, how am I to be pitied!' said a Gastronome of the royal court of the Seine in elegiac tones. 'Hoping to return shortly to my country house, I left my cook there; now business keeps me in Paris, and I am left at the mercy of an officious maidservant whose cooking turns my stomach. My wife will put up with anything, and my children are too young to understand. What with *bouilli* underdone, and roast overdone, I'm dying by both spit and cauldron!'

So he spoke as he sadly crossed the Place Dauphine. Fortunately for the public weal, the Professor overheard his just complaint, and in the plaintiff recognized a friend. 'You shall not die, my dear fellow,' he told the martyred magistrate; 'no, you shall not die of a malady for which I can offer you the remedy. Be my guest tomorrow at a classic dinner, with a few friends; after dinner, we shall have a game of piquet which we shall arrange in such a way that everyone is amused, and so, like all its predecessors, the evening will disappear into the gulf of the past.'

The invitation was accepted, and the mystery accomplished in accordance with the traditional customs, rites and ceremonies; and since that day (23 June 1825) the Professor has been happy to think that he has preserved for the royal court one of the worthiest of its pillars.

19. The Dangerous Effects of Strong Liquor

The factitious thirst which we mentioned in Meditation 8, the thirst which demands to be momentarily allayed with strong liquor, becomes in time so intense and habitual that those who give way to it cannot spend a single night without drinking, and are obliged to leave their beds to slake it.

Such a thirst then becomes an absolute disease, and when an individual has reached that point, it may be confidently prophesied that less than two years of life are left to him.

I was once travelling in Holland with a rich merchant from Danzig who for fifty years had managed the largest brandy shop in that town.

'Monsieur,' this patriarch said to me one day, 'you in France have no idea of the size of the business we have been doing, from father to son, for more than a century. I have closely observed the workmen who come to my shop, and when they give in completely to the craving for strong liquor, which is all too common in Germany, they all come to an end in much the same way.

'At first they only drink a small glass of brandy in the morning, and that amount satisfies them for several years (for I should explain that that habit is universal among the working classes, and any man who went without his glass of brandy would be shunned by his comrades); then they double the dose, that is to say, they drink a small glass in the morning and another at noon. They continue at that rate for two or three years; then they take to drinking regularly three times a day, morning, noon, and evening. Soon they are drinking at all hours, and will have nothing but brandy flavoured with an infusion of cloves: once that stage is reached, it is certain that they have six months to live at the outside; they dry up, fever takes hold of them, they go into hospital, and they are never seen again.'

20. The Chevaliers and the Abbés

I have already referred twice to these two categories of gourmand which have been destroyed by time.

It is over thirty years since they disappeared, so that the greater part of the present generation have never seen them.

They will probably appear again towards the end of this century; but as such a phenomenon requires the coincidence of a great many future circumstances, I believe that very few persons now alive will survive to witness that palingenesis.

It therefore behoves me, in my capacity as a painter of manners and customs, to put the finishing touches to my picture of them; and to do this more easily I have borrowed the following passage from an author who can refuse me nothing:

Strictly speaking, and according to precedent, the qualification of Chevalier should only have been granted to persons decorated with an order, or to the younger sons of titled families; but in fact many chevaliers had found it in their interest to give themselves the accolade; for if the bearer of the title was well bred and of good appearance, so easy-going were the times, that no one ever troubled to investigate his right to it.

The chevaliers were usually fine figures of men; they wore their swords vertical, and strutted along with their heads held high and their noses in the air; they were gamesters, libertines, and brawlers, and no fashionable beauty's suite was complete without them.

They were further distinguished for their extreme courage and the excessive ease with which they drew their swords. Sometimes it was only necessary to look at them, to be challenged to a duel.

So it was that the Chevalier de S—, one of the most notorious of his time, met his end.

He had picked a gratuitous quarrel with a young man newly arrived from Charolles; and the pair had gone to fight at the back of the Chaussée-d'Antin, which at that time was almost all waste ground.

By the way in which the newcomer put himself on guard, S—saw that this was no novice he had to deal with; none the less, he set about putting him to the test; but at the very first pass the Charollais feinted, and then thrust home to such effect that the Chevalier was dead before he hit the ground. One of his friends, who had been his second, silently examined the wound made by that lightning thrust and the course followed by the sword. 'What a perfect thrust in carte,' he said suddenly, walking away, 'and what a wrist that young man must have!' The dead man received no other funeral oration.

When the wars of the Revolution broke out, most of the chevaliers joined one or other of the battalions; others emigrated, and the rest were lost in the crowd. The survivors, who are few in number, may still be recognized by the way they hold their heads, but they are very thin, and walk with difficulty; they have the gout.

When there were a great many sons in a noble family, one was destined for the Church; to begin with he would be granted simple benefices to defray the costs of his education; and later he would become a prince, commendatory abbé, or bishop, according to the degree of his apostolic fervour.

Such was the genuine abbé; but there were also false ones; and many a young man of means, considering a chevalier's career to be too dangerous, gave himself the title of *abbé* when he came to Paris.

Nothing could be more convenient: at the cost of a slight alteration in his appearance he took on the semblance of a beneficed priest; whereupon he became anybody's equal, and was welcomed everywhere, spoiled and sought after; for there was never a house without its abbé.

The abbés were short, plump little men, neatly dressed, amiable, complaisant, full of curiosity, fond of good food, lively and insinuating; those who are left have run to fat and turned very pious.

No life could be pleasanter than that of a rich prior or commendatory abbé; he had position, money, no superiors, and nothing to do.

The chevaliers will reappear if peace lasts a long time, as we have reason to hope it will; but failing a drastic change in ecclesiastical administration, the race of abbés is lost beyond recall; there are no longer any sinecures; and we have returned to the principles of the primitive church: *beneficium propter officium.*

21. Odds and Ends

'Counsellor,' said an old marquise of the Faubourg
Saint-Germain one day, speaking from one end of the table
to the other, 'which do you prefer, Burgundy or claret?'
'Madame,' replied the magistrate in druidic tones, 'that is a
case in which I enjoy examining the evidence so much that I
invariably postpone judgement for a week.'

At the table of a denizen of the Chaussée-d'Antin, there
was served up an Arles sausage of heroic size. 'Please accept a
slice,' said the host to his fair neighbour; 'this is a dish
which, I hope, proclaims a well-stocked house.' 'It is big
enough, certainly,' replied the lady, eyeing it slyly through
her quizzing-glass; 'what a pity that it looks like nothing on
earth!'

It is chiefly people of intelligence who hold gourmandism
in highest esteem; others are incapable of an operation
which consists of a series of judgements and appreciations.

Madame la Comtesse de Genlis boasts, in her Memoirs, of
having taught a German lady who had received her well the
method of preparing as many as seven delicious dishes.

It was Monsieur le Comte de la Place who discovered a
very special way of treating strawberries, by moistening
them with the juice of a sweet orange (the apple of the Hes-
perides).

Another savant has further improved on this recipe by
adding the outer rind of the orange, which he rubs off with a
lump of sugar; and he claims to have proved, through a
fragment of manuscript saved from the torches which destroyed the library of Alexandria, that this was the way
strawberries were seasoned at the banquets on Mount Ida.

'I don't think much of him,' said Monsieur le Comte de M—, speaking of a candidate who had recently obtained an official position; 'he has never eaten black pudding *à la Richelieu*, nor even heard of cutlets *à la Soubise*.'

A heavy drinker was offered grapes at dessert. 'No thank you,' he said, pushing the dish away from him.' 'I am not in the habit of taking my wine in the form of pills.'

A gourmand was being congratulated on his appointment as tax collector at Périgueux; his friends enlarged on the pleasant life he would lead in that paradise of good cheer, the country of truffles, partridges, truffled turkey, etc., etc. 'Alas,' said the melancholy gastronome, 'is it certain that a man can live at all, in a land where the tide never comes in?'

22. A Day with the Monks of St Bernard

It was nearly one o'clock on a fine summer's night when we formed a cavalcade, not without first vigorously serenading those fair ladies who had the good fortune to touch our hearts (this was in 1782).

We were setting out from Belley, and our destination was Saint-Sulpice, a Bernardine Abbey situated on one of the highest mountains in the neighbourhood, at least five thousand feet above sea-level.

In those days I was the leader of a troop of amateur musicians, all friends of joy, and endowed in full measure with all the virtues which go with youth and health.

'Monsieur,' said the Abbot of Saint-Sulpice to me one day, drawing me aside, after dinner, into a window-embrasure; 'you would be doing us a great kindness if you were to come and play for us on St. Bernard's Day; the saint would be all the more completely glorified, our monks would be delighted, and you would have the honour of being the first Orpheuses to penetrate to those lofty regions.'

I did not wait for him to repeat an invitation which held out such pleasant promise, but accepted with a nod which shook the whole room.

Annuit, et totum nutu tremefecit Olympum.[1]

All the necessary measures were taken beforehand, and we set out early; for we had four leagues to travel, along roads that might daunt even those bold explorers who have braved the heights of the lofty Montmartre.

The monastery was built in a valley enclosed to the west by the summit of the mountain, and to the east by a smaller hill.

The western peak was crowned by a forest of pine-trees,

1. 'He nodded, and made the whole of Olympus tremble assent.' [Ed.]

thirty-seven thousand of which were felled one day by a single gust of wind.[1] The bottom of the valley was a vast meadow, divided by clumps of beeches into irregular sections, like large-scale models of those little English gardens which are now so fashionable.

We arrived as day broke, and were greeted by the father cellarer, whose face was quadrangular and nose an obelisk.

'Gentlemen,' said the good father, 'you are very welcome; our reverend abbot will be glad to hear of your arrival; he is still in bed, for yesterday he was very tired; but come with me, and you shall see that we were expecting you.'

With these words he set off, and we followed, rightly suspecting that he was leading us to the refectory.

There all our senses were captivated by the most seductive of breakfasts, a truly classic breakfast.

In the middle of a spacious table stood a *pâté* as tall as a church; to the north it was flanked by a quarter of cold veal, to the south by a huge ham, to the east by a monumental wedge of butter, and to the west by a bushel of raw artichokes, seasoned with pepper and salt.

There were also different kinds of fruit, with plates, napkins, knives, and baskets of silver; and at one end of the table stood lay brothers and servants ready to wait on us, although surprised to find themselves up so early.

In a corner of the refectory we saw a pile of over a hundred bottles, continuously watered by a natural spring which seemed to murmur *Evoe Bacche* as it flowed; and if no smell of Mocha tickled our nostrils, that was because in those heroic times no one drank coffee early in the day.

For a while the reverend cellarer enjoyed our astonishment in silence; then he pronounced the following allocution, which we in our wisdom considered to have been prepared beforehand.

1. Superintendence of Waterways and Forests counted them and sold them; trade profited by the sale, the monks profited, large sums of money were put in circulation, and no one complained about the hurricane.

'Gentlemen!' he said, 'I would like to be able to keep you company; but I have not yet said my Mass, and today is a day full of solemnity. I would invite you to eat, but your youth, your journey here, and our keen mountain air combine to make the invitation superfluous. Accept with pleasure what we offer you with warm hearts. Now I leave you, and go to sing matins.'

With these words he left the room.

It was time for action; and we set to with all the vigour aroused by the three aggravating circumstances so truly indicated by the cellarer. But what could weak sons of Adam do against a meal apparently prepared for the inhabitants of Sirius? Our efforts were in vain; although we ate as much as we could hold, we left only imperceptible traces of our passage.

Then, well fortified till dinner-time, we dispersed; and I for one lay down on a comfortable bed, and went to sleep until it was time for Mass, like the hero of Rocroy and other warriors too who slept until the hour of battle.

I was roused by a muscular brother, who nearly pulled my arm out of its socket, and ran to the church, where I found everyone already at his post.

We performed a symphony during the offertory, sang a motet during the elevation, and finished up with a quartet for wind instruments. And despite all the jokes that are made against amateur music, respect for truth obliges me to state that we gave a very good account of ourselves.

Here let me remark that those who are never satisfied with anything are almost always ignoramuses who only criticize so loudly in the hope that their boldness will gain them credit for accomplishments they lack the courage to acquire.

On this occasion, we received with suitable grace the praises which were lavished on us, and, after the abbot had thanked us, went and sat down at table.

Dinner was served in the style of the fifteenth century, with few side-dishes, and few superfluities of any kind; but an excellent choice of meats and simple and substantial stews, well prepared and perfectly cooked, and above all served with vegetables of a savour unknown to the lowlands, combined to remove all desire for anything we could not see.

My readers will obtain some impression of the abundance prevailing in that excellent fair place, when I say that the second course comprised as many as fourteen different roasts.

Dessert was all the more remarkable in that it was partly composed of fruits which do not grow at that altitude, but which had been brought from the neighbouring valleys; the gardens of Machuraz, Morflent, and other places favoured by the starry source of heat, had been laid under contribution.

Nor was there any lack of liqueurs; but the coffee deserves a special mention.

It was limpid, scented, and wonderfully hot; but above all, it was served, not in those degenerate vessels which they dare, on the banks of the Seine, to call *cups*, but in beautifully deep bowls into which the worthy fathers plunged their thick lips at will, sucking up the life-giving liquid with a noise which would have done credit to two sperm whales fleeing before a storm.

After dinner we went to vespers, and between the psalms we performed antiphons composed by myself expressly for the occasion. They were in the musical style which prevailed at that time, and I shall speak neither ill nor well of them, for fear that I should be held back by modesty or swayed by a father's love.

The official day being thus brought to a close, the neighbours left to go home, and the monks settled down to play a few games together.

For my part, I preferred to go for a walk; and, collecting some of my friends, went out to tread that soft, firm turf which is worth all the carpets made in the Savonnerie, and to breathe that pure mountain air which refreshes a man's soul and turns his thoughts to meditation and romanticism.[1]

1. I have often experienced the same effect in similar circumstances,

It was late when we returned. The abbot came to wish me a good evening and a good night's rest. 'I am leaving you,' he said, 'to finish the evening without me. Not that I believe my presence would be irksome to our monks; but I wish them to know that they have full liberty. It is not always St Bernard's Day; tomorrow we resume our accustomed way of life: *cras iterabimus aequor*.'

In point of fact, after the abbot's departure the company grew more animated, the talk became louder, and there was more cracking of those specifically monastic jokes which are harmless enough, and at which everyone laughs without knowing why.

About nine o'clock supper was served: a choice and dainty meal, several centuries removed from the preceding dinner.

We ate with renewed gusto, chatted, laughed, and sang table songs; and one of the fathers read some verses of his own, which were by no means bad for a tonsured poet.

Towards the end of the evening, a voice was heard crying: 'Father Cellarer, where is your speciality?' 'You are right,' the monk replied. 'I am not cellarer for nothing.'

He went out, to return shortly afterwards accompanied by three servants, the first of whom carried some freshly buttered toast, and the other two a table, on which was a great bowl of sweetened flaming brandy, a drink which was more or less the equivalent of punch, at that date still unknown.

The newcomers were noisily applauded, the toast was eaten and the burnt brandy drunk; and when the clock struck twelve each of us withdrew to his cell, there to enjoy a sleep to which the day's labours had both inclined and entitled him.

N.B. When the father cellarer mentioned in this truly historic narrative was an old man, there was talk one day in his presence of a newly appointed abbot, who was on his way

---

and am inclined to believe that the lightness of the atmosphere in the mountains allows certain cerebral forces to act which its weight oppresses at lower altitudes.

from Paris, and who had the reputation of being very strict.

'I am not worried about him,' said the reverend father: 'let him be as strict as he pleases, he will never have the heart to deprive an old man either of his corner by the fire or of the cellar keys.'

23. Traveller's Luck

One day, mounted on my good horse La Joie, I was cross-ing the pleasant hillsides of Jura.

It was in the worst days of the Revolution, and I was on my way to Dôle to see Representative Prôt and to obtain from him, if possible, a safe-conduct to keep me from going first to prison, and then in all probability to the scaffold.

About eleven o'clock in the morning I arrived at an inn in the small town or village of Mont-sous-Vaudrey; and after attending to the wants of my mount I went into the kitchen, where a sight met my eyes which no traveller could have beheld without a thrill of pleasure.

In front of a blazing fire a spit was slowly turning, most admirably decked with kingly quails, and with those little green-footed landrails which are so very plump. This choice game was yielding its last drops on to a huge round of toast, which looked as if it had been fashioned by a sportsman's hand; and close beside it, already cooked, lay one of those round leverets whieh Parisians never see, and the smell of which would scent a church as sweetly as any incense.

'Good!' I said to myself, greatly cheered by what I saw, 'Providence has not utterly forsaken me. Let me pluck this flower on my way; I can always die a little later.'

Then, addressing the innkeeper, a man of gigantic build, who during my examination had been walking up and down the kitchen with his hands behind his back, whistling: 'My dear fellow,' I said, 'what good things are you going to offer me for dinner?' 'Nothing but good things, Monsieur,' he answered; 'good *bouilli*, good potato soup, good shoulder of mutton, and good haricot beans.'

At this unexpected reply a shiver of disappointment ran through me; the reader knows that I never eat *bouilli*, be-cause it is meat robbed of its juices; beans and potatoes are both fattening; my teeth, I felt, were not strong enough to tear up mutton; in a word, this menu was calculated to break my heart, and all my cares came back to plague me.

The innkeeper gave me a sly look, and seemed to have guessed the cause of my disappointment. . . . 'And for whom are you keeping all this fine game?' I asked, with an air of extreme annoyance. 'Alas, Monsieur,' he answered sympathetically, 'it is not mine to dispose of; it all belongs to some legal gentlemen who have been here these past ten days, working on a valuation for a very wealthy lady; they finished their work yesterday, and are celebrating the happy event with a feast – or revolting, as we say in these parts.'

'Monsieur,' I replied, after a moment's reflection, 'be so kind as to tell these gentlemen that a man of good company begs, as a favour, to be allowed to join them at dinner; that he will pay his share of the cost; and above all, that he will be profoundly indebted to them.' I spoke; he departed, and did not return.

But a little later a short, fat, fresh-complexioned, chubby, stocky, sprightly little man came in, prowled round the kitchen, shifted one or two pots and pans, raised the lid of a casserole, and went out again.

'Good,' I said to myself, 'that was the brother tiler, sent to size me up.' And my hopes revived, for experience had already taught me that my exterior is not repellent.

Nevertheless, my heart was beating like that of a candidate waiting for the last votes in an election to be counted, when the innkeeper reappeared and informed me that the gentlemen were highly flattered by my proposal, and were only waiting for me to join them before they sat down at table.

I danced out of the room, met with the most flattering welcome, and within a few minutes had taken root . . .

What a dinner that was! I will not describe it in detail; but I owe an honourable mention to the superb chicken fricassée, such as can only be found in the country, and endowed with sufficient truffles to rejuvenate old Tithonus.

The roast has been described already; its taste matched its

appearance; it was done to a turn, and the difficulty I had experienced in approaching it further enhanced its savour.

Dessert was composed of a vanilla *crème*, choice cheese, and excellent fruit. All these good things were washed down first with a light, garnet-coloured wine, then with Hermitage, and later with a dessert wine as sweet as it was generous; and the whole was crowned with some excellent coffee, confectioned by the sprightly tiler, who also provided us with certain Verdun liqueurs, which he produced from a sort of tabernacle to which he had the key.

Not only was the dinner good; it was also very gay.

After talking with due circumspection of the affairs of the day, my gentlemen started making jokes at one another's expense, in a manner which enlightened me in part as to their lives; they said little of the business which had brought them together, but told a few good stories and sang some songs, to which I responded with some unpublished verses of my own. I even recited some impromptu verses, which were loudly applauded; here they are:

> *To the tune of 'The Farrier'.*
>
> A pleasant thing it is and sweet
> Friendly travellers to meet,
> To sing and laugh and merry make
> With wine a manly thirst to slake.
> Gladly would I linger here,
> Free from worry, care, and fear,
> Four days,
> Fifteen days,
> Thirty days,
> A year or two,
> Enjoying very bliss with you.

If I record these verses here, it is not that I think highly of them; I have written better in my time, thank heaven, and could improve these if I wished; but I prefer to leave them in their impromptu form in the hope that the reader will agree with me that a man who could make so merry, with a revolutionary committee on his heels, had the head and heart of a true Frenchman.

We must have been at least four hours at table, when we began to consider how best to finish the day: my companions decided to take a long walk to help their digestion, and then to play a game of loo while waiting for the evening meal, which was to consist of a dish of trout and the still very desirable remnants of our dinner.

To all these proposals I was obliged to say no; the sun descending towards the horizon warned me to set off.

My companions pressed me to stay, as warmly as politeness would allow, and only gave way when I assured them that my journey was not entirely a matter of pleasure.

As the reader will have guessed, they refused to let me pay my share of the reckoning; taking care to ask no awkward questions, they came out to see me mount; and we parted after exchanging the warmest farewells.

If any one of those who treated me so hospitably that day is still alive, and this book falls into his hands, I wish him to know that after more than thirty years this chapter was penned with the liveliest gratitude.

Strokes of luck never come singly, and my journey was crowned with almost unhoped-for success.

I found Representative Prôt, in fact, strongly prejudiced against me; he eyed me with a sinister air, and I thought that he was going to have me arrested; however, I was let off with nothing worse than a fright, and after a few explanations his features seemed to relax a little.

I am not the sort of man whom fear embitters, and I do not believe that that man was evil; but he was a person of small ability and did not know what to do with the formidable powers entrusted to him; he was like a child armed with the club of Hercules.

Monsieur Amondru, whose name I record here with extreme pleasure, found it no easy matter to persuade him to come to a supper-party at which it was planned that I should be a guest; but in the end he came, only to greet me in a way that was anything but reassuring.

By Madame Prôt, however, to whom I hastened to present my respects, I was rather less coldly received. The circumstances in which I was introduced to her justified at least a certain curiosity.

We had no sooner begun conversing when she asked me whether I was fond of music. Oh, unhoped-for luck! It seemed that she adored it, and as I am myself a competent musician, from that moment our hearts beat in unison.

We talked until supper, by which time we had covered the whole subject. She spoke of the manuals on composition, I knew them all; she spoke of the operas of the day, I knew them all by heart; she named the best-known composers, I had seen most of them with my own eyes. She talked on and on, because it was a long time since she had met anyone with whom to discuss music; and although she seemed to approach the subject as an amateur, I have since learned that she had once been a professional singing-teacher.

After supper she sent for her portfolio; she sang, I sang, we sang; never have I put more zeal into my singing, and never have I enjoyed it more. Monsieur Prôt had already suggested leaving several times, but she had refused to hear of it, and we were blaring, like two trumpets, the duet from *La Fausse Magie*, 'Do you recall that happy day?' when he finally gave the order for departure.

This time he had to be obeyed; but as we were separating, Madame Prôt said: 'Citizen, when a man cultivates the arts as you do, he does not betray his country. I know that you want something from my husband: you shall have it, I promise you.'

When I heard these comforting words, I kissed her hand with all my heart; and sure enough, the very next morning, I received my safe-conduct, duly signed and magnificently sealed.

Thus was the purpose of my journey accomplished. I returned home with head held high; and thanks to harmony, that sweet child of Heaven, my ascension was postponed for a goodly number of years.

24. Poetical

> *Nulla placere diu, nec vivere carmina possunt,*
> *Quae scribuntur aquae potoribus. Ut male sanos*
> *Adscripsit Liber Satyris Faunisque poetas,*
> *Vina fere dulces oluerunt mane Camoenae.*
> *Laudibus arguitur vini vinosus Homerus;*
> *Ennius ipse pater nunquam, nisi potus, ad arma*
> *Prosiluit dicenda: 'Forum putealque Libonis*
> *Mandabo siccis; adimam cantare severis.'*
> *Hoc simul edixit, non cessavere poetae*
> *Nocturno certare mero, potare diurno.*[1]
>
> HORACE. *Epistles* I, 19.

If I had had the time, I would have made a methodical selection of gastronomical poems from the Greeks and Romans down to the present day, dividing them into historical periods, to show the intimate connexion which has always existed between the art of speaking well and the art of eating well.

What I have left undone, someone else will do.[2] We shall find that the table has always set the tone for the lyre, and thus we shall have one more proof of the influence of the physical on the moral.

Up to the middle of the eighteenth century, such poems were chiefly made in praise of Bacchus and his gifts, because in those times to drink wine, and to drink it in large quantities, was the highest degree of gustative exaltation to

1. 'No poems can please nor live long which are written by water drinkers. Ever since Bacchus enrolled poets, as half-crazed, amongst his Satyrs and Fauns, the sweet Muses have usually smelt of wine in the morning. Homer is convicted as a wine-lover by his praise of wine, Father Ennius himself never leapt up to tell of arms unless he had been drinking: "The Forum and well of Libo I'll award to the sober, the power of song I'll deny to the staid." Ever since he said this, poets have never ceased to rival each other in drinking at night, and continuing to drink by day.' [Ed.]

2. This, unless I am mistaken, makes the third work which I am bequeathing to students of Gastronomy: 1. *Monograph on Obesity*; 2. *Essays on the Theory and Practice of Shooting-luncheons*; and 3. *Chronological Selection of Gastronomical Verse*.

which anyone could attain. However, to break the monotony and enlarge the field, Cupid was linked with Bacchus, though it is by no means certain that the association was a happy one for love.

The discovery of the New World, and the acquisitions which resulted, ushered in a new order of things.

Sugar, coffee, tea, chocolate, alcoholic liqueurs, and all the resulting mixtures have made of good cheer a more comprehensive whole, of which wine is now simply a more or less indispensable accessory; for tea can easily take the place of wine at breakfast.[1]

Thus a wider field has been opened up to the poet of today; he can sing of the pleasures of the table without being obliged to wallow in drink; and already charming poems have been written in praise of the new treasures of gastronomy.

Like other readers I have enjoyed the fragrance of these ethereal offerings. But, while admiring the authors' talent and savouring the harmony of the verses, I felt more satisfaction than other readers when I found that all these poets adhered to my favourite system; for most of these pretty things were made for dinner, at dinner, or after dinner.

I hope skilled hands will one day exploit that part of my domain which I am leaving to them; meanwhile, I shall content myself with offering my readers a few pieces chosen at random, which I have accompanied with very short notes, so that nobody need rack his brains to discover the reason for my choice.

SONG OF DEMOCARES AT THE FEAST OF DENIAS

Let us drink, and let us sing the praises of Bacchus.

He delights in our dances, he delights in our songs; he stifles envy, hatred, and sorrow. He is the begetter of the enchanting Graces and the bewitching Loves.

Let us love, let us drink, and let us sing the praises of Bacchus.

The future is not yet; soon the present is no more; life's only moment is the moment of delight.

1. The English and Dutch eat bread and butter, fish, ham, and eggs, and rarely drink anything but tea for breakfast.

Let us love, let us drink, and let us sing the praises of Bacchus.
Wise in our follies, rich in our pleasures, let us trample the earth
and its vain grandeur underfoot; and in the sweet drunkenness
with which such sweet moments fill our souls,
Let us drink, and let us sing the praises of Bacchus.

This song is taken from the *Travels of Young Anacharsis*:
no further reason is required.

The following song is by Motin, who is said to have been
the first poet to write drinking-songs in France. It belongs to
the golden age of inebriation, and is not lacking in spirit:

> Tavern, how dear you are to me;
> Nothing on earth or under sky
> Was ever quite so good to see,
> For every need you do supply.
> Even your dishclouts are so fair
> They can with Holland cloth compare.
>
> When the fierce sun displays its power
> I'd rather to your shelter go
> Than to a green and leafy bower.
> And when the earth is cloaked in snow,
> A faggot there delights me then
> More than the forests of Vincennes.
>
> You grant me all that I could wish;
> Thistles as roses do appear,
> And tripe tastes like a royal dish,
> While fights are fought with mugs of beer.
> I could no greater bliss desire
> Than I find by a tavern's fire.
>
> Bacchus we thank who gave us wine
> Which warms the blood within our veins;
> That nectar is itself divine.
> The man who drinks not, yet attains
> By godly grace to human rank
> Would be an angel if he drank.
>
> Wine beckons me, invites my kiss,
> It drives my sadness far away,
> And fills me with unending bliss;

We love each other more each day.
I burn for it, it does me burn;
I drink it up, am drunk in turn.

When I have sampled too much cheer
My steps in every sense I bend;
With jolly smile and tingling ear
I take a stranger for a friend;
And I who never danced before
Cut a fine caper on the floor.

For my part 'tis my firm desire
That claret and white wine reside
Within me until I expire,
Provided they in peace abide;
For if in concord they are lacking,
Then I shall surely send them packing.

The next is by Racan, one of our oldest poets; it is full of grace and philosophy, has served as a model for many others, and seems much younger than its years.

TO MAYNARD

Maynard, let us not yield to care,
But drink instead this nectar rare,
Let us each ruby droplet sup
Which does in excellence precede,
Even that wine which Ganymede
Pours in the gods' immortal cup.

This wine will make a century
Seem but a day, so, drinking, we
Regain our youth and shed our years,
It banishes far from our mind
Regret for things we left behind,
And conquers all tomorrow's fears.

Let us drink, Maynard, long and deep,
For stealthily the years do creep
Until we reach our dying day;
To pray or cry is all in vain:
The years, like rivers on the plain,
Never return the other way.

Spring may come, all clothed in green
Where winter with its snows had been;
The sea has ebb and flow tides too;
But once sweet youth gives place to age
And Father Time has turned the page,
The good years never come anew.

The laws of death hold equal thrall
O'er palace royal or stately hall,
Or the poor peasant's reed-roofed hut.
The king the peasant's lot dictates,
But both are subject to the Fates,
Who with their scissors both threads cut.

Their edicts all things do efface
And undo in the shortest space
Whatever we have raised on high;
And they will take us off to drink
Beyond the dark shore's sombre brink
Of Lethe's waters by and by.

The next is the Professor's own, and he has also set it to
music. He shrank from the ordeal of publishing it, despite
the pleasure he would have derived from the knowledge that
he was on every piano; by an unheard-of stroke of luck it
can be sung and *will be sung* to the tune of the 'Vaudeville
de Figaro':

THE CHOICE OF THE SCIENCES
Let us Fame no more pursue,
For she sells her favours dear;
History we'll forfeit too,
With her string of tales so drear.
Like our ancient forbears who
Drank mightily when knights were bold,
Let us drink a wine that's old. (*Twice*)

I have left Astronomy
With her highways in the sky;
Chemistry is not for me,
The cost is far too high.
But for dear Gastronomy
I feel love I know is true.
Gourmandise, I worship you! (*Twice*)

Reading did I never cease
Till my hair turned steely grey;
Yet the sages that were Greece
Had not much of note to say.
Now I spend my days in peace,
Learning laziness instead.
Ah, what bliss to lie in bed! (*Twice*)

I was once a doctor grave,
Then I bade my drugs goodbye.
Drugs and physic do not save,
Only help a man to die.
So to food my heart I gave
Cooking does much more than books:
There are no better men than cooks. (*Twice*)

This my work is somewhat rude,
But as night invades the sky,
Lest melancholy should intrude,
I let love come stealing nigh.
For despite the sharp-tongued prude,
Love's a pretty game to play:
Let us play it while we may! (*Twice*)

I witnessed the birth of the following lines, which is why I
am planting them here. Truffles are the gods of our time,
and it may be that our idolatrous devotion to them is not
altogether to our honour.

IMPROMPTU

Truffle, we greet you from above,
   For let us not ungrateful be
   To you who in the war of love
   Bring us a certain victory.
      To ease the way
      For loving play,
Heaven sent us down this treasure
To fortify us in our pleasure,
So give us truffles every day.

*By Monsieur B— de V—, a distinguished
gastronome and a favourite pupil of
the Professor's*

I conclude with a poem which really belongs to Meditation 26.

I tried to set it to music, but did not succeed to my satisfaction; someone else will do better, especially if he gives free rein to his imagination. The accompaniment should be forceful, and should indicate in the second couplet that the patient's condition is worsening.

THE DEATHBED
A physiological Ballad

In all my senses life grows faint,
My eye is dull, my body weak;
My Louise weeps without restraint
And gently strokes my pallid cheek.
My friends have called, but not to feast;
They bade me all a last goodbye;
The doctor came and then the priest:
The time has come to die.

I try to speak, my lips are still;
I try to pray, but all in vain.
A bell I hear that bodes me ill;
Each movement brings me added pain.
I see no more. Caught in a vice,
My breast expels a rattling sigh
Which lingers on my lips of ice:
The time has come to die.

By the Professor.

25. Monsieur Henrion de Pansey

In all good faith I believed myself to be the first, *in our own day*, to have conceived the idea of an Academy of Gastronomes; but I very much fear that, as sometimes happens, I have been forestalled. This may be seen from the following anecdote, recounting an incident which goes back nearly fifteen years.

In 1812, Monsieur le Président Henrion de Pansey, whose genial wit has braved the frosts of time, addressing three of the most distinguished scientists of the day (Messieurs de Laplace, Chaptal, and Berthollet), said: 'I consider the discovery of a new dish, which sustains our appetite and prolongs our pleasure, a far more interesting event than the discovery of a star; we can see enough stars already.

'Nor,' the Judge continued, 'shall I ever consider the sciences sufficiently honoured, or adequately represented, until I see a cook take his seat as a full member of the Institute.'

The good President always expressed a delighted interest in my work; he wished to provide me with a motto, and used to say that it was not his *Esprit des Lois* which opened the doors of the Academy to Monsieur de Montesquieu. It was from him that I discovered that Professor Berriat Saint-Prix had written a novel; and it was he, too, who suggested to me the chapter which deals with the alimentary activities of the *émigrés*. Therefore, since honour must be paid where honour is due, I have written the following quatrain about him, which contains at once his history and his eulogy:

LINES TO BE INSCRIBED BENEATH THE PORTRAIT
OF MONSIEUR HENRION DE PANSEY

Hard did he labour night and day,
And filled his office worthily,

> Yet though a scholar wise and grey,
> He kept his amiability.

In 1814 Monsieur le Président Henrion was appointed Minister of Justice, and those who served under him in that ministry like to recall the reply he made to them, when they came to see him in a body to present their respects, on the occasion of his taking office:

'Gentlemen,' he said, in the paternal tones which so well became his imposing stature and his advanced years, 'it is unlikely I shall stay with you long enough to do you any good; but at least you may rest assured that I shall do you no harm.'

26. Recommendations

My work is over; but to prove that I am not quite out of breath, I shall proceed to kill three birds with one stone.

I am going to supply my readers of all nations with some recommendations which will be to their advantage; I am going to give my favourite artists a memorial which they deserve, and the public a brand from the fire at which I warm my own hands.

1. *Madame Chevet*, provision-merchant, at No. 220, Palais-Royal, near the Théâtre-Français. I am rather a faithful customer of hers than a large consumer: our relations date from her first appearance on the gastronomical horizon, and she was once kind enough to mourn my death, on the occasion of what was fortunately a false alarm.

Madame Chevet is the essential link between extreme comestibility and great fortunes. She owes her prosperity to the purity of her commercial faith; whatever time has tarnished disappears from her premises as if by magic. The nature of her business requires her to make a considerable profit; but once the price is agreed upon, the purchaser is sure of obtaining something of the highest quality.

This faith will be hereditary; already her daughters, who as yet have scarcely emerged from childhood, invariably adhere to the same principles.

Madame Chevet has representatives in every land where the wishes of the most capricious gastronome can possibly be gratified; and the more rivals she has, the higher stands her reputation.

2. *Monsieur Achard*, pastrycook and confectioner, No. 9 rue de Grammont, a native of Lyons, set up shop about ten years ago and gained his reputation through his biscuits and vanilla waffles, which defied imitation for a long time.

Everything in his shop has an air of perfection and even of

coquetry about it which would be vain to look for elsewhere. The hand of man is nowhere to be seen; you would take his creations for the natural products of some enchanted land; and for this reason everything he makes is carried off the same day, and may be said to have no future.

At the height of summer, not a moment passes but some brilliant carriage draws up in the rue de Grammont, usually bearing a handsome Titus and his befeathered lady. The former dashes into Achard's, there to arm himself with a large bag of dainties. On his return, he is greeted with '*O mon ami! Que cela a bonne mine!*' or 'O my dear! How good that looks!' And off speeds the horse, taking them towards the Bois de Boulogne.

Gourmands are so ardent and good-natured that for a long time they have put up with the asperities of an ungracious shopgirl. This blot has been removed; now a new face has appeared behind the counter, and Mademoiselle Anna Achard's dainty hands lend fresh merit to preparations which are already recommendation in themselves.

3. On *Monsieur Limet*, at No. 79 rue de Richelieu (and thus my neighbour), who is baker to several highnesses, I have likewise fixed my choice.

Taking over a business of no great distinction, he quickly raised it to a high degree of prosperity and fame.

His standard bread is very fine; and it is difficult to achieve, in the most expensive bread, such whiteness, savour and lightness.

Foreigners, as well as people from the remotest departments, always find the bread they are used to at Monsieur Limet's; his customers accordingly come to his shop in person, and quite often line up in a queue.

His success will astonish nobody, when it is known that Monsieur Limet avoids the rut of routine, strives perpetually to discover new resources, and is advised by scientists of the highest reputation.

27. Privations

First parents of the human race, whose gourmandism is historical, you lost all for an apple, what would you not have done for a truffled turkey? But in the earthly paradise there were no cooks or confectioners.

How I pity you!

Great kings who laid proud Troy in ruins, your valour will go down from age to age; but your table was pitiful. Reduced to ox-thighs and the backs of swine, you never knew the charms of fish-stew, nor the bliss of chicken fricassée.

How I pity you!

Aspasia, Chloe, and all you others whom Grecian chisels made eternal for the despair of the beauties of today, never did your charming mouths taste the suavity of rose or vanilla meringue; you scarcely even advanced as far as gingerbread.

How I pity you!

Sweet priestesses of Vesta, loaded with such honours, but also threatened with such fearful tortures, ah, if you had only tasted those delicious syrups which refresh the soul, those crystallized fruits which scorn the seasons, those fragrant creams, the marvels of today!

How I pity you!

Roman financiers, who bled the known world white, your famous halls never saw those tasty jellies which delight the idle, nor those varied ices which would brave the torrid zone.

How I pity you!

Invincible paladins, celebrated in the songs of troubadours, when you had smitten giants hip and thigh, set damsels free, and wiped out armies of the foe, no black-eyed captive maiden brought you sparkling champagne, Madeira malvoisie, nor our great century's liqueurs; you were reduced to ale or Suresnes wine.

How I pity you!

Mitred and croziered abbots, dispensers of the grace of heaven, and you fierce Templars, who took up arms to fight the Saracens, you never knew that sweet reviver, chocolate, nor the Arabian bean which kindles thought.

How I pity you!

Proud dames who raised your almoners and pages to the highest rank, to fill the void of the crusades, you never shared with them the charm of biscuits, nor the bliss of macaroons.

How I pity you!

And you too, gastronomes of 1825, sated already in the midst of plenty, and dreaming now of novel dishes, you will never know the mysteries science shall reveal in 1900, mineral esculences perhaps, liqueurs distilled from a hundred atmospheres; you will never see what travellers as yet unborn shall bring from that half of the globe which still remains to be discovered or explored.

How I pity you!

Envoy to the Gastronomes
of the Two Worlds

Excellencies:

The work which I humbly submit to you seeks to unfold before the eyes of all men the principles of that science of which you are the ornament and the support.

I would also offer up incense to Gastronomy, that young goddess who, though only lately adorned with her crown of stars, already overtops her sisters, just as Calypso rose head and shoulder above the charming nymphs around her.

Soon the temple of Gastronomy shall raise its mighty portals heavenwards, to adorn the world's metropolis; you shall set it echoing with your voices; you shall enrich it with your gifts; and when the Academy promised by the oracles shall have been established on the unshifting corner-stones of pleasure and necessity, you, O enlightened gourmands and charming guests, shall be its members or correspondents.

In the meantime, lift your radiant faces heavenwards; go forward in your might and majesty; the world of esculence lies open before you.

Work, then, Excellencies; spread the word for the sake of the culinary art; digest well for your own sakes; and if in the course of your labours you happen to make some notable discovery, be so kind as to communicate it to

Your Humble Servant,

THE AUTHOR OF THE
GASTRONOMICAL MEDITATIONS

Penguin Handbooks of Cookery and Wine

*Not for sale in the U.S.A. or Canada
†Not for sale in the U.S.A.